LITERARY TEXTS
IN AN ELECTRONIC AGE

SCHOLARLY IMPLICATIONS
AND LIBRARY SERVICES

PAPERS PRESENTED AT THE
1994 CLINIC ON LIBRARY APPLICATIONS OF DATA PROCESSING
April 10-12, 1994
GRADUATE SCHOOL OF LIBRARY AND INFORMATION SCIENCE
UNIVERSITY OF ILLINOIS AT URBANA-CHAMPAIGN

Clinic on Library Applications of Data Processing: 1994

LITERARY TEXTS
IN AN ELECTRONIC AGE
SCHOLARLY IMPLICATIONS
AND LIBRARY SERVICES

Edited by
BRETT SUTTON

GRADUATE SCHOOL OF LIBRARY AND INFORMATION SCIENCE
UNIVERSITY OF ILLINOIS AT URBANA-CHAMPAIGN
1994

Printed in the United States of America
on acid-free paper

CONTENTS

Introduction

The explosive rate of technological progress in the development of information systems has not benefited all users to the same degree. Even with the appearance of advanced information retrieval systems and the availability of previously printed texts in electronic form, for many library users, the main purpose of computers in libraries is still to provide fast and precise access to printed documents, not electronic files. In academic settings, this is particularly true for humanistic scholars for whom the traditional print-oriented library is laboratory, toolkit, and the single most important source of scholarly materials. Although there has been no shortage of fantasizing about the all-electronic library, even in the more technologically advanced academic institutions, literary work is practiced by many scholars using techniques differing little from those in use a century ago. These patterns, however, are changing. Literary scholars no longer have to learn computer programming in order to gain useful access to literature in electronic form: programs are now available that are capable of performing in minutes analytical tasks that used to take months; scholars are beginning to create electronic editions of classic literary works and are pooling their efforts to make those texts available to others; new fast and efficient delivery systems for electronic texts are beginning to appear; working prototypes of fully electronic libraries are now in operation in academic library settings. Scholarly work in the humanities that bypasses print altogether is now possible.

The papers in this volume explore the potential of electronic texts in the humanities and describe the possible roles for libraries as electronic books take the place of printed ones. This apparently simple topic embodies a considerable amount of complexity, however. Glancing over these papers, it is easy to see that the question of literary texts in the humanities spans many areas of interest, reflecting the various needs of librarians, publishers, system administrators, scholars, readers, and writers. It is one purpose of this collection to bring these diverse perspectives into conjunction. Given this assortment of points of view, it is perhaps not surprising that a number of different themes emerge. A few, however, stand out.

One significant theme is the pivotal role that humanities scholars themselves have played in the development of electronic approaches to literary studies. Over the last several decades, researchers in the humanities have educated themselves about computers and applied them to their own unique text processing needs, sometimes under adverse conditions and often alone because there was no one else to do it. This work, small in scale at first, has had significant consequences, transforming both research and education in the literary disciplines. Humanists have come to realize that not only can computer technology provide better, faster ways of accomplishing traditional scholarly tasks, but it also constitutes a way of articulating and solving new kinds of scholarly problems, answering questions that had never been asked before. Many of the basic concepts upon which full-text information systems in the humanities are based have their roots in this research, and the scholarly community continues to play a leading role in this work.

These efforts have not been without obstacles, however. Many scholars have experienced the problem, all too common in the academic world, of freeing themselves from the restrictions of print only to find themselves subject to new and more perplexing forms of electronic bondage. Developing an expertise in information technology, however necessary, is not always a high priority for literary scholars, nor should it be. To become distracted by computers is to risk being drawn away from scholarly pursuits. Here is where librarians, whose role in humanities scholarship has traditionally been one of archiving, organizing, and disseminating texts, have become significant contributors. Collaborations involving library organizations such as RLIN and the Library of Congress, not to mention several university libraries that have taken a leading role in this area, and scholarly societies such as the Association for Computers and the Humanities and the Association for Literary and Linguistic Computing, have been fruitful in advancing the cause of electronic approaches to humanities research. More recently, electronic publishers such as Chadwyck-Healey and software developers such as the Open Text Corporation have provided useful electronic products. The collective result of these efforts has been a quickening of the pace at which texts are converted into electronic formats, the development of software for textual analysis suitable to the needs of literary scholars, broader sharing and dissemination of electronic texts, and new possibilities for humanities education.

Another theme that emerges in these papers is the importance of standards. In the earlier years of humanities computing, scholars had to adapt whatever hardware and software was at hand in order to create electronic editions and develop analytical tools. There was a great deal of reinvention of the wheel, and many of the resulting systems were incompatible, making it difficult for one scholar to reuse electronic texts produced by another. Today, scholars working with electronic texts in the humanities must continue to make choices among various hardware platforms, operating systems, markup systems, file types, storage media, processing tools, character sets, and delivery systems. But because of progress in the development of standards, the choices are safer, and the possibilities for reuse are much improved. The Text Encoding Initiative's application of Standard Generalized Markup Language is one example. Another is the recent work in adapting the MARC record for the description and cataloging of electronic texts. The latter project has been a particular challenge because of the unique features of electronic texts, which do not possess a physical form in the usual sense, exist potentially in multiple formats, and are susceptible to rapid and unannounced modification. But success in this area is essential if libraries are going to be able to retain bibliographic control over this new medium.

The incorporeality of the electronic book leads to another significant issue: the development of new delivery mechanisms. The publication of texts in magnetic and optical formats creates certain new problems for libraries, but it remains possible to treat such documents as if they were books, since they remain, after all, tangible objects. Purchasing, cataloging, marking, storing, and circulating these items are possible with existing library systems. Some electronic texts, however, do not exist in any particular place or take any lasting tangible form but may instead be disseminated on demand over computer networks. Libraries are beginning to realize the revolutionary potential of the Internet in providing a form of remote storage that includes the possibility of fast transfer of documents directly into the hands of the users at the moment the request is made, supplementing or even replacing local ownership. With interfaces such as Mosaic capable of delivering not just text but full-color images, sound, and motion pictures, the electronic book begins to diverge in significant ways from the printed monograph. It is even possible for a "book" requested and received by the reader to be assembled on the fly at the moment of the request from various components stored in separate locations. Such remote archives will certainly benefit from

all-electronic systems of publications that are currently under
development. By streamlining the chain of events that leads from author
to reader, these systems will radically alter certain traditional roles,
among them the role of librarians in acquiring and organizing texts.
But at the same time, there are likely to be new roles for librarians,
requiring familiarity with new technologies and an interest in
developing new kinds of delivery services that are radically different
from those that have been offered in the past.

Traditionally, librarians have provided texts, and scholars were
responsible for the analysis of those texts. Another consequence of
electronic text processing systems has been the blurring of these two
roles. Systems are now available that not only deliver literary texts but
that provide analytical utilities as well. There is no exact analogue
in the traditional library for documents that come with their own
processing tools, but is perhaps best viewed as a novel and powerful
extension of the reference function. With such systems in place, is it
unreasonable for libraries to consider taking over some of the analytical
tasks of humanistic research? Although we may well expect that not
every library will choose to do so, this is an interesting area for the
expansion of library services. Such a scenario adds to the two familiar
library functions of ownership and archiving a third area of
responsibility—processing. The academic library is evolving under the
effect of these changes. At some institutions, it has meant the installation
of computer centers that resemble laboratories or classrooms. Effective
implementation of these new services will depend on librarians'
understanding of the diverse needs of the library's users, who may include
researchers, educators, students, and the general reading public, and
their successful handling of new versions of old questions about equity
of service and budget priorities.

For every opportunity, there is a problem to solve, and these papers
bring to light a number of these problems. One of the most vexing
is the problem of copyright, a principle born of the age of mechanical
printing and increasingly problematic in a world dominated by fast-
moving and easily duplicated electronic commodities. The new
technologies seem at nearly every point to undercut the control applied
by copyright, encouraging the creation of new forms of control that
frustrate the efforts of libraries to provide the free and open service
that is traditionally their mission. The copyright problems are only
a part of larger economic questions raised by electronic media. How
these will affect the role of academic presses, the ability of authors
to make a fair profit from their work, and, more generally, the structure
of the information cycle are questions that are as yet unresolved.

Ultimately, as humanities scholars themselves have pointed out,
the development of electronic texts may affect not just the future of

libraries but the evolution of reading and literacy. There is evidence that the electronic text is in some settings less concrete, less linear, more interactive, and more mutable than printed text. Moreover, electronic communication has the potential of changing the relationship between writer and reader and altering control mechanisms and power relationships. We know that when traditional texts are converted into electronic form, new possibilities emerge; what are the possibilities for literary works created specifically for electronic media? Does the hypertext book represent, as some suggest, an important new form of human literary expression? It is at least becoming more difficult to view electronic texts as mere transformations of traditional codices and increasingly reasonable to see them as a new evolutionary stage in the history of human expression that includes the emergence of alphabetical writing and printing. The consequences of these new technologies for literary culture and for libraries are only dimly perceived at this early stage, but these papers help suggest the directions that these changes may take.

BRETT SUTTON
Editor

JAY DAVID BOLTER

Professor
School of Literature, Communications, and Culture
Georgia Institute of Technology
Atlanta, Georgia

Authors and Readers in an Age of Electronic Texts

ABSTRACT

Electronic hypertext is the latest in a series of technologies of writing; it is a technological innovation that is both revolutionary and evolutionary. Hypertext challenges our sense that any book is a complete, separate, and unique expression of its author. In addition to hypertextual writing, the computer also supports new forms of graphic representation and communication. As all forms of electronic communication become increasingly important in our society, we must learn how to combine these two orthogonal information spaces: the visual space of computer graphics with the semantic space of hypertext.

INTRODUCTION

These proceedings address a range of issues under the rubric of electronic literacy. Some of the authors consider the problems of transferring texts recorded in earlier technologies of writing to the new electronic medium. Others consider how to use these texts once they have been transferred. Some address the challenges that electronic technology poses for publishers as the traditional providers of texts, others the challenges faced by libraries as the traditional centers for collecting and organizing texts. These issues in turn entail larger questions: How does the computer change the nature of symbolic representation and communication, the nature of writing itself? What does it mean to be an author in an electronic environment? What does

7

it mean to be an electronic reader? At the outset, it may be useful to reflect briefly on these larger questions.

HYPERTEXT AND THE HISTORY OF WRITING

What makes electronic writing interesting and novel are the qualities of fluidity, multiplicity, and dispersed control—in other words, its hypertextual qualities. Hypertext systems are by no means as widely used as word-processing programs. However, the word processor is only a transitional tool, because the results of word processing are still meant to be read in the conventional way, as ink on paper. In a fully electronic or hypertextual document, the writing and the reading occur in the computer medium. When the writer writes and the reader reads on the computer screen, then the computer can display the qualities that distinguish it from the older technology of print. Unlike print, the computer allows the writer to define units of text of any size and to present those units in a variety of orders, depending upon the needs and wishes of the reader. This capacity for fluid presentation is what characterizes hypertext.

Electronic writing is the latest in a series of technologies of writing; regarding electronic writing as part of a technological tradition helps us to see that the technological innovations in writing are always revolutionary and evolutionary at the same time. It is common to compare electronic media to the printed book, but the comparison is usually limited to the printing and publishing industry as it exists today. Our historical field of view needs to be wider. The state of print technology today is the latest phase of what we might call the "industrial period of print," which began in the early nineteenth century with the development of the steam-driven press and continued with such innovations as paper from wood pulp, mechanized typesetting, and effective photo-offset lithography. It is equally important to consider printing in the "Gutenberg period," from the fifteenth to the eighteenth centuries. This craft period in the history of printing had rather different qualities from the industrial era that followed. Indeed, in order fully to appreciate the nature of electronic writing, we should look at the long period before Gutenberg. When we do, we can identify a number of ways in which electronic writing resonates with early technologies and with the earlier genres and practices that grew up around these technologies.

Since the invention of the Greek alphabet, there have been three principal writing media in ancient and Western societies—the papyrus roll, the handwritten codex, and the printed book—and each has fostered certain attitudes toward the act of writing and the nature of written text. The electronic medium is likely to do the same. As Elizabeth Eisenstein (1979) explains in *The Printing Press as an Agent of Change,* the introduction of printing was a technical change that also changed the way science was practiced and the attitude of humanists toward the ancient and modern texts that they studied. The printing press affected styles of writing and genres of literature. In fact, each technology of writing has had this effect. In describing the changes brought about by printing, Eisenstein stresses the ability of the press to preserve and stabilize both words and images with a greater degree of accuracy than handwriting could provide. It was the fixity of the printed text that encouraged exacting textual criticism in humanistic scholarship and the drive for greater mathematical precision and descriptive accuracy in the sciences. Now, however, the computer is calling the idea of fixity into question: in place of the stable printed text, the computer offers us a fluid and interactive one. The computer promises, therefore, to reverse at least some of the qualities that Eisenstein identified in the printing revolution (see Bolter 1991, 1-43).

That reversal comes from the hypertextual character of the electronic writing. Hypertext is the essence of electronic writing. The definition of hypertext should not be limited to systems with explicit links and paths for navigation, although there are now many such applications in use—everything from George Landow's (1991) pedagogical hypertext on Charles Dickens to Michael Joyce's (1989) fiction *afternoon.* The hypertextual qualities of fluidity and dispersed control are also present in a variety of computer applications, including electronic mail, textual databases, electronic encyclopedias and handbooks, presentation programs, and computer-assisted instruction. My definition of hypertext extends to all those applications that promote the topical division and interrelation of texts as well as dispersed access and control. This definition includes most of the initiatives described at this conference. Textual databases—such as those of the Center for Electronic Texts in the Humanities under the direction of Susan Hockey and Project Gutenberg headed by Michael Hart—provide the foundation for hypertextual division, commentary, and dispersal. The Text Encoding Initiative, whose editor is C. M. Sperberg-McQueen, will allow further segmentation and hypertextual treatment of text.

Perhaps the best example of hypertext by another name is the Internet itself. The Internet is a physical embodiment of hypertext, with computers serving as nodes and cables or satellite connections as links. These physical connections become the surface upon which hypertexts are written and read; these hypertexts may take the form of listservs and newsgroups. Each newsgroup on the USENET is a disorganized, collaborative hypertext. The whole Internet consisting of hundreds of newsgroups and probably millions of messages is a text that spreads its reticulations over the United States and around the world. It is a hypertext that changes minute by minute, as users add messages and as moderators and systems delete them. No one writer contributes more than a tiny fraction of the messages, and no one reader can read more than a fraction. Of course, the World Wide Web and Mosaic do constitute an explicit hypertext system. With its blocks of text and graphics and its point-and-click interaction, Mosaic functions as a simple unified interface for the hypertextualization of all the various resources of the Internet.

ELECTRONIC WRITING AND CRITICAL THEORY

A hypertext is different in important ways from a printed book. Hypertext challenges the traditional notion of the book as a writing that is complete in itself and is the unique expression of an author. Hypertext encourages us to remember that all texts are connected. Once we begin to understand writing as connecting, we have less sympathy for traditional distinctions between the individual book, the encyclopedia, and the library as a great collective book. Hypertext suggests new kinds of collective works and libraries as well as new individual works, and in suggesting new kinds of text, hypertext compels us to reconsider the relationship among the text, the author, and the reader. The computer as hypertext raises fundamental questions of literary theory because it undermines both the fixity of the text and the authority of the author.

There is now a body of scholarship on hypertext fashioned by Stuart Moulthrop (1989), Michael Joyce (1988), George Landow (1992), Landow and Delany 1991), Richard Lanham (1989), Jane Douglas (1991), and many others. A broad area of agreement has emerged that hypertext seems in a curious way to embody poststructural literary theory. Hypertext is the operational realization of major theoretical work of the past two decades. Theorists from the reader-response critics to the deconstructionists have been talking about text in terms that are strikingly appropriate to hypertext in the computer (Bolter 1991, 147-68). When the deconstructionists emphasize that a text is unlimited, that it expands to include its own interpretations, they are describing a hypertext, which grows with the addition of new links and elements. When Roland Barthes draws his famous distinction between the work and the text, he is giving a characterization of the difference between writing in a printed book and writing by computer (Bolter 1991, 161).

Barthes's and Foucault's critique of traditional notions of authorship is borne out by the practice of hypertext (see Landow 1992). In hypertext, the reader assumes something of the role of a traditional author; that is, the reader constitutes the text in the act of reading. In a hypertext of any significant size, each reading and therefore each text is unique. By participating in the creation of the textual structure, the reader becomes both author and audience at the same time. And if we arrange the writing space so that the reader's choices can be saved, then the reader may give the newly constituted text to others to read. The first reader becomes an author for a second reader, and the chain of authors and readers may then continue indefinitely. The author too has a new relation to the text, since he or she is creating not one text but a whole family. The author sets up the outlines and defines the limits of possible thought and action in the text, but the author leaves to the reader the responsibility of exploring the space within those limits.

Hypertext, then, permits levels of authorship—without suggesting that one level is more important or worthy than others. There is the author of the program or system that constitutes the writing environment. There is the author who creates the structure of text and links. There is the reader as author who follows the links to call forth the text. As I have just mentioned, this reader as author may also have the ability to alter the text itself or make new links. Furthermore, any of these authors may work in collaboration rather than alone. In itself, this multiplicity of authorial roles is nothing new. Writing in the age of print has been characterized by multiple roles: authors, publishers, editors, proofreaders, typesetters, binders, and so on. But print technology is also characterized by a fairly rigid hierarchy, with authors and publishers at the top, and by a radical separation of authors from their readers. The hierarchy was perhaps not so rigid prior to the invention of the printing press, when publication was not an event. Publication simply meant making a copy of one's work by hand and sending it to a colleague.

In this sense at least, the electronic writing space more closely resembles the space of the manuscript than that of the printed page. In this new space, too, it is easy to pass from reader to author. It is easy in a technological sense; it merely involves entering a few commands at the keyboard. It is also easy in a cultural sense, for there is (as yet) no great divide between electronic authors and their readers. Again, electronic mail and newsgroups on the Internet are good examples here. One can move easily from reading a newsgroup article to writing and posting one's own article; anyone with full Internet access can be a contributor as well as a reader.

With hypertext, writing is connecting. The idea that writing should be a kind of creation *ex nihilo* seems to belong to or at least to be fostered by the technology of print. The legal notion of copyright, which grew up in the age of print, assumes that each writer will create something new and unique, without more than a limited debt to other writers. Other constructions of the idea of writing are certainly possible. One thinks, for example, of the Platonic dialogue in which the text is a product of collaboration. The philosophical value of the text depends upon the agreement and contributions of two interlocutors. For Plato, the sophist, who creates his text by himself and delivers it in a continuous speech, cannot attain true wisdom. Another construction of writing is provided by medieval writers such as Bonaventura, cited by Elizabeth Eisenstein (1979) in *The Printing Press as an Agent of Change* (pp. 121-22). For him, compilers and commentators are writers too. What compilers and commentators do is to link together textual units, so that their writing practices have always been hypertextual. Electronic technology encourages us to return to that kind of writing, indeed to see writing in a radical sense as connecting—connecting verbal ideas, connecting one text to others in a tradition, connecting texts together to form a new composite. And once we begin to understand writing as connecting, we are carried easily from the individual texts to collective texts, from the individual book to the encyclopedia and library as a collection of texts. Hypertext suggests new kinds of collective works and libraries as well as new individual works.

Once again, a historical perspective seems important to me. Libraries are very old—depending upon our definition, we can date them back to ancient Alexandria in the third century B.C. or to ancient Nineveh centuries earlier. Libraries are great books: organized collections of text whose principles of organization depend both upon the structure of knowledge in their contemporary society and upon the contemporary technology of writing. For our society and with electronic technology, a hypertextual library would be a great book that dissolves and reconstitutes itself to meet the needs of each user.

AUTHORSHIP, COPYRIGHT, AND HYPERTEXT

Just as electronic technology seems likely to change the institution of the library, there are other institutions and institutional practices in our society that are also threatened. Let us return to the question of authorship. In her article, "The Genius and the Copyright," and in subsequent work, Martha Woodmansee (1984, 1992) has shown how the notion of author evolved in the eighteenth and nineteenth century and how this affected the budding theory of copyright. Peter Jaszi (1992) has carried that analysis on into the legal language and decisions of the twentieth century. Both have reached the conclusion that there is a discord between current legal theory and current literary theory. Legal theory in the United States and Europe still seems wedded to the nineteenth-century notion that an author is a solitary, independent, creative agent; that creativity is practically synonymous with originality; and that the value of a text is measured by its originality.

Hypertext calls all these propositions into question. Literary theory had already been questioning these propositions for the past quarter of a century. The character of the author, the nature of originality, the independence of one text from other texts—all these are familiar targets of poststructuralist literary theory. My point is simply this. If hypertext (and therefore the computer as a writing technology) embodies or realizes poststructural theory, then it too must come into conflict with current legal theory. And if, as Woodmansee and Jaszi both argue, legal theory is having difficulty dealing fairly with the current practices of writers in print, it will have infinitely greater difficulty dealing with hypertextual writing. The ironies abound when we try to measure hypertext by the legal terms that have been defined for printed text. Copyright law recognizes fixed verbal expressions. Yet hypertext is not a single fixed text; nor is a hypertext fully characterized by the words it contains. In a hypertext, linking is writing. What legal status does a link have? What happens if a subsequent reader changes the structure of a hypertext by adding new links? No verbal text has been changed, but the hypertext is different, because new possible readings have been created. To whom do these readings belong?

Let me offer the following, somewhat subversive thoughts on hypertext and the notions of copyright and intellectual property. First, I would like to make a distinction—one that may at first seem frivolous but in fact seems to me useful in discussing the ambiguities and ambivalences that now surround copyright. It is a distinction between the legal speed limit and what I might call "the cultural speed limit." The legal speed limit is of course whatever the white rectangular road sign indicates—say, 55 miles per hour for urban expressways. But in most American highways, the cultural speed limit is not 55 but rather somewhere between 65 and 70. That is, most drivers do not think they are traveling too fast until they are going perhaps 10 to 15 miles per hour over the legal limit. Perhaps there are many such gaps between the legal and cultural definitions of what is right or appropriate. Certainly, such a gap already exists with regard to copyright for printed materials and now especially for computer materials. The photocopier, the tape recorder, and the computer disk drive have made it easy to make copies, and our cultural assumption seems to be that we should be able to make copies in limited quantities for most any use. I think the very ease of making copies has raised the cultural speed limit here.

In the coming decades, fully electronic writing promises to have a much greater effect on our cultural notion of protected expression. As we come to use the computer for more and more of our reading and writing, as we come to regard hypertext as the "natural" way to write, we will necessarily be more and more estranged from traditional theories of copyright. The gap between the cultural and the legal speed limits here will widen, and I suppose that such a gap can only grow so wide before one has to change the legal limit. If people continue to ignore certain aspects of the laws of copyright, then eventually the courts may have to recognize what they do as fair use. I admit that for the present that does not seem to be happening. Instead, corporations and individuals seem to be in a frenzy to claim everything as intellectual property—to copyright, patent, and trademark the world. This frenzy itself may point to a cultural concept that is approaching crisis.

If our culture were to be consistent as it moves towards a period in which electronic text becomes ubiquitous, then it would just throw the notion of copyright out. Copyright is incompatible with hypertext or with electronic writing in general. We would retain the notion for printed products but not for computer-mediated writing. There would be no such thing as copyright: people would be free to copy, link, alter, and appropriate texts as they saw fit. Society would have to evolve other means of encouraging and remunerating various kinds of writing, as indeed was the case before the institution of copyright. Clearly, this is not what will happen in the short run, yet in the long run, the gap between the cultural and legal speed limits may well become intolerable.

SYMBOLIC COMMUNICATION AND
PERCEPTUAL MANIPULATION

I have now touched on various aspects of hypertextual reading and writing and offered an optimistic assessment of what the future holds— optimistic for those at this conference who are committed to exploring and elaborating the possibilities of electronic writing. There is a caution that needs to be expressed: the computer and electronic media can also be used in ways that do not foster literacy in any form, electronic or traditional.

We have been considering the computer as a means of symbolic representation and communication. This is the principal role that the computer has played in the almost fifty years since its invention. The original inventors and users of computers were scientists and engineers who needed a powerful calculator for numerical analysis. But it was soon realized that numerical analysis was only part of the larger sphere of symbolic manipulation: that the computer could manipulate letters of the alphabet or arbitrary systems as well as numbers. Since that realization, there has been a development from databases for business purposes to word processors and outline processors to textual databases to hypertext.

In all these applications, the computer is a tool for symbolic writing. In the past couple of decades, however, the computer has been serving as a tool for a different kind of representation: graphic representation. The great success of computer-generated graphics and computer-controlled multimedia has exposed a new mass audience to electronic technology. Viewing computer graphics is also a quite different experience from reading text in a word processor. The viewer is not interacting with a symbolic structure; he or she is instead enjoying a perceptual experience provided by the machine. In graphics applications (and often in multimedia as well), the computer is functioning as a perceptual manipulator, creating or re-creating for us a world of sight and sound. When the computer is used to control recorded video clips, it is presenting segments of a televised world, and television is a medium that advertises itself as a re-creation of perceived reality. Computer graphics and animation are also attempts to create a perceptual world. Sometimes, this world resembles the real one; sometimes, it is intentionally distorted—for example, in cartoon animation. The appeal is to visual and aural perceptions: what communication goes on is through perception rather than through mathematical or alphabetic symbols. In these applications, the computer is much closer in spirit to television than to its traditional uses as a writing technology—for broadcast television too is a perceptual medium.

Perhaps the most compelling demonstrations of computer-mediated perception come from three-dimensional graphics and virtual reality. Three-dimensional environments and virtual reality present the user with a visual world that is wholly created and controlled by the machine: the user is immersed in a synthetic perceptual world. The virtual room or landscape is drawn in perspective, and when the user changes his or her view by a movement of the head, the perspective is redrawn to match. The computer has replaced our familiar perceptual world with another that has its own convincing visual logic. Virtual reality is at the moment the highest of high tech, but the goal of re-creating the perceptual world is centuries old. Its origins can be traced back at least to the development of linear perspective and realism in Renaissance painting—techniques meant to convince the viewer that the painting was a view into a real, or at least possible, world. Realism in some form dominated Western painting until the development of photography in the nineteenth century. Photography then led to animated photography, that is, film. Film was more lifelike in the sense that the image now moved. Then came electronic photography or television, which was not

more precise than film but again more lifelike in the sense that it could
be immediate. Film is always recorded, but television can be "live."
With virtual reality, the view is "live" in a different sense: the virtual
world responds to the viewer's movements.

Virtual reality allows the viewer to step into the picture and move
around in it. In realistic painting and in photography, what you get
is only a framed view, a view that looks onto another world. There
is a sense of depth, but there is only one perspective, the one originally
defined by the artist or by the lens of the camera. And the viewer remains
separated from the view. Film puts the framed world in motion, but
the world is still separated from you. The same is true of television.
Because television cannot be more visually precise than film, it tries
another avenue. Broadcast television claims to be your window on the
world, bringing you news and events as they happen: a summit meeting,
the Olympics, a failed coup in Russia. The Persian Gulf War was an
extraordinary example of television's attempt to put you there: live
coverage was coming at times from both sides of the battle. But even
with live television, what the viewer sees is a flat, framed image.

In order to put the viewer in the scene, one has to define a common
space for the viewer and the image. Virtual reality takes the radical
approach of surrounding the viewer with the image. It permits the
viewer to pass through the frame into the depicted world. The goal
of virtual reality is to replace the world as we know it through our
senses with another world. This is the whole point of virtual reality
for telepresence (operating a robotic device at a safe distance), for
simulation (such as flight simulation), and for entertainment uses. What
virtual reality attempts to eliminate is any sense of difference or
separation between the viewer and the view. And computer-controlled
multimedia is often conceived in the same spirit as virtual reality.
Multimedia on a computer screen or separate monitor does not surround
the viewer, but it is responsive to the viewer's actions. The viewer can
press a button or type a command and get a new view. Multimedia
puts the viewer operationally at the center of a changing world, whereas
virtual reality puts the viewer visually at the center. In either case, the
emphasis is on creating a world that the user can both visit and (to
some extent) control.

Multimedia, virtual reality, interactive, and even conventional linear
television are all examples of electronically mediated perception. There
is nothing inherently wrong with this technology. What concerns me
is first that users may tend to misconstrue the experience that the
technology offers. It remains a mediated experience. Yet there is a strong
tendency to forget the mediating character of the technology, to imagine
that what the screen shows is reality. This complaint has of course

been made about broadcast television for decades—that users tend to assume that what they see is unmediated perceptual reality. The same problem exists with the new computer-controlled manifestations, particularly virtual reality. So we get the strange notion that virtual reality can put the user into immediate experiential contact with a world of his or her choosing. One enthusiast for virtual reality, Jaron Lanier, has suggested that "in virtual reality you can visit the world of the dinosaur, then become a Tyrannosaurus. Not only can you see DNA, you can experience what it's like to be a molecule" (Ditlea 1989, 97). Lanier speaks as if there were such an experience—as if you as a human subject could enter into an immediate intuitive relationship with the creatures of the Jurassic Period or with inanimate molecules. It is odd enough to ask what it would be like to be a Tyrannosaurus, but it is utterly incoherent to ask what it is like to be a molecule. A molecule is a mathematical and scientific construct. In other words, it belongs far more obviously to the world of symbolic representation than to the world of perception. The danger is that electronic media of perception will encourage some to think that they can replace symbolic representation with pure perception. If that danger seems remote, consider the fact the Lanier has already made precisely that claim: that virtual reality will usher in an era of what he calls "post-symbolic communication" (see Bolter 1991, 229-31). This is really a new version of the myth of presence—that one can forget the mediating technology and place oneself in direct contact with an objective reality. With the myth of presence and the reliance on media of perception, the whole notion of reading and writing is challenged—and not as hypertext challenges the traditional definition by providing new opportunities for symbolic interaction. The myth of presence suggests that we can do without reading and writing altogether. It suggests that symbolic structures of our culture (electronic texts as well as conventional printed books) can be replaced with electronic imagery.

Here is an important dichotomy. The computer as hypertext belongs to the tradition of the printed book or earlier forms of writing technology. The computer as graphics engine belongs to the tradition of television, radio, photography, and even realistic painting. These different traditions correspond to different forms of communication and ultimately to different kinds of knowledge: abstract or symbolic knowledge on the one hand and perceptual or procedural knowledge on the other. There is the familiar adage that a picture is worth a thousand words. In fact, no amount of verbal description can contain or constrain a picture, for a picture is simply a different form of communication. Yet the same is true in reverse. A paragraph of prose cannot be translated into a picture. Even descriptive prose is a form of symbolic communication in language that has no visual equivalent, although it may have visual analogues.

In the computer, too, text and graphics are complementary forms of communication. The question is how can we combine these two orthogonal information spaces: the visual space of graphics with the semantic space of text. In the business world, we are witnessing a number of attempted mergers: attempts to bring together the computer, the television, and the telephone into attractive packages for office or home use. Hardware and software manufacturers, entertainment companies, and telecommunications companies are busily forming alliances. All are eager to market products like the Personal Digital Assistants, combinations of faxes, telephones, databases, and notepads; two-way television for the home; video-telephones; and so on.

Many of these proposals emphasize graphics and video at the expense of textual and symbolic communication. The real challenge, I would suggest, is to insist on the importance of symbolic representation and communication in the coming development of electronic applications. In this way, we can achieve new forms of communication that combine graphics with the symbolically dense character of computerized text. The desktop metaphor of today's personal computers already points the way to such a combination: graphic elements or icons are used in conjunction with conventional alphabetic text. Hypermedia applications also show how text, graphics, animation, and video can coexist in the space of the computer. But here I would distinguish, as some others do, between multimedia and hypermedia. In hypermedia, the point is not merely to present sounds and images but to establish and present sounds and images as part of a hypertextual web. Multimedia images are related to one another and also often to elements of ASCII text. In other words, the multimedia elements are themselves textualized: they no longer pretend to be simple recorded perceptions and become instead part of a larger symbolic structure.

AN ECLECTIC FUTURE

The future of electronic communication promises to be even more eclectic than the present situation. Two- and three-dimensional graphics and animation may soon become as common in the electronic writing space as the textual databases and hypertextual documents with which we are now familiar. There will likely be two-way video and interactive television. There will likely be virtual reality games that offer the viewer the experience of being a dinosaur. There should also be applications that integrate computer graphics into symbolic structures. These applications can define a new typography, a new kind of book that can flourish only in electronic writing space. The work of the researchers here at this conference will help to insure that this new writing space remains rich in symbolic content. If we can retain and enhance the symbolic richness of this space, then the essence of reading and writing will be preserved, and readers and writers in the electronic age will remain in touch with the five-thousand-year-long tradition of symbolic communication.

ACKNOWLEDGMENTS

Portions of these remarks were delivered at the SIGDOC '93 conference held at the University of Waterloo in London, Ontario, in October 1993.

REFERENCES

Bolter, Jay David. 1991. *Writing Space: The Computer, Hypertext, and the History of Writing*. Hillsdale, N.J.: Erlbaum.

Ditlea, Steve. 1989. Another World: Inside Artificial Reality. *PC Computing* 2(11): 90-99, 102.

Douglas, Jane Yellowlees. 1991. Understanding the Act of Reading: The WOE Beginner's Guide to Dissection. *Writing on the Edge* 2(2): 112-25.

Eisenstein, Elizabeth. 1979. *The Printing Press as an Agent of Change*. 2 vols. Cambridge: Cambridge University Press.

Jaszi, Peter. 1992. On the Author Effect: Contemporary Copyright and Collective Creativity. *Cardozo Arts and Entertainment Law Journal* 10(2): 293-320.

Joyce, Michael. 1988. Siren Shapes: Exploratory and Constructive Hypertexts. *Academic Computing* 3(4): 10-14, 37-42.

Joyce, Michael. 1989. *afternoon, a story*. [Computer software]. Watertown, Mass.: Eastgate Systems.

Landow, George P. 1991. *Dickens Web*. [Computer software]. Watertown, Mass.: Eastgate Systems.

Landow, George P. 1992. *Hypertext: The Convergence of Contemporary Critical Theory and Technology*. Baltimore: Johns Hopkins University Press.

Landow, George P., and Paul Delany, eds. 1991. *Hypermedia and Literary Studies*. Cambridge, Mass.: MIT Press.

Lanham, Richard. 1989. The Electronic Word: Literary Study and the Digital Revolution. *New Literary History* 20(2): 265-90.

Moulthrop, Stuart. 1989. In the Zones: Hypertext and the Politics of Intrepretation. *Writing on the Edge* 1(1): 18-27.

Moulthrop, Stuart. 1992. *Victory Garden*. [Computer software]. Watertown, Mass.: Eastgate Systems.

Woodmansee, Martha. 1984. The Genius and the Copyright: Economic and Legal Conditions of the Emergence of the 'Author'. *Eighteenth-Century Studies* 17(4): 425-48.

Woodmansee, Martha. 1992. On the Author Effect: Recovering Collectivity. *Cardozo Arts and Entertainment Law Journal* 10(2): 279-92.

SUSAN HOCKEY

Center for Electronic Texts in the Humanities
Rutgers and Princeton Universities
New Brunswick, New Jersey

Electronic Texts in the Humanities: A Coming of Age

ABSTRACT

Electronic texts have been used for research and teaching in the humanities ever since the end of the 1940s. This paper charts the development of various applications in literary computing including concordances, text retrieval, stylistic studies, scholarly editing, and metrical analyses. Many electronic texts now exist as a by-product of these activities. Efforts to use these texts for new applications led to the need for a common encoding scheme, which has now been developed in the form of the Text Encoding Initiative's implementation of the Standard Generalized Markup Language (SGML), and to the need for commonly used procedures for documenting electronic texts, which are just beginning to emerge. The need to separate data from software is now better understood, and the variety of CD-ROM-based text and software packages currently available is posing significant problems of support for libraries as well as delivering only partial solutions to many scholarly requirements. Attention is now turning to research towards more advanced network-based delivery mechanisms.

INTRODUCTION

It is now forty-five years since Father Roberto Busa started work on the first-ever humanities electronic text project to compile a concordance to the works of St. Thomas Aquinas and related authors (Busa 1974-). Since that time, many other electronic text projects have begun, and a body of knowledge and expertise has gradually evolved. Many lessons have been learned from these activities, and it is now possible to make some realistic projections for the future development of electronic text usage in the humanities. Until recently, almost all work has been done on electronic transcriptions of text rather than on digitized images. The discussion in this paper will concentrate on transcriptions, which are referred to as text, but the implications for images will be noted briefly.

The focus of the paper is on primary source material in the humanities. This can be literary text, which is prose, verse, or drama, or a combination of these. It may also be documentary and take the form of letters, memoranda, charters, transcripts of speeches, papyri, inscriptions, newspapers, and the like. Other texts are studied for linguistic purposes, notably collections of text forming language corpora and early dictionaries. Many humanities texts are complex in nature, and the interpretation of the complex features within them is often the subject of scholarly debate. Some texts contain several natural languages and/or writing systems. Others have variant spellings, critical apparatus with variant readings, marginalia, editorial emendations, and annotations, as well as complex and sometimes parallel canonical referencing schemes. An adequate representation of these features is needed for scholarly analysis.

APPLICATIONS IN LITERARY COMPUTING

The earliest and most obvious application was the production of printed word indexes and concordances, often with associated frequency lists. A word index is a list of words in a text where each word (keyword) is accompanied by a reference indicating the location of the occurrences of that word in the text. In a concordance, each occurrence of each word is also accompanied by some surrounding context, which may be a few words or up to several lines. A word frequency list shows the number of times that each word occurs. Words would normally appear in alphabetical order, but they could also be alphabetized or sorted by their endings, which is useful for the study of morphology or rhyme schemes, or in frequency order where the most common words or the *hapax legomena* (once-occurring words) can easily be seen. Specialized concordances show words listed by their references (for example, by speaker within a play) or sorted according to the words before or after the keyword, or by the number of letters they contain. It can be seen that the production of concordances was typically a mechanical batch process that could generate vast amounts of printout.

Early on, attention was also paid to defining the alphabetical order for sorting words in a variety of languages, for example, transcriptions of Greek and Russian as well as Spanish where *ch, ll,* and *rr* are separate letters of the alphabet. Ways of dealing with hyphens, apostrophes, accented characters, editorial emendations, and the like were soon devised, and in most cases, the choice was left to the user. A major strength of two of the most widely used concordance and retrieval programs today, Micro-OCP and TACT, is their flexibility in alphabet definitions. More detail on alphabetization and different types of concordances may be found in Howard-Hill (1979), Hockey (1980), and Sinclair (1991).

By the mid-1950s, a number of other concordance-based projects had begun. Brandwood's (1956) work on Plato formed the basis of a stylistic study. In France, plans for the Trésor de la Langue Française, a vast collection of literary works since the time of the revolution, began in 1959 to aid the production of the new French dictionary (Quémada 1959). These texts form the basis of the ARTFL (American Research on the Treasury of the French Language) database at the University of Chicago. Other groups or projects of note in the 1960s include Howard-Hill's (1969) Oxford Shakespeare Concordances, word frequency counts of Swedish (Gothenburg) (Allén 1970), Classical Latin texts at Liège (Delatte and Évrard 1961), Medieval Latin in Louvain-la-Neuve (Tombeur 1973), and work on various Italian texts at Pisa under the direction of Antonio Zampolli (1973). At that time, the only means of input was uppercase-only punched cards or, sometimes, paper tape. Burton (1981a, 1981b, 1981c, 1982) describes these projects and others in her history of concordance making from Father Busa until the 1970s, which makes interesting reading.

The interactive text retrieval programs that we use today are a derivative of concordances, since what they actually search is a precompiled index or concordance of the text. Besides their obvious application as a reference tool, concordance and text retrieval programs can be used for a variety of scholarly applications, one of the earliest of which was the study of style and the investigation of disputed authorship. The mechanical study of style pre-dates computers by a long time. Articles by T. C. Mendenhall at the end of the last century describe his investigations into the style of Shakespeare, Bacon, Marlowe, and many other authors, using what seems to have been the first-ever word-counting machine. Mendenhall (1901, 101-2) notes

> the excellent and entirely satisfactory manner in which the heavy task of counting was performed by the [two] ladies who undertook it. . . . The operation of counting was greatly facilitated by the construction of a simple counting machine by which the registration of a word of any given number of letters was made by touching a button marked with that number.

Mendenhall's findings were not without interest, since he discovered that Shakespeare has more words of four letters than any other length, whereas almost all other authors peak at three. Many other stylistic studies have based their investigations on the usage of common words, or function words. These are independent of content, and authors often use them unconsciously. Synonyms have also been studied as have collocations or pairs of words occurring close together. The work of Mosteller and Wallace (1964) on the *Federalist Papers* is generally considered to be a classic authorship study, since the twelve disputed papers were known by external evidence to be either by Hamilton or by Madison and there was also a lot of other material of known authorship (Hamilton or Madison) on the same subject matter. A study of common words showed that Hamilton prefers "while," whereas Madison almost always uses "whilst." Other words favored by one or the other of them included "enough" and "upon."

Anthony Kenny's (1978) investigation of the *Aristotelian Ethics* was based on function words, which he divided into categories such as particles and prepositions, that were derived from his reading of printed concordances. He was able to show that the usage of common words in three books that appear in both the *Nicomachean* and the *Eudemian Ethics* is closer to *Eudemian Ethics*. More recently, John Burrows's (1987) examination of Jane Austen's novels has become something of a landmark study in literary computing. By analyzing their usage of common words, he was able to show gender differences in the characters in the novels and to characterize their idiolects. These and similar studies employ some simple statistical methodologies for which Kenny (1982) is a useful introduction. They also show the need to index every word in the text and to distinguish between homographic forms.

Concordances can also be a valuable tool for the historical lexicographer, and several large textbases were originally compiled for this purpose. The Dictionary of Old English (DOE) in Toronto created the complete Corpus of Old English, which totals some three million words. Lexicographers at the DOE have created complete concordances of all this corpus and select citations from the concordances for the dictionary entries (Healey 1989). The most frequent word in Old English occurs about 15,000 times, and it was just possible for a lexicographer to read all the concordance entries for it. This is obviously not feasible for much larger corpora such as the Trésor de la Langue Française. A notable modern example of what has become known as corpus lexicography is Collins's *COBUILD English Dictionary*, which was compiled using a twenty-million-word corpus of English (Sinclair 1987).

Other electronic texts have been created for the analysis of meter and rhyme schemes. In the 1960s, scansion programs existed for Greek and Latin hexameter verse (Ott 1973). Metrical dictionaries were compiled for authors as diverse as Hopkins (Dilligan and Bender 1973) and Euripides (Philippides 1981). Sound patterns have been studied in Homer

(Packard 1974), some German poets (Chisholm 1981), and Dante (Robey 1987).

The traditional scholarly editing process has also led to the creation of some electronic texts. In simple terms, this process has consisted of collating the manuscripts, establishing the textual tradition, compiling an authoritative text, compiling the critical apparatus, and then printing text. In the 1960s, computer programs to collate manuscripts began to appear, and it was soon realized that collation could not be treated as a completely automatic process and that, because of the lineation, verse was easier to deal with than prose. Robinson's (forthcoming) COLLATE program was developed after a study of earlier systems. It has a graphical user interface and is by far the most flexible collation program.

Many early humanities projects were hampered by design forced upon them by the limitations of hardware and software. Until disk storage became more widely available in the 1970s, texts and associated material were stored on magnetic tape, which could only be accessed sequentially. Disk storage allowed random access, but data were still constrained within the structures of database programs, particularly relational databases where the information is stored as a set of rectangular tables and is viewed as such by the user. Very little humanities-oriented information fits this format without some restructuring, which, more often than not, results in some loss of information.

Hypertext has provided a solution to data modeling for the humanities. It offers flexible data structures and provides a web of interrelated information, which can be annotated by the user if desired. An obvious application in the humanities is the presentation of primary and secondary material together. Images, sound, and video can be incorporated to aid the interpretation of the text. The traditional scholarly edition can be represented very effectively as a hypertext, but hypertext is a more obvious medium for presenting multiple versions of a text without privileging any particular one of them (Bornstein 1993). Other experiments have used hypertext to model the narrative structure of literature with a view to helping students understand it better (Sutherland forthcoming).

ELECTRONIC TEXTS TODAY

Many of the electronic texts that are in existence today were created as a by-product of research projects such as those described above. Large collections of text have been assembled by a few research institutes, mostly in Europe where public money has been provided for the study of language and its relation to the cultural heritage. Most other texts have been compiled by individuals for their own projects. These texts reflect the interests of those research groups or individuals, and it is perhaps questionable as to how many of them can be used for other scholarly purposes. These texts are ASCII files, not files that have been indexed for use by specific programs. Initial estimates show that 90 to 95 percent of texts fall into this category. For a variety of reasons, few of them have been made available for other scholars to use, and these scholars may find that they are not well suited to their purposes.

However, it was soon realized that considerable time and effort is required to create a good electronic text. Many existing texts have been keyboarded, and this is still the normal means of input. Optical character recognition (OCR) of some material became feasible in the early 1980s, but in general, it is only suitable for modern printed material. OCR systems tend to have difficulty with material printed before the end of the last century, newspapers, or anything else where the paper causes the ink to bleed, as well as material containing footnotes and marginalia, nonstandard characters and words in italic, or small capitals. Those systems that are trainable can be more suitable for humanities material, but these require some skill on the part of the operator. Hockey (1986) and the collection of papers assembled by the Netherlands Historical Data Archive (1993) give further information. More importantly, OCR also generates only a typographic representation or markup of the text, whereas experience with using texts has shown that this is inadequate for most kinds of processing and analysis. Most large data entry projects are choosing to have their data keyed, which allows some markup to be inserted at that time.

Recognizing the need to preserve electronic texts, the Oxford Text Archive (OTA) was established in 1976 to "offer scholars long term storage and maintenance of their electronic archives free of charge." It has amassed a large collection of electronic texts in many different formats and is committed to maintaining them on behalf of their depositors. Depending on the conditions determined by their depositors, OTA texts are made available to other individuals for research and teaching purposes at little cost. However, there is no guarantee of accuracy, and users of OTA texts are encouraged to send any updated versions that they may have created back to Oxford. Proud (1989) reports on the findings of a British Library sponsored project to review the Oxford Text Archive.

There have been a few systematic attempts to create or collect and archive texts for general-purpose scholarly use. The most notable one for a specific language is the Thesaurus Linguae Graecae (TLG), which began at Irvine, California, in 1972. It is now nearing completion of a databank of almost seventy million words of Classical Greek (Brunner 1991). The texts are distributed on a CD-ROM that contains plain ASCII files. They are not indexed in any way. In the late 1980s, the Packard Humanities Institute (PHI) compiled a complementary CD-ROM of all Classical Latin, which is about eight million words. The Women Writers' Project at Brown University is building a textbase of women's writing in English from 1330 to 1830 and contains many texts that are not readily accessible elsewhere. Begun in the 1980s, the Dartmouth Dante Project (DDP) is aiming to make available the text of the *Divine Comedy* and all major commentaries. The texts are stored and indexed using BRS-Search and can be accessed via Telnet to lib.dartmouth.edu then, at the prompt, type "connect dante."

A few other collections of text should be noted here. The Istituto di Linguistica Computazionale in Pisa has a large collection of literary and nonliterary works in Italian. Institutes funded by the German government at Bonn and Mannheim have been building text collections for many years. Bar-Ilan University in Israel is the home of the Responsa Project, and the Hebrew Academy in Jerusalem also has a substantial collection. Material in Welsh and other Celtic languages has been built up at Aberystwyth and elsewhere. The International Computer Archive of Modern English at Oslo concentrates on English-language corpora, and groups in various English-speaking countries are compiling corpora of their own usage of English. The British National Corpus is nearing completion of a hundred-million-word corpus of written and spoken English. Many other similar activities exist. The Georgetown University Center for Text and Technology maintains a catalog of projects and institutes that hold electronic texts but not the texts themselves. This catalog can be accessed most easily by Gopher to guvax.georgetown.edu. Lancashire (1991) is the most comprehensive source of information in print about humanities computing projects in general.

The Rutgers Inventory of Machine-Readable Texts in the Humanities is the only attempt to catalog existing electronic texts using standard bibliographic procedures (Hoogcarspel 1994). The Inventory is held on the Research Libraries Information Network (RLIN) and is maintained by the Center for Electronic Texts in the Humanities (CETH). It contains entries for many of the texts in the Oxford Text Archive, plus material from a number of other sources. The Inventory is now being developed by CETH staff who have prepared extensive guidelines for cataloging monographic electronic text files using *Anglo-American Cataloguing Rules*, 2d ed., (*AACR2*) and RLIN.

In the last few years, more electronic texts have begun to be made available by publishers or software vendors. These are the texts that are more likely now to be found in libraries. They are mostly CD-ROMs and are usually packaged with specific retrieval software. Examples include the *Global Jewish Database* on CD-ROM, the *New Oxford*

English Dictionary on CD-ROM, the CETEDOC CD-ROM of the Early Christian Fathers, and the WordCruncher disk of American literature. The CD-ROM versions of the *English Poetry Full-Text Database* and *Patrologia Latina* published by Chadwyck-Healey also fall into this category, although these texts are also available on magnetic tape for use with other software. Oxford University Press also publishes electronic texts, which are ASCII files. Their texts are particularly well documented, and most can be used with the Micro-OCP concordance program, which they also publish.

Some of these packaged products are relatively easy to use, but prospective purchasers might want to be aware of a number of issues before they launch into acquiring many of them. Almost every one of these products has its own user interface and query language. They are mostly designed for scholarly applications on what are complex texts. Therefore, it can take some time to understand their capabilities and to learn how to use them. If this proliferation of products continues, the cost of supporting them will not be insignificant. Librarians are not normally expected to show patrons how to read books, but they can expect to spend some considerable time in learning how to use these resources and showing them to users. Those that are easy to use may not satisfy many scholarly requirements. For example, on the WordCruncher CD-ROM, which is one of the easiest to use, the texts have been indexed in such a simple way that there is no way to distinguish between I in act and scene numbers (e.g., Act I) and the pronoun I. Several of these products are designed for the individual scholar to use on his or her own machine rather than for access by many people. They provide good facilities for storing search requests for future use, but this is not much help if twenty other people have stored new requests or modified existing ones in between. Another issue is just what words have been indexed and how. A response to any search request is only as good as the words that have been indexed. In some cases, this seems to have been determined by software developers who have little understanding of the nature of the material and the purposes for which it might be used. Other institutions have chosen to acquire texts in ASCII format and provide network access to them, usually with Open Text's PAT system. In this case, the burden of deciding what to index falls on the librarian, who is thus assuming some responsibility for the intellectual content of the material.

CREATING ELECTRONIC TEXTS FOR THE FUTURE

Creating an electronic text is a time-consuming and expensive process, and it therefore makes sense to invest for the future when doing it. Texts that are created specifically for one software program often cannot easily be used with others. The need to separate data from software is now well recognized. Data that are kept in an archival form independent of any hardware and software stand a much better chance of lasting for a long time because they can be moved from one system to another and because they can be used for different purposes and applications.

Experience has shown that an archival text needs markup and documentation for it to be of any use in the future. Markup makes explicit for computer processing things that are implicit to the human reader of a text. Markup is needed to identify the structural components of a text (chapter, stanza, act, scene, title) and enables specific areas or subsets of text to be searched and text that has been retrieved to be identified by references or other locators. It may also be used to encode analytic and interpretive features. Many humanities texts are complex in nature, and many different markup schemes have been created to encode their properties. Ones that have been in common use are COCOA, which is used by Micro-OCP and TACT, the beta code used by the Thesaurus Linguae Graecae, and the three-level referencing system used by WordCruncher. These markup schemes concentrate on the structure of a text, as opposed to schemes such as TeX and troff, which contain formatting instructions.

Following a planning meeting in 1987, a major international effort to create guidelines for encoding electronic texts was launched by the Association for Computers and the Humanities, the Association for Computational Linguistics, and the Association for Literary and Linguistic Computing. This project, known as the Text Encoding Initiative (TEI), brought together groups of scholars, librarians, and computer professionals to examine many different types of texts and to compile a comprehensive list of the features within those texts.

The TEI soon determined that the Standard Generalized Markup Language (SGML) was a sound basis for the development of the new encoding scheme. SGML became an international standard in 1986. It is a metalanguage within which encoding schemes can be defined. It is descriptive rather than prescriptive and thus can form the basis of the reusable text. It permits multiple and possibly conflicting views to be encoded within the same text. It is incremental so that new encodings can be added to a text without detriment to what is already there. SGML-encoded texts are also ASCII files, and so their longevity can be assured. The TEI's application of SGML is very wide ranging. It provides base tag sets for prose, verse, drama, dictionaries, transcripts of speech, and terminological data. To these can be added tag sets for textual criticism, transcription of primary sources, language corpora, formulae and tables, graphics, hypermedia, analytical tools, and names

and dates. The application has been designed so that other tag sets
can be added later. The first definitive version of the TEI guidelines
has very recently been published (Sperberg-McQueen and Burnard 1994).

Many existing electronic texts have little or no documentation
associated with them. Often, it is difficult to establish what the text
is, where it came from, and, in a few cases, even what language it is
in. There seem to be two main reasons for this. In some cases, the
text was created by an individual who was so familiar with that text
that he or she did not find it necessary to record any documentation
about it. In other cases, the person who created the text did not have
any model to follow for documenting the text and thus recorded only
minimal information about it. Where documentation does exist, it is
in many different formats, making the task of compiling information
about electronic texts extremely difficult.

As part of its recommendations, the TEI has proposed an electronic
text file header to meet the needs of librarians who will manage the
texts, scholars who will use them, and computer software developers
who will write programs to operate on them. The TEI header consists
of a set of SGML elements that include bibliographic details of the
electronic text and the source from which it was taken, information
about the principles that governed the encoding of the text, any
classificatory material, and a revision history that records the changes
made to the text.

DIGITAL IMAGING

Many of the lessons learned from the creation and use of electronic
texts can also be applied to digital imaging of manuscripts and textual
material. The potential of digital imaging for preservation and access
is now being exploited in numerous projects. From this point of view,
the archival role is obviously very important. Most of the cost in digital
imaging is in taking the object to and from the camera, and so it makes
sense to digitize at the highest resolution possible. Storing the image
in a proprietary format linked to some specific software will lead to
all the same problems that have been experienced with text stored in
a proprietary indexing program. It will not be possible to guarantee
that the image will be accessible in the future or that it can be used
for other purposes. Documentation and provenance information are just
as important for images. SGML can be used to describe material that
is not itself textual. The TEI header would need only a slight modification to be used for images and offers a route to using both text
and image together. The TEI's hypertext mechanisms allow pointers
from the text to the image and can form the basis of a system that
operates on the transcription of the text but displays the image to the user.

ANALYSIS TOOLS

Experience of working with electronic literary texts has highlighted a number of analysis tools and features that have been found to be useful. The most obvious is the need to index every word and not to have a stop list. This is important for many stylistic and linguistic studies that have concentrated on the usage of common words. It also avoids the omission of some homographic forms; for example, the English auxiliary verbs "will" and "might" are also nouns. The punctuation is often important in early printed texts, and some scholars may want to search on that. In other languages, it provides a simple key to the examination of the ends of sentences, for example, clausulae in Classical Latin. Words that are not in the main language of the texts need to be indexed separately to avoid homographs such as "font" in English and French, or "canes" in English and Latin. The ability to search on the ends of words is also useful, particularly for verse and in languages that inflect heavily. A very small number of resources provide an index by endings. For others, this kind of search can take some time as it can only be handled by a sequential search on the word index. A good text will also have structural encoding, and the user may want to have the option of restricting proximity searches to within certain structural boundaries or allowing them to extend beyond a boundary. For example, finding "tree" within ten words of "flower" may not be useful if "tree" is the last word of a chapter and "flower" occurs at the beginning of the next chapter.

There has not been as much progress in the development of tools to analyze text. Essentially, we are still able to search text only by specifying strings of characters, possibly linked by Boolean operators, whereas most users are interested in concepts, themes, and the like. String searches cannot effectively disambiguate homographic forms, for example, "bank" as in money bank as opposed to "bank" of the river or the verb "bank" (used of an airplane), or Latin "canes" as "dogs" or "you will sing."

Computer programs to perform morphological analysis, lemmatization, syntactic analysis, and parsing have been used experimentally for some time, but our understanding of these is still only partial. The most successful parsing programs claim accuracy of about 95 percent. Morphological analysis has been done reasonably well for some languages, for example, Ancient Greek, but there are no widely available general-purpose programs that are suitable for literature. Father Busa recognized the need to lemmatize his concordance to St. Thomas Aquinas in order to make it more useful to scholars, but this was done manually, which is still the only way to ensure accurate data.

In Busa 1992, he reflects on the lack of intellectual progress and on how little the computer can still do.

Because of its nature, literature is harder to deal with than many other types of text, and there have been relatively few attempts to apply more sophisticated language analysis algorithms to it. After years of working with rule-based systems, researchers in computational linguistics are turning to the compilation of large-scale lexical resources and knowledge bases for use by natural language understanding systems. The usual method has been to create an electronic version of a printed dictionary and restructure that within the computer as a lexical database that contains morphological analyses, lemmas, frequent collocations, and other information that would help to disambiguate homographic words. However, printed dictionaries are designed for humans not for computers to use. They exist to document the language and thus contain many citations for uncommon usages of words but very few (in proportion to their occurrences) of usual usages. A computer program must look every word up in the dictionary and thus needs more information about common words. This has led to the current interest in language corpora, which are large bodies of text from which information can be derived to augment electronic dictionaries. In many ways, this development represents another coming of age, since the initial methodologies used by computational linguists to analyze large corpora are concordance based and are very similar to those that have been used in literary computing for many years. Once information about word usage has been derived, it can be encoded within the text (using SGML markup) and used to train and refine future programs, which will eventually perform more accurate analyses. We can only hope that this coming of age will lead to better access technologies and to the computer doing more for us.

REFERENCES

Allén, Sture. 1970. Vocabulary Data Processing. In *Proceedings of the International Conference on Nordic* and *General Linguistics,* ed. Hreinn Benediktsson, 235-61. Reykjavik: Visindafelag Islendiga.

Bornstein, George. 1993. What is the Text of a Poem by Yeats? In *Palimpsest: Editorial Theory in the Humanities,* ed. George Bornstein and Ralph G. Williams, 167-93. Ann Arbor: University of Michigan Press.

Brandwood, Leonard. 1956. Analysing Plato's Style with an Electronic Computer. *Bulletin of the Institute of Classical Studies 3*: 45-54.

Brunner, Theodore F. 1991. The Thesaurus Linguae Graecae: Classics and the Computer. *Library Hi Tech 9*(1): 61-67.

Burrows, J. F. 1987. *Computation into Criticism: A Study of Jane Austen's Novels and an Experiment in Method.* Oxford: Clarendon Press.

Burton, Dolores M. 1981a. Automated Concordances and Word Indexes: The Fifties. *Computers and the Humanities 15*(1): 1-14.

Burton, Dolores M. 1981b. Automated Concordances and Word Indexes: The Early Sixties and the Early Centers. *Computers and the Humanities 15*(2): 83-100.

Burton, Dolores M. 1981c. Automated Concordances and Word Indexes: The Process, the Programs, and the Products. *Computers and the Humanities 15*(3): 139-54.

Burton, Dolores M. 1982. Automated Concordances and Word-Indexes: Machine Decisions and Editorial Revisions. *Computers and the Humanities 16*(4): 195-218.

Busa, Roberto, S. J. 1974-. *Index Thomisticus*. Stuttgart-Bad, Connstatt: Fromann-Holzboog.

Busa, Roberto, S. J. 1992. Half a Century of Literary Computing: Towards a 'New' Philology. (Reports from Colloquia at Tübingen). *Literary & Linguistic Computing 7*(1): 69-73.

Chisholm, David. 1981. Prosodic Approaches to Twentieth-Century Verse. *ALLC Journal 2*(1): 34-40.

Delatte, L., and É. Évrard. 1961. Un Laboratoire d'Analyse Statistique des Langues Anciennes à l'Université de Liège. *L'Antiquité Classique 30:* 429-44.

Dilligan, R. J., and T. K. Bender. 1973. The Lapses of Time: A Computer-Assisted Investigation of English Prosody. In *The Computer and Literary Studies,* ed. A. J. Aitken, Richard W. Bailey, and N. Hamilton-Smith, 239-52. Edinburgh: Edinburgh University Press.

Healey, Antoinette diPaolo. 1989. The Corpus of the Dictionary of Old English: Its Delimination, Compilation and Application. Paper presented at the Fifth Annual Conference of the UW Centre for the New Oxford English Dictionary, St. Catherine's College, Oxford, England.

Hockey, Susan. 1980. *A Guide to Computer Applications in the Humanities.* London: Duckworth; Baltimore: Johns Hopkins University Press.

Hockey, Susan. 1986. OCR: The Kurzweil Data Entry Machine. *Literary & Linguistic Computing 1*(2): 63-67.

Hoogcarspel, Annelies. 1994. The Rutgers Inventory of Machine-Readable Texts in the Humanities. *Information Technology and Libraries 13*(1): 27-34.

Howard-Hill, T. H. 1969. The Oxford Old-Spelling Shakespeare Concordances. *Studies in Bibliography 22:* 143-64.

Howard-Hill, T. H. 1979. *Literary Concordances: A Guide to the Preparation of Manual and Computer Concordances.* Oxford: Pergamon Press.

Kenny, Anthony. 1978. *The Aristotelian Ethics: A Study of the Relationship between the Eudemian and Nicomachean Ethics of Aristotle.* Oxford: Oxford University Press.

Kenny, Anthony. 1982. *The Computation of Style.* Oxford: Pergamon Press.

Lancashire, Ian., ed. 1991. *The Humanities Computing Yearbook 1989-90: A Comprehensive Guide to Software and Other Resources.* Oxford: Clarendon Press.

Mendenhall, T. C. 1901. A Mechanical Solution of a Literary Problem. *Popular Science Monthly 60* (December): 97-105.

Mosteller, Frederick, and David L. Wallace. 1964. *Inference and Disputed Authorship: The Federalist.* Reading, Mass.: Addison-Wesley.

Netherlands Historical Data Archive. 1993. *Optical Character Recognition in the Historical Discipline: Proceedings of an International Workgroup.* Netherlands Historical Data Archive, Nijmegen Institute for Cognition and Information.

Ott, Wilhelm. 1973. Metrical Analysis of Latin Hexameter: The Automation of a Philological Research Project. In *Linguistica Matematica e Calcolatori (Atti del Convegno e della Prima Scuola Internazionale, Pisa 1970),* ed. Antonio Zampolli, 379-90. Florence: Leo S. Olschki.

Packard, David W. 1974. Sound-Patterns in Homer. *Transactions of the American Philological Association 104:* 239-60.

Philippides, Dia Mary L. 1981. *The Iambic Trimeter of Euripides.* New York: Arno Press.

Proud, Judith K. 1989. *The Oxford Text Archive.* British Library Research and Development Report. London: British Library.

Quémada, Bernard. 1959. La Mécanisation dans les Recherches Lexicologiques. *Cahiers de Lexicologie 1:* 7-46.

Robey, David. 1987. Sound and Sense in the Divine Comedy. *Literary & Linguistic Computing 2*(2): 108-15.

Robinson, Peter M. W. Forthcoming. COLLATE: A Program for Interactive Collation
    of Large Manuscript Traditions. In *Research in Humanities Computing*, vol. 3, ed.
    Susan Hockey and Nancy Ide, 32-45. Oxford: Oxford University Press.
Sinclair, John M., ed. 1987. *Looking Up: An Account of the COBUILD Project in Lexical
    Computing*. London: Collins.
Sinclair, John M. 1991. *Corpus, Concordance, Collocation*. Oxford: Oxford University
    Press.
Sperberg-McQueen, C. M., and Lou Burnard, eds. 1994. *Guidelines for the Encoding
    and Interchange of Electronic Texts*. Chicago and Oxford: Association for Computers
    and the Humanities, Association for Computational Linguistics, Association for
    Literary and Linguistic Computing.
Sutherland, Kathryn. Forthcoming. Waiting for Connections: Hypertexts, Multiplots,
    and the Engaged Reader. In *Research in Humanities Computing*, vol. 3, ed. Susan
    Hockey and Nancy Ide, 46-58. Oxford: Oxford University Press.
Tombeur, P. 1973. Research Carried Out at the Centre de Traitement Electronique des
    Documents of the Catholic University of Louvain. In *The Computer and Literary
    Studies*, ed. A. J. Aitken, Richard W. Bailey, and N. Hamilton-Smith, 335-40.
    Edinburgh: Edinburgh University Press.
Zampolli, Antonio. 1973. La Section Linguistique du CNUCE. In *Linguistica Matematica
    e Calcolatori (Atti del Convegno e della Prima Scuola Internazionale, Pisa 1970)*,
    ed. Antonio Zampolli, 133-99. Florence: Leo S. Olschki.

C. M. SPERBERG-M^CQUEEN

Editor
Text Encoding Initiative
University of Illinois at Chicago

The Text Encoding Initiative: Electronic Text Markup for Research

ABSTRACT

This paper describes the goals and work of the Text Encoding Initiative (TEI), an international cooperative project to develop and disseminate guidelines for the encoding and interchange of electronic text for research purposes. It begins by outlining some basic problems that arise in the attempt to represent textual material in computers and some problems that arise in the attempt to encourage the sharing and reuse of electronic textual resources. These problems provide the necessary background for a brief review of the origins and organization of the Text Encoding Initiative itself. Next, the paper describes the rationale for the decision of the TEI to use the Standard Generalized Markup Language (SGML) as the basis for its work. Finally, the work accomplished by the TEI is described in general terms, and some attempt is made to clarify what the project has and has not accomplished.

INTRODUCTION

This paper describes the goals and work of the Text Encoding Initiative (TEI), an international cooperative project to develop and disseminate guidelines for the encoding and interchange of electronic text for research purposes. In the simplest possible terms, the TEI is an attempt to find better ways to put texts into computers for the purposes of doing research that uses those texts.

The paper will first discuss some basic problems involved in that process, then some practical aspects of the reuse and reusability of textual resources. With the context thus clarified, the origins and organization of the TEI itself can then be described briefly, along with the reasons behind the decision of the TEI to use the Standard Generalized Markup Language (SGML) as the basis for its work. Finally, the work accomplished by the TEI can be described in general terms, and some attempt made to clarify what the project has and has not accomplished.

REPRESENTING TEXT ELECTRONICALLY

In the introductory paragraph of this paper, the TEI was described as an international cooperative effort to find better ways "to put texts into computers." The first problem encountered when one tries to set about this task is that, in a literal sense, it cannot be done. Texts *cannot* be placed inside computers—if only for the pedantic but simple reason that texts are abstract linguistic, literary, aesthetic, referential, historical, and cultural objects, while computers are physical objects controlled by complex electronic circuitry. Abstract objects cannot be "put into" physical objects. In this respect, text is on the same footing as numbers, which, being abstract mathematical objects, similarly elude any efforts to place them inside physical devices. The solution is the same in both cases: the best one can do is to make the physical object mimic the salient features of the abstract object and to manipulate this physical *representation* of the abstract object.

The value in this admittedly pedantic quibble is that it forces us to face squarely the critical fact that our problem is thus one of *mimesis* (or to put it into computational terms, one of finding a suitable *representation* for the data). Instead of a simple mechanical or quasi-mechanical process that can be carried out without reflection, the representation of texts in electronic form involves the same complications and limitations that inhere in any act of representation. Representations never reproduce all aspects of their objects with perfect fidelity; they invariably omit some aspect or other of the object represented and, by this omission, distort it. Designing a method for representing some object by means of some other object therefore ineluctably requires the designer not simply to decide what is salient and must be included but equally what is expendable and gets tossed off the sled in an emergency. It is no wonder, then, that systematic schemes for the representation of whole classes of objects reflect the biases, preconceptions, and preoccupations of their designers.

And yet for all their flaws, representations are absolutely essential to any intellectual work at all, because they are essential to understanding. Because they are selective reproductions of what is thought salient about some object, representations serve to reify our understanding of the object represented, and they allow us to test that understanding and compare it with different views of the object—themselves reified by different representations.

These issues are familiar, in a restricted form, to any computer programmer who has had to consider whether to represent a numeric quantity as a short integer, a long integer, or a real number at single or double precision; they are much less widely familiar when it comes to the representation of textual data in electronic form, even though textual data are intellectually much more complex and much less well defined than integers and real numbers—perhaps in part *because* text is less well defined.

If, as Niklaus Wirth has put it, "programs = algorithms + data structures," then a suitable method of representing textual data might be expected to represent a significant step forward in computational work with language and literature. Such a representation should make it easier to use computers to work with texts and thus contribute to the success of textual research and indirectly to the understanding of texts and of textual information.

If one asks oneself about the nature of a suitable representation for texts in electronic form, what it would mean to "represent a text" in a machine, one discovers a second advantage of the pedantic quibble with which this paper began. For, being forced to pose this question in terms of representations, one is equally forced to recognize that—since representations are typically utilitarian in character—the answer will inevitably be "it depends; suitable for what?" Before defining the qualities of a "suitable representation," one must specify what use is to be made of it. One is thus led to ask what it is that those interested in text in electronic form want to *do* with it.

A first simple answer is that we want to use it in the normal manner. Since it is text and we are readers, we will want to read it. Users will want to disseminate it to friends, colleagues, or the public across the network. As researchers, they will want to study it: literary scholars will want to study its themes, images, style, narrative structure, vocabulary, and diction; linguists will want to study its lexicon, morphology, parts of speech, syntax, or discourse structure. Textual critics will want to edit it, to study the variants in different manuscripts or early editions of the work, collate the various versions, and annotate it. Even those who work most intensively with computers will probably want to print the text out, nicely formatted, on paper. As time passes, the chances are good that people will want to link the text to related material, be it other versions of the same text, commentary, graphics or illustrations, images of manuscripts, or yet other materials, either locally or in a network environment.

Equally important, we will want to *reuse* it. The costs of getting material into an acceptable electronic form are high enough to make reuse of data an important goal in virtually every computational field, from the natural sciences to the social sciences to the humanities. In the humanities, this fact is reflected in the increasing numbers of projects whose aim is to create generally usable bodies of electronic textual material intended for use by others; in computational linguistics, it is reflected in the growth of projects to develop standard reference corpora for use in all areas of natural-language processing, as well as in efforts to create "opportunistic corpora" gathering together as much textual material as can be obtained.[1]

Third, because many of those interested in electronic text are researchers, it is a safe prediction that they will eventually want to do things with this electronic text that no one has yet invented or imagined. It is in the nature of research that not only the answers to the questions but frequently the questions themselves are not known at the outset of a project.

In other words, there is no satisfactory answer to the question of what we want to do with texts, once we put them into electronic form. In the long run, we want to do *everything*. This is not a wholly vacuous answer to the question; it does have the consequence that we want a representation that, as far as possible, does not constrain what we can do with the text. Anything we can do with the text, we would like to be able to do with the representation. It also serves to warn us that we should resist the temptation to design the electronic representation of text with any single application in mind. Since any given application for the electronic text is only one among many, there is not much point in designing characteristics into our data representation that make sense only in one application: a more general representation will make better sense in the long run, even if we must sacrifice some modest amount of short-term convenience or efficiency in a single application.

Paradoxically, experience seems to show that the best way to ensure that one can process the text in any way one wants is to ignore processing as far as possible and focus on saying what one thinks the text *is*. That is, one needs to find a *declarative* way of representing the text, not a *procedural* way. This involves adding a level of indirection to processing and so is sometimes disparaged as inefficient, but it's very important.

The basic problem of putting text into computers thus turns out to be that one must find a representation of the text that captures the essentials of the text and omits only the aspects one agrees to believe are negligible. In the practice of the forty-five years during which practitioners have been creating machine-readable texts for research purposes, one can identify some elements of a consensus regarding what is involved in such a representation. It is not enough to transcribe just the characters of the text; it is necessary to be able to include further information in the electronic text as well. This control information should ideally be readily distinguished from the text itself. Borrowing a term from traditional publishing, one can distinguish *markup* (the control information) from *content*.[2] By means of explicit markup or otherwise, electronic representations of text must solve five problems.

First, they must find a method of representing the characters or symbols of the text. This is relatively simple in the case of the characters of the Latin alphabet, the Arabic numerals, and common punctuation marks; it is less simple for accented characters, special symbols, and scripts other than the Latin alphabet, because these are not well supported by common data-processing hardware or software. The situation is improving of late, with the development of ISO 10646 and Unicode, which provide a standard and very large repertoire of scripts and characters, but even with these standards, it will still be necessary to find ways to represent nonstandard symbols and characters (e.g., the special symbols of a personal shorthand invented by the writer of a manuscript or nonstandard characters omitted from ISO 10646 because they are nonstandard).

Second, they must represent, or choose to ignore, the overall logical and typographic structure of the text, including things like act and scene divisions and at least some phenomena like emphasis, quotation, bibliographic citation, and annotation. The history of typography offers persuasive evidence that these phenomena are important enough to thinking about texts that generations of scribes, authors, and typesetters have been forced to find print representations for them. Electronic representations of text would ignore the history of typography at their peril.

Third, the two-dimensional character of text in printed books and manuscripts must be reduced to a linear form in order to be represented in conventional computer file systems. This may involve changing the order of material (e.g., transcribing notes at their point of attachment), omitting material (e.g., running titles and page numbers, which are often omitted from electronic versions of texts), and finding methods of linking material that is physically separate but logically connected (e.g., endnotes).

Fourth, interpretive or analytic information is often explicitly represented, as in language corpora that tag each token with its part of speech. Such interpretive information may or may not be considered part of the text strictly speaking, but it is essential to certain kinds of serious work with the text. It is sometimes urged that creators of electronic texts eschew interpretation and limit themselves to the transcription of "the text itself." On this logic, for example, some would object to procedures like the provision of part-of-speech information in language corpora like the tagged Brown and Lancaster-Oslo-Bergen corpora on the grounds that it represents a subjective interpretation of the objective linguistic facts constituted by the wording of the texts.

As usually formulated, this objection to interpretation is intellectually problematic in itself, since no clear boundary can be drawn between interpretation and "the text itself." The "objective linguistic facts" about the wording of the text are themselves often the subject of hot disputes among textual critics, and even the reading of the characters in a manuscript (or in a printed book) can be controversial. That is, what constitutes objective fact for one reader may seem to another to involve illicit interpretation of the text. Those who create electronic text primarily for the use of others will of course do well to distinguish between information on which there is likely to be broad agreement and information more likely to be controversial, and to allow the user of the electronic text to disregard the controversial information in a systematic way. But it is impossible to distinguish consistently and firmly between controversial and noncontroversial information. And even if such a distinction were possible, it does not follow that electronic texts can or should be kept devoid of analytic or interpretive (i.e., controversial) information: as long as researchers use electronic texts in their work, they will find it convenient to record their interim or final results in the text, for further processing later on. Any general method of text encoding must therefore provide methods for recording such interpretations.

Finally, it is often useful to record certain auxiliary information about the text, even though it may not in any way be considered part of "the text itself." Control information identifying the author and title of the text, providing a bibliographic description of the source, identifying those responsible for the electronic version, and providing other useful information about the text, is commonly recorded in electronic texts or in accompanying documentation. A strong case for providing this information within the text itself can be made from the simple observation of how frequently electronic materials are found separated from the paper documentation that originally accompanied them. In language corpora, such ancillary control information may often include characterizations of the text as a whole—e.g., demographic descriptions of the speakers in a corpus of spoken material or classification by subject matter and text type in corpora of written materials.

From the descriptions just given, it may be observed that in practice, the researchers who have thus far put texts into electronic form have been by and large more interested in texts per se than in the details of the pages on which the texts were written. The page is one representation of a text; the electronic transcription is another. The electronic version can of course represent the page, but it can also represent the text, without the intermediary of the page. For purposes of research with texts, what are needed are text *description* languages, not page *description* languages, and not just images of pages.

In emphasizing the text over the page this way, I follow the unspoken but unambiguous practice of standard practice in most textual work. New editions, even critical editions, very rarely preserve the pagination and lineation, let alone the typeface, leading, and gathering structure of earlier editions. This is only defensible if the text is not the same as the page. Often, students are given modern-spelling editions to read. This practice is defensible only if the text is not the same as the accidentals of the early printings or manuscripts.

Even though any scholar recognizes the potential importance of layout, typeface, etc., and is open to their overt or subliminal influence, still it is an unusual work of scholarship in language or literature (let alone the other disciplines that concern themselves with text) in which the argument hinges on typographic or bibliographic analysis. An obvious exception, of course, are works devoted to paleography, codicology, analytic bibliography, and the history of printing and binding. Practitioners in these fields will require methods of recording the details of the physical presentation of a text in a given edition or manuscript. Like other specialized information, however, this may not be of great utility to researchers in other fields.

RESOURCE SHARING

Machine-readable texts have been in use for research for over forty-five years; this is about as long as computers have been commercially available.[3] In general, computer-assisted projects of text analysis have historically followed a common pattern: first, the text to be analyzed is recorded in electronic form, and then the analysis itself is performed and the results published.

For at least thirty years, the observation has been made that when multiple projects work with the same text, the first step need not be repeated for each project. Once the machine-readable text is created, it can be used for many different analyses without further encoding work. For thirty years, that is, there have been calls for machine-readable texts to be *shared*.

These calls for resource sharing, however, have been only moderately successful. Those concerned with encouraging sharing and reuse of resources might do well to ponder the reasons.

In the first place, some people don't want to share their texts. If one has gone to all the pain and trouble of creating an electronic text and is about to perform an analysis on it, one may well be reluctant to share it with others. These others may take it, perform their own analysis of it, and possibly even publish before the text's creator, receiving all the attendant glory. The creators of electronic texts may, however, wish to retain as much glory as possible for themselves, for use when they next come up for tenure, promotion, or a raise. The sharing of texts, however, confers much less glory than publication, and so creators of electronic texts have no incentive to share their texts and some incentive to retain them for private use.

It may be noticed that while in one light this line of argument is discouraging as to the prospects of achieving widespread reuse of resources, in another it is rather encouraging. The argument relies on the implicit claim that relative to the analysis the task of creating the electronic text is large and onerous. In other words, it really would save time and trouble for the research community overall if a way could be found to make it easier and more common to share electronic texts.

A second reason for the community's failure to achieve widespread text sharing is that when researchers do use each other's texts, they discover that they don't always understand them, because the methods used to encode the texts are so often idiosyncratic. This results in part from the newness of the medium. Faced with the task of representing a text in electronic form, without established conventions for the result, scholars find themselves in an Edenic position. Like Adam and Eve, the creator of an electronic text has the privilege of giving something a name, and having the name so given be *the* name of that thing. If one decrees, for example, that an asterisk is used to mark an italic word, and that a percent sign will precede and follow each personal name, and that a commercial at-sign is used to mark each place name, then that is what those things mean. The blankness of the slate gives to the encoder a kind of euphoric power, which is understandably slightly intoxicating. The result is that over the last forty years virtually every scholar who has created an electronic text has used the opportunity to wield that power and to invent a new language for encoding the text.

Electronic texts thus are, and have always been, in the position of humankind after the Tower of Babel. The result, predictably, has been pretty much what the Yahweh of Genesis had in mind. The cooperation of the research community has been hindered and delayed by the needless misunderstandings and the pointless work of translating among different systems of signs, makework that would be unnecessary if there existed an accepted common language for use in the creation of electronic texts. Three distinct difficulties may be identified in the attempt by one researcher to use electronic texts created by someone else.

First, when one researcher (call her A) gets a text from another researcher (call him B), first of all, she may not understand what all the special marks in it mean. If B has invented a new language, a special system of signs, that is, for this specific text, then A may find that B's text contains signifiers that are opaque because A doesn't know their significance.

The second difficulty is that once A does understand B's signs, it may become clear that the signifieds of B's text don't tell her what she wants to know. It's good that A now understand that the at-sign means a place name, but if A is interested not in place names but rather in the use of the dative case (which B has not marked in the text), then B's text may not be as much use to A as she may have hoped before learning what all those special marks in the text meant.

The third difficulty is that, after swallowing her disappointment and beginning to *add* information to B's text, specifically by marking the occurrences of the dative case, A will all too frequently find

- that the markup language B used has no method of marking the dative case,
- that it also has no provision for graceful extension of its vocabulary, and thus
- that it does not scale up well.

THE TEXT ENCODING INITIATIVE

These three difficulties are not equally soluble, but they are all soluble at least in part. The TEI is an attempt to solve them, as far as possible.

The second is soluble only within very restricted bounds. Without violating the autonomy of the individual researcher, it is impossible to decree that we must all mark the dative case. Some of us, as it happens, are not interested in the dative case but concern ourselves instead with place names. It's hard enough to create texts suitable for our own purposes; we cannot hope to create texts suitable at the same time for everyone else's, too. Within limits, however, a tenuous consensus can be formed regarding some minimum set of textual features that everyone, or almost everyone, regards as being of at least potential interest. No one should hope for too much from this consensus; the simple political fact is that very few features seem useful to absolutely everyone. Thus, I would not recommend to anyone that they should encode a text recording only the features that the universal consensus regards as useful. Almost no one would be happy with such a text; everyone regards other features as desirable, though we can reach no agreement as to what those other features are.

The first difficulty, that of understanding what it is the encoder is saying about a text, can be solved much more satisfactorily. The TEI will provide a large, thoroughly defined lexicon of signs (*tags* is the technical term) for use in marking up texts, and the published text of the TEI guidelines will suffice for virtually all the signifieds that workers with electronic text now record in their texts. By using this set of documented signs, one cannot guarantee that one will find the encoding work of others useful or interesting, but it can at least be made probable that secondary users of the text can understand what features the encoding of a text does and does not record.

Because such a vocabulary of tags must necessarily be rather large, almost no one will be interested in using every item in it. The first task of the encoder who uses TEI markup will therefore be to make a selection among the signs defined in the scheme and to begin making local policy decisions as to how those signs are to be used. The TEI provides, in the TEI header, a place to record those policy decisions, so that later users of the text can know what was done when the text was created.

The third difficulty, graceful extension and scale-up to more elaborate, information-rich versions of a text, the TEI handles in three ways.

First, the TEI itself is designed to be used both for rather sparse markup, which captures only a little information, and also for richer markup. That is, the TEI markup language itself scales up and down.

Second, the predefined vocabulary of the TEI includes a number of "built-in extensions," by means of which new varieties of known classes may be integrated into the markup scheme without any change to its formal definition at all. For example, many markup languages (TeX, LaTeX, Script, troff, Scribe) provide tags for marking enumerated lists, bulleted lists, and possibly one or more other styles of list. In general, however, one is limited to the varieties of list foreseen in the design of the system. One cannot add a new type of list to LaTeX without modifying LaTeX. The TEI defines one basic list element and provides a *type* attribute to allow different varieties of list (e.g., bulleted or enumerated) to be distinguished. Since the values of the *type* attribute are not constrained, a new kind of list can be introduced simply by providing a suitable value for the *type* attribute.

Third, the definition of TEI conformance explicitly envisages the formal modification of the markup language itself, in cases where this is needed. The design and integration of such modifications do require a certain technical skill, though possibly less than is required to modify LaTeX or Scribe. But it is expected that, as with those systems, a local guru will usually be found who can help the user who needs help in changing the formal markup language.

The TEI thus builds a finite vocabulary but explicitly plans for its growth, both by means of formal modifications to the markup language and without such modifications, by means of built-in extensions. That is, the TEI explicitly recognizes that *no finite vocabulary is complete.*

The effort to solve the problems of interchange outlined above, by building such a scheme, began with a planning conference, held in Poughkeepsie, New York, at Vassar College in November of 1987. Thirty-one representatives of professional societies, research centers, text archives, and corpus projects met to discuss the desirability and feasibility of creating a single common scheme for encoding machine-readable texts. There was a clear consensus that such a scheme was both possible and desirable. Somewhat to the surprise of the organizers, this view was shared even by the participants responsible for several of the large existing archives of electronic text, many of which have thousands of dollars and tens of staff years invested in their own locally developed encoding schemes.

At the meeting, three organizations active in the application of computers to natural-language and textual material agreed to sponsor an effort to develop a new text encoding scheme, suitable for use both in local processing and as an interchange language between sites that preferred to use their own locally developed markup languages for local processing. These were the Association for Computers and the Humanities, which under the leadership of Nancy Ide had sponsored the planning conference, the Association for Literary and Linguistic Computing, and the Association for Computational Linguistics. Each of these associations named two delegates to a Steering Committee for the TEI, which began to meet almost immediately after the Planning Conference.

The Steering Committee, in turn, named the author as editor (later, Lou Burnard of Oxford University Computing Service was named as associate editor), with the responsibility of planning and coordinating the work of the project; sought and received funding from the National Endowment for the Humanities, the Andrew W. Mellon Foundation, the Commission of the European Communities (now the European

Union), and the Social Science and Humanities Research Council of Canada; and invited other professional societies to join in an Advisory Board. The Advisory Board met in February 1989, reviewing and approving the overall planning and design work done to that time. Following a plan for division of labor enunciated at the planning meeting, four working committees were appointed, with the task of addressing problems of

- text documentation (especially bibliographic control information and the like),
- text representation,
- text analysis and interpretation, and
- metalinguistic issues and syntax of the encoding scheme.

Of these, the first committee had the most clearly circumscribed area of responsibility, and the second and third had an essentially unbounded scope of activity. The slightly artificial distinction between representation and interpretation of a text was drawn for reasons of practical convenience. As a rule of thumb, the text representation committee was to be responsible for developing markup capable of recording the textual features signaled overtly (e.g., by italics, boldface, or special layout) by conventional printed books, while the committee on analysis and interpretation dealt with everything else that might be thought useful. The latter committee was instructed to concentrate its initial work on the problems of linguistic analysis, both because linguistic analysis seemed more successfully formalized than other textual disciplines and because linguistic understanding is a precondition of so many other areas of textual work.

The working committees met in 1989 and 1990, and the result of their labors was released in June of 1990 as TEI document TEI P1 ("public proposal no. 1"). In 300 letter-sized pages, this draft covered issues of characters and character-set documentation, defined a header for in-file bibliographic description of electronic texts and documentation of the encoding practices used in them, described SGML markup for a large set of features common to many text types and for the provision of analytic and interpretive information with particular reference to linguistic analysis, sketched SGML tag sets for corpora, literary texts, and dictionaries, and defined methods of extending the TEI tag sets.

After the publication of TEI P1, work immediately began on its extension and revision, and work groups were appointed to work on specialized topics such as character sets; textual criticism; hypertext and hypermedia; formulae, tables, figures, and graphics; language corpora; manuscripts and codicology; verse; drama and other performance texts; literary prose; linguistic description; spoken text; literary studies;

historical studies; printed dictionaries; machine lexica; and terminological data.

These work groups met over a period of two years, and the resulting draft, TEI P2, was issued chapter by chapter beginning in early 1992 and continuing through the end of 1993. At that time, all the published chapters were revised, several essential new chapters were added, and the resulting cumulative document was published in the first half of 1994 under the document number TEI P3. This version of the guidelines has grown from 300 pages to 1,300 pages, in part by the addition of an alphabetical reference list of SGML tags and in part by the addition of a great deal of new material. The following is the table of contents for TEI P3:

Part I: Introduction
    1 About These Guidelines
    2 A Gentle Introduction to SGML
    3 Structure of the TEI Document Type Definition

Part II: Core Tags and General Rules
    4 Characters and Character Sets
    5 The TEI Header
    6 Elements Available in All TEI Documents
    7 Default Text Structure

Part III: Base Tag Sets
    8 Prose
    9 Verse
    10 Drama
    11 Transcriptions of Speech
    12 Print Dictionaries
    13 Terminological Databases

Part IV: Additional Tag Sets
    14 Linking, Segmentation, and Alignment
    15 Simple Analytic Mechanisms
    16 Feature Structures
    17 Certainty and Responsibility
    18 Transcription of Primary Sources
    19 Critical Apparatus
    20 Names and Dates
    21 Graphs, Networks, and Trees
    22 Tables, Formulae, and Graphics
    23 Language Corpora

Part V: Auxiliary Document Types
    24 The Independent Header
    25 Writing System Declaration
    26 Feature System Declaration
    27 Tag Set Documentation

Part VI: Technical Topics
    28 Conformance
    29 Modifying the TEI DTD

The design goals for the project were early formulated: The TEI encoding scheme should be

- sufficient for the needs of research;
- simple, clear, and concrete;
- usable without special software;
- rigorous and efficient to process;
- extensible; and
- conformant to existing and emerging standards.

These goals have not all been met in equal measure. The very size and subtlety required of the scheme by the first goal is partly at odds with the demand of the second goal that the scheme be simple, for example. In some measure, however, all of these goals have found some reflection in the final specification of the TEI encoding scheme:

- The list of topics given above, and the broad base of researchers who participated in the development of the guidelines, provide the best indication of the effort to ensure that the TEI guidelines would suffice to meet the needs of most researchers.
- In the interests of concreteness, the TEI formulated not general advice on the construction of SGML tag sets but a concrete TEI document type declaration (DTD), which can be used as is for the vast majority of research projects using electronic text.
- Because SGML is human-readable, software-independent, and requires no non-ASCII characters, TEI-encoded texts can in principle be used without special-purpose software, and interested projects can develop their own software to process TEI-encoded texts. Experience has shown, however, that work with TEI texts is materially aided by the use of SGML-aware software. This is particularly true of texts with complex encoding. To that extent, the third goal might plausibly be regarded as having been achieved only in part.

- Since the TEI scheme is formulated using SGML, it provides an explicit and rigorous document grammar and defines a tree-structured model of text (extended with pointers to allow the representation of directed graphs) that lends itself to efficient manipulation. To simplify the task of ad hoc software development, the TEI defines an "interchange format" that restricts the syntax of SGML to a manageable subset of the full syntax, which is thought by some to be marred by an excessive number of special cases and ad hoc rules.
- Extension of the TEI tag set is explicitly allowed in TEI-conformant texts—although this complicates the life of software developers materially and may make interchange more difficult and so is not actively recommended.
- The standards most relevant to text encoding are ISO 8879, which defines SGML, and the various character-set standards. SGML conformance is a condition of TEI conformance, but for pragmatic reasons, no single standard character set is mandated for TEI-encoded texts.

TEI AND SGML

As noted, the TEI uses SGML as the basis for its encoding scheme; this section describes the basis for that choice. First of all, SGML is nonproprietary, an international standard formulated by ISO (the International Organization for Standardization) and thus not within the control of any one software developer. This helps ensure the vendor- and platform-independence of SGML applications and of SGML-encoded data. With SGML, there is no user lock-in to specific systems; information is owned by the user, not by the propriety systems used to manipulate it. This is sufficiently important for industry to have led to wide adoption of SGML for strategic data. It is even more important for the research community, since computer systems commonly have lives measured in years, while major literary and linguistic research projects have lives measured in decades. Even for projects of shorter duration than the *Oxford English Dictionary* or its various counterparts in other languages, longevity is a major issue. Work in the textual disciplines may remain relevant and important for decades or centuries. When that work takes the form of electronic texts or work with such texts, it is important that the electronic forms of the texts remain usable for a much longer life span than any software has ever yet possessed.

Second, SGML provides a reasonably good model of text. Fundamentally, it allows text to be represented in a labeled tree structure, with extensions to allow pointing and the creation of directed or undirected graph structures. A variety of mechanisms are available for handling information that does not fit well into a purely hierarchical model (discussed at length in one chapter of the guidelines). SGML is general, in contrast to markup languages like TeX or troff, which are focused on the production of printed output. It is extensible, in contrast to schemes like the Office Document Architecture (later renamed the Open Document Architecture), which do not allow for user extensions to the markup language. SGML-based markup languages are generally declarative, rather than procedural, and SGML encourages the use of analytic or descriptive, rather than appearance-oriented or presentational, markup. This helps achieve the reusability of SGML data.

THE TEI ENCODING SCHEME

The TEI encoding scheme is defined as an *application* of SGML, and its formal specification takes the form of an SGML "document type definition" or DTD. This specification is characterized by

- an emphasis on logical, rather than physical, structure of the text, on texts rather than on pages, for the reasons described above;
- the frequent application of Occam's Razor—for example, in the provision of a single tag for lists, with an attribute to specify the type, rather than separate tags for ordered, bulleted, and simple lists;
- a modular architecture that groups tags into easily understood sets, which may be combined more or less freely for use with particular texts;
- the explicit provision of methods of adding new tags, and even new tag sets, to the encoding scheme, so as to ensure that the TEI markup language remains open to improvement and extension.

Particular attention has also been paid to ensuring that information of varying types can be included in the same document, and that documents can be gradually enriched by the addition of new information and analysis, without the new information getting in the way of the old. SGML software can readily ignore the markup not of interest to the user at any given moment, effectively filtering the document into a form suitable for the particular task in hand. It is possible using the TEI scheme, for example, to combine in a single document:

- orthographic transcription of the text;
- pointers to a digital or analogue recording of a speech signal or a videotape of an event;
- markup of proper nouns, dates, times, etc.;
- part-of-speech tagging;

- analysis of surface syntactic structure, including multiple analyses of ambiguous structures;
- analysis of the discourse structure;
- cross references to other material on the same topic;
- links to figures and graphics stored in any suitable notation (which need not be SGML).

A simple example may be used to show what the TEI scheme looks like in practice; most SGML-aware display software, however, will not show the tags to the user in this form, instead using font, type size, and layout guided by user-defined style sheets to signal the nature of the information being displayed.

A TEI-encoded version of Franklin Delano Roosevelt's first inaugural address, for example, might look like this:

```
<!DOCTYPE TEI.2 system 'tei2.dtd' [
<!ENTITY % TEI.prose 'INCLUDE' >
<!ENTITY wsd.en SYSTEM 'teien.wsd' SUBDOC>
]>
<TEI.2>
<teiHeader>
<fileDesc>
<titleStmt>
    <title>First Inaugural Address: An Electronic Version.</>
    <author>Franklin Delano Roosevelt.</>
    <respStmt><resp>tagged from the Project Gutenberg edition
      by</> <name>C. M. Sperberg-McQueen</> </>
<publicationStmt>
    <authority>C. M. Sperberg-McQueen</authority>
    <pubPlace>Chicago</>
    <availability> <p>This electronic text may be freely redistributed; it
      should not however be confused with the Project Gutenberg version
      of the same text, from which this version derives in part. The inaugural
      speech itself is in the public domain.</availability>
    <date>1994</>
</publicationStmt>
<sourceDesc>
<bibl> <title>"The only thing we have to fear. . .is fear itself." President
Franklin Delano Roosevelt's First Inaugural Speech</title> [Originally
delivered March 4th, 1933] ([Champaign, IL]: Project Gutenberg, 1994)
[file fdr10.txt]</bibl>
</sourceDesc>
</fileDesc>


<encodingDesc>
<projectDesc>
    <p>This tagged version of Roosevelt's inaugural was prepared as a
demonstration of SGML tagging by C. M. Sperberg-McQueen. The
untagged text from which it derives was produced by Project Gutenberg.
<editorialDecl>
```

```
<correction status=silent> <p>Corrected by CMSMcQ against the text
of the speech as given in Henry Steele Commager's <title>Documents
of American History.
</title>
</p> </correction>
</editorialDecl>
</encodingDesc>

<profileDesc>
<langUsage>
<language id=en>U.S. English</language>
</langUsage>
</profileDesc>

<revisionDesc>
<list>
<item>26 March 1994 : CMSMcQ : complete header, tag
paragraphs of text, reformat paragraphs.
<item>10 March 1994 : CMSMcQ : add skeleton file in TEI form, begin
tagging header.
</list>
</revisionDesc>
</teiHeader>
<text>
<front>
<titlePage>
<docTitle>
<titlePart>Inaugural Speech of Franklin Delano Roosevelt</>
<titlePart>Given in Washington, D.C.</>
</docTitle>
<docDate>March 4th, 1933</docDate>
</front>
<body>

<p>President Hoover, Mr. Chief Justice, my friends:

<p>This is a day of national consecration, and I am certain that my
fellow-Americans expect that on my induction into the Presidency I will
address them with a candor and a decision which the present situation
of our nation impels.

<p>This is pre-eminently the time to speak the truth, the whole truth,
frankly and boldly. Nor need we shrink from honestly facing conditions
in our country today. This great nation will endure as it has endured,
will revive and will prosper.

<p>So first of all let me assert my firm belief that the only thing we
have to fear is fear itself &mdash; nameless, unreasoning, unjustified terror
which paralyzes needed efforts to convert retreat into advance.

<!— text omitted to conserve space ... —>

<p>In this dedication of a nation we humbly ask the blessing of God.
May He protect each and every one of us! May He guide me in the days
to come!
```

```
</body>
</text>
</TEI.2>
```

The document begins with an SGML document type declaration, indicating that the main DTD is found in a system file called "tei2.dtd"; on the second and third lines, entity declarations identify the identifiers "TEI.prose" and "wsd.en" with, respectively, the string "INCLUDE" and the system file "teien.wsd." The former indicates that the TEI base tag set for prose is to be included; the latter identifies an externally stored writing system declaration, which in this case documents the language (English) and character set used to encode the text. The string "]>" on the fourth line of the example ends the document type declaration.

The document instance itself begins on the fifth line. Each SGML element is delimited by a start-tag and an end-tag, themselves delimited by angle brackets or angle-bracket-slash and angle bracket. The "<TEI.2>" on line 5 and the "</TEI.2>" on the last line of the example show the beginning and end of the entire document instance. The root element, <TEI.2>, contains in turn two subelements: a TEI header, tagged <teiHeader>, and a <text>. The text itself contains merely a series of paragraphs, tagged <p>; the TEI header, on the other hand, has a fairly elaborate substructure used to document the electronic text, including its bibliographic source and the encoding practices used in creating it.

The allowable content (i.e., the syntax) and the semantics of the elements like <TEI.2>, <teiHeader>, and <p> are given by the TEI guidelines, as part of the predefined vocabulary of SGML elements provided by the TEI encoding scheme.

The TEI defines a single unified encoding scheme, which is scalable, allowing both very light text markup and extremely dense, information-rich markup. It provides explicit support for analysis of the text, without requiring adherence to any particular linguistic approach or other theory, and allowing the peaceful coexistence of many different types of analysis. Using standard SGML techniques, it makes possible the linkage of text to speech or other nontextual data at any desired level of granularity. With its wealth of flexible analytic mechanisms and its support for information filtering, the TEI encoding scheme provides a computationally tractable representation of rich text that has few serious competitors within or outside the SGML community. Above all, the work of the many volunteers on its work groups has ensured that the TEI defines a compendious inventory of textual phenomena of interest to researchers, for the description of the physical, formal, rhetorical, linguistic, and other aspects of the text.

CONCLUSION

By providing a common public vocabulary for text markup, we will have taken one major step toward making electronic texts as important and useful as they ought to be, but only one step. Other steps are still required.

First of all, we must as a community make a serious commitment to allowing reuse of our electronic texts. This will require either a massive upsurge in the incidence of altruism or much stronger conventions for the citation of electronic texts, and giving credit for the creation of electronic materials, both in bibliographic practice and at promotion, tenure, and salary time.

Second, we must cultivate a strict distinction between the format of our data and the software with which we manipulate it, because software is short-lived, but our texts are, or should be, long-lived. Our paper archives are full of documents 15 or 20 years old, or 150 to 200 years old, or even 1,500 or 2,000 years old. But I cannot think of a single piece of software I can run that was written even 100 years ago. To allow our texts to survive, we must separate them firmly from the evanescent software we use to work on them. SGML and other standards encourage such a distinction, but proprietary products typically obscure it. In some operating systems, every document is tied, at the operating system level, to a single application—precisely the wrong approach, from this point of view.

Third, we need to cultivate better, more intelligent software, with better understanding of the nature of text structures, in order to make the texts contained in our archives more useful in our work.

Finally, we need, if possible, to come to a richer consensus about the ways in which we encode texts. We should try to move beyond an agreement on syntax and achieve more unity on the specific features of text that are widely useful. Such a consensus will make the TEI less of merely syntactic convention and more of a real common language.

The TEI's contribution to the success of electronic textual research will, I hope, be that it provides us with a common language, to allow us to escape our post-Babel confusion. As the list just concluded makes clear, such a common language is not all we need. But as the Yahweh of Genesis says:

> If as one people speaking the same language they have begun to
> do this, then nothing they plan to do will be impossible for them.
> (Gen. 11:6, New International Version)

NOTES

¹ Among humanities projects, one might mention the Brown University Women Writers' Project, which is creating a corpus of women's writing in English from 1330 to 1830; the Nietzsche Nachlass project now at Dartmouth; the Leiden Armenian Database, collecting primarily medieval Armenian texts; the Global Jewish Databank at Bar Ilan, an outgrowth of the earlier Responsa Project, a collection of rabbinical responses to questions on points of Jewish law; and the Thesaurus Linguae Graecae at the University of California at Irvine. This is by no means an exhaustive list but indicates the breadth of current activity. Among corpus projects, the Brown and Lancaster-Oslo-Bergen corpora of the 1960s, and their various analogues in other languages, are now being succeeded by a new wave of larger projects, for example, the British National Corpus, which will encode 100,000,000 (one hundred million) words of written and spoken British English, and the Network of European Reference Corpora. The most prominent of what I am referring to as "opportunistic projects" may be the ACL Data Collection Initiative (DCI) and the European Corpus Initiative (ECI).

² There are occasional efforts to argue that markup is not necessary and, indeed, is actively harmful. Perhaps the most widely known proponent of this view at the moment is Michael Hart of Project Gutenberg, which distributes ASCII-encoded public-domain texts by means of anonymous File Transfer Protocol (FTP) servers. Each Project Gutenberg text, however, appears to contain an extensive header, giving the text's version number, filename, and date, providing a contact address, appealing for funds, and including a lengthy legal disclaimer. This header provides metatextual information, which is not strictly part of the text being transcribed, and so by definition constitutes markup of the text. Thus, even those who resist the use of formal markup languages do recognize in practice the need for markup to provide meta-information. One drawback of providing such meta-information without a formal markup scheme is that there is no convenient method to recognize automatically the boundaries between the text and the meta-information or markup.

³ I take Father Roberto Busa's *Index Thomisticus* project, which began in 1948, as marking the first use of machine-readable text for research.

REFERENCE

Association for Computers and the Humanities (ACH), Association for Computational Linguistics (ACL), and Association for Literary and Linguistic Computing (ALLC). 1994. *Guidelines for Electronic Text Encoding and Interchange*, TEI P3, ed. C. M. Sperberg-McQueen and Lou Burnard. Chicago; Oxford: Text Encoding Initiative.

ANITA K. LOWRY

Head, Information Arcade
University of Iowa Libraries
Iowa City, Iowa

Electronic Texts and Multimedia in the Academic Library: A View from the Front Line

ABSTRACT

Electronic texts and hypermedia databases can be invaluable resources for helping students engage and understand primary sources in the humanities. In addition, the ability not only to interact with existing electronic resources but also to manipulate and create information in digital forms contributes a unique dimension to the learning process. The Information Arcade at the University of Iowa Libraries provides a model for the role of the academic library in integrating electronic resources and interactive technologies into research and teaching.

ELECTRONIC PRIMARY SOURCES AND INTERACTIVE LEARNING

Primary sources in the humanities—whether the creative works of the human imagination or the documentary records of human affairs—do not yield their secrets readily. They do not come to students with their multiple layers of meaning pre-digested and transparent or their contradictions and paradoxes neatly rationalized; they may reflect a time or place far removed from the student's experience and learning or provide evidence of a world inaccessible to the student's senses. Teaching students about the nature and use of primary source materials and teaching them the special analytical skills that these sources demand are among the challenges that faculty face in both graduate and undergraduate courses. Just getting undergraduates interested in primary sources may be the first and greatest hurdle.

57

While I would not argue that electronic resources are a panacea for teaching students to appreciate primary sources, I am convinced that they can be an invaluable tool for this purpose. Electronic texts with text analysis programs and hypermedia databases that link texts with other primary source materials as well as with commentary and reference sources—these present source materials to students in completely new ways. They make source materials both *more* accessible to students and, paradoxically, *less* accessible, and it is by virtue of *both* of these seemingly contradictory characteristics that they make such excellent teaching tools.

On the one hand, electronic databases can bring together materials from a great variety of sources, many of them obscure or difficult to locate, and put them literally at the fingertips of scholars and students. At Stanford University, in an undergraduate English course nicknamed "Electronic Chaucer," Professor Mary Wack and her students used a large collection of images in an online database, the *Stanford Humanities Image Archive,* to explore manuscripts, art works, maps, and other documents of medieval culture. In this database, each image can be accompanied by up to thirty-five pages of information, commentary, and bibliography, and the images and text may rapidly be retrieved, displayed, juxtaposed, and examined, inside or outside of the classroom. Here is how Professor Wack describes one of the ways her class has profited from this database in the classroom setting:

> When my class informed me that they really didn't understand the concept of "ordinatio" after our first session on it, I was able to show them a page from Ellesmere juxtaposed with pages from both the Kelmscott Chaucer and an Ovid MS. On the spur of the moment I could illustrate by comparison and contrast how the elements of page design contribute to a reader's interpretation of the text. . . . The quality and flexibility in the reproduction of images goes far toward reducing the logistical problems of access to the sorts of objects that medievalists often study (manuscripts, objects in European collections) . . . *it opens students to the many possibilities for concentrated engagement with medieval objects more typical heretofore of graduate work* [emphasis added]. (Wack 1993, 9)

In a very different sense, however, texts or other sources in electronic databases are *not* as immediately accessible as those in print, because they are not laid out neatly on a page for browsing or casual perusal. The text retrieval or analysis software that is used with a text database forces the student to formulate a question or series of questions in order to retrieve information from the source and organize it in a meaningful way; this makes explicit the close attention and questioning stance that must be brought to bear on primary source materials. And so, with these electronic resources, an instructor can give students vivid and dynamic lessons in the interrogation and interpretation of primary source materials.

For example, students in Columbia University's renowned "Contemporary Civilization" course must come to grips with seminal works of the Western intellectual tradition from Plato to Freud—no mean feat for undergraduates. In his "Contemporary Civilization" class, Professor W. D. Van Horn used a full-text database containing key works by Jean-Jacques Rousseau (1990) to teach his students strategies for examining some of the difficult paradoxes in Rousseau's thought by searching through the database for pairs of opposing concepts, such as nature versus society or freedom versus obligation. On the one hand, this exercise with the electronic text enabled students quickly to locate relevant sections of the texts for closer study; at the same time, the interactive and iterative process of identifying concepts, of selecting the words and combinations of words to define them, and then of further refining those definitions as a result of searching the database helped students to focus closely on the words and structure of the texts and to re-create for themselves the terms of Rousseau's arguments (Van Horn 1991).

Reference librarians are all familiar with the undergraduate student who has to write a paper on a theme or motif in a literary work, let's say a play by Shakespeare, or is asked to compare and contrast some aspect of the writings of two authors. This student immediately heads to the library to try to find books and articles on the topic, hoping to find in the writings of others the answers to the riddles of the primary text. The *MLA Bibliography* on CD-ROM has been a godsend to these students and to the reference librarians who must help them try to locate, in the enormous haystacks of Shakespeare criticism, just the needle that will pierce their specific topics. But might these students not also discover that the *WordCruncher Disc* CD-ROM (*WordCruncher* 1990), which contains the complete full-text of the Riverside edition of Shakespeare's works, is an attractive tool for interrogating the text directly, thus helping them to seek answers in their own engagement with the words of the author?

And, last but not least, *hypermedia* text databases, which contain not only primary source texts but also a variety of other related source materials in different media, can help students to understand some of the relationships between the text and its broader literary, historical, and cultural context. It is the goal of the developers of the *Perseus* (*Perseus* 1992) hypermedia database to create an "electronic environment . . . [that will] allow individuals to use more varied kinds of evidence than they normally would . . . to ask more questions and pursue problems to a deeper level than would otherwise be possible" (Crane 1990, 150). To that end, *Perseus* contains many original texts in Greek and in English translation, thousands of photographs of art objects and archeological artifacts, maps, site plans, photographs, and video images of the remains of sanctuaries and other sites, reference tools, and explanatory essays and annotations written especially for *Perseus;* subsequent editions will add new materials in each category. Because of the breadth and depth of its source collections and its wealth of hypermedia links, the *Perseus* database provides a rich and complex environment for the exploration of primary sources, including texts. In addition, the software allows faculty or students to write their own commentary and annotations into the database and to create and save their own links and pathways among its treasures; this ability to "customize" a database for individual or group study is an exciting feature of many hypermedia databases.

I have seen undergraduate students use electronic texts with enthusiasm and success. I share the conviction expressed by the creators of *Perseus* and the other faculty I have just quoted that electronic texts and hypermedia text databases hold great promise for undergraduates as well as for graduate students. But I also know that these innovative materials will not have a significant impact on undergraduate education unless there is adequate planning, commitment, and support from the library, the computer center, the university administration, and, last but certainly not least, the faculty. The infrastructure and support services that are sufficient to accommodate the use of electronic texts by faculty and graduate students may not suffice for use by undergraduates, if for no other reason than the sheer numbers of undergraduate students.

In order to integrate electronic primary source materials successfully into the undergraduate academic experience, access to these materials must be as transparent and hassle-free as possible and point-of-use assistance must be readily available. As Gregory Crane, the general editor of the Perseus Project, found when he used an early version of the database in a class that he taught:

> When asked to abandon a familiar type of written assignment for an electronically annotated pathway through the database, most students expressed doubts as to whether the pedagogical gains outweighed the anxiety, frustration, and inconvenience posed by first having to overcome the problems of limited access to the materials, which were only available in the computer laboratory, and then having to deal with an unfamiliar system to complete the assignment. (Mylonas et al. 1993, 152)

For librarians, acquiring and cataloging a hypermedia database on CD-ROM or subscribing to an online electronic text database constitutes merely the first step in the process of helping faculty and students realize the potential benefits of using electronic primary source materials.

Libraries must also address complex issues of access and service in order to lower the barriers to widespread and equitable use of electronic resources in research and teaching.

THE ROLE OF THE ACADEMIC LIBRARY

Several years ago at the University of Iowa, the Libraries decided to take on the challenges of providing access to electronic texts, hypermedia, and other electronic resources, with a special emphasis on the applications of interactive technologies to undergraduate education. The University Libraries, the Office of Information Technology, and the University of Iowa administration jointly submitted a proposal and received a three-year, $752,432 grant from the Roy J. Carver Charitable Trust to establish what was initially called the Interactive Information Learning Center and is now called the Information Arcade. While the Information Arcade was not established exclusively as a pedagogical facility, the planning and implementation of the Arcade has been strongly influenced by the desire to fully support and strongly encourage new applications of electronic resources for teaching and independent learning. I should make it clear that the scope of the Arcade includes but is not limited to electronic texts and that the Arcade seeks to serve teaching and research needs in all disciplines; however, to date, its collections are strongest in the humanities and social sciences (which are the disciplines served by the Main Library). Its classroom and lab area, however, are used by faculty and students in a wide range of disciplines, including the sciences.

Let me briefly describe the Information Arcade and then examine some of the assumptions and rationale for this particular model for integrating information technologies into the curriculum. And then let me venture some preliminary conclusions, or at least observations, about what we have learned since we opened our doors in August of 1992.

The Information Arcade is located in the Main Library, just inside the building's north door and next to the Information and Instructional Services Department (formerly known as the Reference Department), with which it shares a common door. I am quite glad that this space on the first floor was chosen, because it is both prominent and directly adjacent to the Information and Instructional Services Department, whose collections and services it both complements and extends. The Arcade occupies approximately 6,000 square feet of renovated space that includes a large electronic classroom, a lab area with clusters of microcomputers that we call information stations and multimedia stations (I'll get to the distinction between them in a moment), a large service desk, a semiprivate faculty cluster, and staff offices and workroom. All microcomputers in the Information Arcade are on a local area network, whose file server is located across the street at the Weeg Computing Center; network management services constitute one of the primary contributions of the Office of Information Technology to this joint project.

What are some of the basic assumptions that went into the design of the Information Arcade? We first assumed that the classroom is still a central locus for undergraduate learning. So electronic source materials must be available in an electronic classroom, where the instructor can use them to enhance lecture and discussion and where students can use them on individual stations for guided and collaborative in-class explorations. For these very same reasons, the electronic classroom is an invaluable resource for library instructional programs that involve information technologies. From the day it opened, the Information Arcade's electronic classroom has been heavily booked for undergraduate and graduate courses that meet there either regularly or occasionally and for library instruction.

Outside the classroom, there are clusters of what we call information stations and, in another part of the room, what we call multimedia stations. These two names reflect a crucial distinction and commitment. The purpose of the information stations is to enable faculty and students to use existing information resources: electronic texts, hypermedia databases, courseware, software, and the Internet. The purpose of the multimedia stations is to enable them actually to create and manipulate source materials in digital formats; accordingly, the multimedia stations have powerful microcomputers and large screens, with a variety of peripherals like scanners, CD-ROM and laserdisc players, VCRs, tape deck, and removable storage media. At the multimedia stations, students have access to special software for digitizing, editing, and manipulating text, images, sounds, and moving images, as well as a variety of presentation and authoring programs. The multimedia stations reflect a fundamental conviction that in the electronic age students will learn not only by interacting with existing resources but also by creating their own multimedia documents.

One of the primary exponents of this active approach to learning is Professor Brooks Landon of the English Department. Professor Landon teaches a course titled "Literature and Culture of Twentieth Century America," which focuses on the impact of technology on literary culture in the twentieth century. A central concern of this course is the meaning and implications of the 1893 World's Columbian Exposition in Chicago, a great cultural event that exposed millions of Americans to large-scale applications of outdoor electric lighting and other new technologies for the first time and served as a kind of official introduction to the twentieth century (Landon 1993). Professor Landon is creating an ambitious hypermedia database about the Columbian Exposition called *The White City;* his class meets in the electronic classroom of the Information Arcade, where he can use his database to guide his students hypertextually through the White City that he has re-created with primary source text documents, images and photographs, old moving picture clips, and contemporary accounts and modern interpretations of the fair. The students read classic and popular literature of the late nineteenth and early twentieth centuries. But instead of writing term papers, the students in the class research, write, and prepare their own hypermedia mini-databases on topics relating to the exposition. They locate and digitize selections from a variety of source documents, including articles in the press of the time, publications from the fair, and other writings on the fair or on the topics they've chosen. These documents, along with the hypertext essays the students write, may even be incorporated into the ongoing development of *The White City* database.

Professor Landon has been teaching this course for several years, but the spring term of 1993 was the first time that he taught it in this fashion, because of the facilities newly made available in the Information Arcade. Discussing the course with a colleague, Professor Landon expressed particular pleasure with the quality of the students' work that semester. And what did he consider to be one of the most impressive indicators of the success of this new "electronic" course and its unorthodox assignment? It was the fact that the students in this class had done a great deal more bibliographic and historical research and made greater use of primary source materials than undergraduate students are usually inclined to do. Motivated by the technology and the possibilities it opened up for them, they had sought out a wide range of contemporary source materials on turn-of-the-century America from the library's stacks and special collections in order to analyze, digitize, and synthesize them into their hypermedia projects in a meaningful way.

The development of Professor Landon's *White City* database has been made possible by Second Look Computing, the multimedia development studio at the Weeg Computing Center. At Second Look, the latest in multimedia equipment and software and an expert staff of multimedia specialists are available to assist faculty with multimedia projects for a variety of research, educational, and information applications around campus. Complementing the mission of Second Look, the Information Arcade provides a place for faculty to integrate these projects into the classroom or into course assignments, as well as a place for students to work on smaller scale projects of their own.

Other courses that not only use the Arcade electronic classroom but that also require the students to create multimedia documents include courses in political communication and cognition, music and multimedia, interactive media in libraries, women in film, design and management of civil engineering projects, and computer applications for clinical practice in nursing.

Our experience has been that the more people know about multimedia, the more they want to do with it. A commitment to multimedia production in the library brings with it substantial costs for equipment, software, and, most of all, staff support. The kinds of expertise that are required to help students manage the multiple steps and the decisions that must be made at each step simply for scanning alone are formidable. Whether we are dealing with texts, still or moving images, numeric data, or other electronic primary source materials, the difference between supporting faculty and students in the use and limited manipulation of existing resources and supporting them in the creation of their own resources is enormous.

So how has the Information Arcade approached the issue of staff support? Our "front line" staff consists of lab monitors, who handle basic informational questions, dispense printouts from the networked laser printer, check out manuals and other materials from behind the desk, and perform a variety of clerical and simple technical tasks throughout the Arcade. In addition, six graduate assistants, who hold half-time year-long appointments analogous to a university research or teaching assistantship, provide the majority of the public services in the Information Arcade. Competition for these positions is keen, and graduate assistants are chosen for their interpersonal and communication skills, subject expertise in areas other than computers, broad experience with and interest in academic computing applications and electronic information sources, and their ability quickly to learn things that they don't already know. A lab monitor and at least one graduate assistant are on duty at all times the Arcade is open, and during busy times, we schedule two graduate assistants—even then, the graduate assistants and lab monitors can be pretty harried during the week before a major multimedia assignment is due.

So far, the participation of reference librarians and bibliographers in the public service activities of the Information Arcade has consisted primarily of teaching workshops on the online catalog, the Internet, and on electronic resources in various fields; this spring, we have had presentations for faculty and graduate students on such topics as electronic texts, primary sources in the social sciences, and electronic sources in classics. In each of these sessions, we have made a point of including electronic primary source materials that are especially appropriate for undergraduate teaching. I am strongly convinced of the importance of these kinds of programs for faculty and graduate students and feel that they should be focused by discipline and targeted at specific departments or at a group of individuals from various departments who are likely to have an interest in a particular electronic text or other resource. I also think that there are other significant opportunities yet to be realized for librarians to be involved in supporting the creation and use of electronic primary source materials in research and teaching— opportunities that draw on their specialized subject and language knowledge and their expertise in information retrieval and management.

What have been some of our biggest challenges to date? First of all—access. With some exceptions, electronic primary source publishing in the humanities is currently split between two computer platforms: DOS or Windows for electronic texts and text analysis software, and Macintosh for hypermedia text databases like *Perseus*. And CD-ROMs that tie their texts to nonstandard markup systems and proprietary software are still the distribution medium of choice for most publishers. I think that this will begin to change under the influence of projects like the Center for Electronic Texts in the Humanities and the Text Encoding Initiative. But I am sure that multiple platforms and CD-ROMs will be with us for quite awhile. So if there is a technical wizard in the crowd who can guarantee me that you can successfully network *all* of our diverse DOS, Windows, and Macintosh CD-ROMs, including our multimedia titles, there is a job in Iowa waiting for you. And if you can successfully negotiate reasonably priced network licenses for each and every one of them, then you can name your price! Because until we can successfully deliver electronic texts and software to workstations throughout the Information Arcade, the Libraries, and the campus, we cannot really meet the needs of students or scholars for access to these resources and cannot promote widespread integration of them into the undergraduate curriculum.

The second challenge on my list? Staff—having enough of it and making sure that staff members can keep up with burgeoning collections of electronic information sources housed locally, available over the Internet, and being created by faculty and students on campus. This is a topic that deserves a paper in itself and cannot be considered in isolation from the fundamental rethinking of the roles of professional and nonprofessional staff that is taking place throughout academic librarianship. But, as I said before, we must recognize that supporting the *creation* of electronic source materials rather than just their *usage* makes unprecedented demands on library staff and has significant ramifications for the kinds of staff expertise and the numbers of staff that are needed.

In conclusion, I think that in the first year and a half of its existence the Information Arcade has begun to make a difference in the ways that undergraduates confront primary source materials, including electronic and hypermedia texts in the humanities. But the facilities and services of the Arcade constitute only part of the solution to the issue of interactive resources and methods in undergraduate education—which, nevertheless, is better than being part of the problem! Ultimately, the solution requires a campus-wide strategy to address issues relating to the campus network infrastructure, the design and equipping of classrooms, facilities for individual and group access to electronic resources beyond word processing and electronic mail, incentives for experimental pedagogical efforts by faculty, copyright and licensing, personnel in the libraries and computing facilities, and the allocation and reallocation of scarce resources within the framework of university priorities. We are already grappling with many of these issues at the University of Iowa, and I hope and believe that the Libraries can be a catalyst for the development of a campus-wide strategy and will play a central role in its formulation and implementation.

REFERENCES

Crane, Gregory. 1990. 'Hypermedia' and Scholarly Publishing. *Scholarly Publishing 21*(3): 131-55.

Landon, Brooks. 1993. Literature and Culture of Twentieth Century America [Course description]. (January). University of Iowa, Iowa City.

Mylonas, Elli, Gregory Crane, Kenneth Morrell, and D. Neel Smith. 1993. The Perseus Project: Data in the Electronic Age. In *Accessing Antiquity: The Computerization of Classical Studies*, ed. J. Solomon, 133-56. Tucson: University of Arizona Press.

Perseus: Interactive Sources and Studies on Ancient Greece Ver. 1.0 [Computer file on CD-ROM and laserdisc]. 1992. New Haven: Yale University Press.

Rousseau, Jean-Jacques. 1990. *Discourse on the Origin of Inequality* and *On the Social Contract*. In *Political Philosophy: Machiavelli to Mill* [Computer file on disk]. Pittsboro, N.C.: InteLex Corp.

Van Horn, W. D. 1991. Class notes and conversation with author. (October). Columbia University, New York.

Wack, Mary. 1993. Electronic Chaucer. *Computers and Texts 5:* 8-9.

WordCruncher Disc Vol. 1 [Computer file on CD-ROM]. 1990. Orem, Ut.: Electronic Text Corp.

MARK TYLER DAY

Co-Director, Library Electronic Text Resource Service
Indiana University
Bloomington, Indiana

Humanizing Information Technology: Cultural Evolution and the Institutionalization of Electronic Text Processing

ABSTRACT

This paper examines the process by which new academic library services are created in response to a changing academic ecology with reference to a particular case study—that of Indiana University's still developing Library Electronic Text Resource Service (LETRS). It explains the recent rise of interest in electronic texts as a product of social forces generated by the evolution of industrial capitalism. This evolution has resulted in the creation of complex social organizations and information technologies designed to control the complex processes of industrial expansion. We are only now beginning to develop adequate scientific explanations of this evolution.

INTRODUCTION

The role of the academy as a haven of pure research and learning has become a major area of contention in the new postindustrial, postmodern, electronic information age. Contemporary intellectual theories both within and without the academy question the validity and reliability of traditional humanistic discourses and the effectiveness and efficiency of the institutions that those discourses legitimize. This raises the question of whether, within the context of a turbulent and often hostile environment, modern information technologies can be used to further humanistic ends, and of how the pursuit of these ends can be re-institutionalized in culturally reproducible forms. The development of socially viable answers to these questions will itself be accomplished by a process of cultural evolution. Achieving a better understanding of how cultural evolution works may therefore assist us in arriving at more adequate answers.

Today, academic libraries face problems of control and communication on the same scale as those faced by industrial enterprises and national governments, yet their parent organizations can still be characterized as "...monolithic, capital-and labor-intensive institutions that manage their internal economies through a curious mixture of state socialism and buccaneer capitalism" (O'Donnell 1994). This situation makes the task of mobilizing support for the application of electronic technologies to the humanities extremely difficult. A variety of approaches are being taken, some of which show more chance of success than others. The collaborative organizational structure of Indiana University's Library Electronic Text Resource Service (LETRS), its role in the movement to establish electronic text centers on university campuses, and its mission to support humanities computing makes LETRS a useful case study for investigating how electronic technologies may not only be changing the form and function of literary texts, but also of those institutions designed to support literary scholarship. Our viewpoint in this endeavor will be that of a participant observer, our theoretical stance will be that of the social sciences, and our ultimate concern will be the quality of human life.

POSTMODERN HUMANISTS IN CYBERSPACE AND THE PROBLEM OF CULTURAL REPRODUCTION

Because change involves destruction as well as creation, it naturally arouses human fears that what is essential to a valued way of life will disappear and be "replaced" with something worse rather than something better. When change appears to be inevitable, it takes away our sense of autonomy, giving us no choice but to adapt one way or another. Arguments for or against change ultimately revolve around the issue of what I will call cultural reproduction: will electronic texts, although different from printed texts and perhaps even improved in some aspects, still be the same in other essential features? The issue becomes particularly complex when attempting to assess possible changes to literary texts, because both the term literature and the term text represent "essentially contested concepts" (Gallie 1955-56). No consensus exists on what their "essential features" might be. In part, this is because postmodern culture has, as Lyotard puts it, "...altered the game rules for science, literature, and the arts" (Lyotard 1984, xxiii)— increasing our incredulity toward traditional humanistic assumptions about our ability to define, let alone achieve, the true, the good, and the beautiful. These new rules have altered our cultural games to such an extent that many of them can no longer be recognized. The unexpected audience resistance to our keynote speaker's claim that he was preaching to the converted came not so much from a resistance to the idea that printed books will disappear as from the fear that traditional concepts by which we interpret the meaning of writing and reading will be negated by new theories of textuality. Professor Bolter has presented this argument more fully in his book *Writing Space:*

> The traditional Western view is that we can reach the signified, that we can get beyond the forest of signs to what the signs stand for. All of deconstruction's work is to show that the transcendental signified cannot be achieved. . . .
> The new view of signs is embodied unambiguously in electronic hypertext. Here the writer and reader know that there is no transcendence, because they know that the topical elements they create are arbitrary sequences of bits made meaningful only by their interconnecting links. All this suggests again that the computer takes us beyond deconstruction, which for all its ambivalence, is still incapable of acquiescing in the arbitrary and limited character of writing. . . . Electronic readers and writer have finally arrived at the land promised (or threatened) by post-modern theory for two decades: the world of pure signs. . . . While traditional humanists and deconstructionists have been battling over the arbitrary, self-referential character of writing, computer specialists, oblivious to this struggle, have been building a world of electronic signs in which the battle is over (Bolter 1991, 204).
> A great deal is philosophically at stake here. . . . A philosophy of mind for the coming age of writing will have to recognize the mind as a network of signs spreading out beyond the individual mind to embrace other tests, written in other minds and on conventional writing surfaces. Something like Peirce's vision of the mind as a sign should prevail. The most radical solution would dispense altogether with the notion of intentionality: there is no privileged author but simply textual networks that are always open to interpretation. Such a philosophy may be nothing less than the end of the ego, the end of the Cartesian self as the defining quality of humanity. The radical view would also seem to vindicate symbolic artificial intelligence (Bolter 1991, 221).

The essential feature that Bolter wants to preserve in an electronic world is literacy, defined as pure, symbolic communication. In this, he wants to strengthen the use of the computer as a symbol-manipulating device to which "the immediate perception of the world is not open" (Bolter 1991, 224) in order to counteract what he sees as the false consciousness of alternative modern media such as television whose

essential feature is to promote the illusion that we can achieve such
immediate perception. "Unlike the computer, which is a technology
of literacy, television therefore works against literacy in favoring image
over idea, emotional response over analysis" (Bolter 1991, 226).

In line with the postmodern valorization of semiosis as the Queen
of the sciences, Bolter here follows Paul de Man's argument in his essay
on "The Epistemology of Metaphor," which deconstructs our Western
belief, culturally inherited from John Locke, that we can directly perceive
reality. Specifically, de Man focuses on Locke's attempt to establish the
priority of experience over language so that we can "speak of things
as they are" when we seek human understanding and can restrict the
uses of figurative speech to "discourses where we seek rather pleasure
and delight than information and improvement" (de Man 1979, 13).
De Man then shows how Locke's attempt to define "man" (i.e., human
being) using the concept of "substances . . . as the support, the ground
of the properties (*hypokeimenon*)" fails (de Man 1979, 17). He concludes
that the "proliferating and disruptive power of figural language"
imparts to all texts an unstable epistemology that calls into question
the distinctions that we use to fix meanings and to classify texts—
including his own (de Man 1979, 28). Thus, those texts that we consider
especially rigorous in their attempt to control terminology and relate
it to "truth"—i.e. those discourses that we label philosophic, scientific,
and technical—nevertheless depend upon figural language. Likewise,
those that we consider especially playful in their attempt to invent
imaginary worlds—i.e. those that we label literary, humanistic, and
poetic—depend upon philosophic or epistemological assumptions.

According to Bolter, the new postmodern view of signs has arisen
and is embodied in the social structures of contemporary postindustrial
societies as well. Processes begun during the Enlightenment have
gradually destroyed the possibility of maintaining a common cultural
heritage:

> As our written culture becomes a vast hypertext, the reader is free
> to choose to explore one subnetwork or many, as he or she wishes.
> It is no longer convincing to say that one subject is more important
> than another. Today even highly educated readers, especially but
> not exclusively scientists, may know only one or a few areas well.
> Such ignorance of the shared textual tradition is in part the result
> of the specialization of the sciences that has been proceeding since
> the 17th century. But even the humanities are now utterly
> fragmented. . . . [S]pecialization has gone too far to be recalled.
> In the sciences it is indispensable. In the humanities and social
> sciences it is institutionalized. The intellectual world is now defined
> by numerous "special interest groups" pulling this way and that....

> Within the hypertextual libraries that are now being assembled, individual intellectual communities can retreat into their subnetworks and operate with as much or as little connection to each other as they desire. . . . We are hard put to criticize any of these choices: they are simply questions of taste. (Bolter 1991, 234-235)

MANAGING CULTURAL REPRODUCTION
IN A POSTINDUSTRIAL ECONOMY

Within the academy, the operation of these trends over the last several decades has been reflected in a general decline in the relative position of the humanities to the point of precariousness. Arguments about the future of books, the humanities, and libraries revolve around the issue of whether these trends will continue or abate, whether their results will diminish or enhance the distinguishing features of our concern, and whether there is anything we can do about it. Answers to all of these questions, it seems to me, require us first to find out the underlying causes of these trends. Two approaches recommend themselves: a pragmatic approach using the ancient arts of dialogue and rhetoric; and a theoretical approach using modern information technologies and scientific models.

The Orator and the Manager

The ancient art of rhetoric has been revived in our postmodern age as a practical method for arriving at decisions in a context of dissent, incredulity, and pluralism. In this case, agreement on what we mean by a human being, a literary text, or an electronic text center derives from a process of real-life negotiation, not from a process of discovering some transcendent or immediately perceived truth. Authors such as Lanham and Lyotard—while agreeing that the networked realm of cyberspace provides writing space for private, playful self-expression within a society that has fragmented into competing interest groups holding fundamentally different beliefs and values—also emphasize the need to pragmatically promote a broader community of interest with the classical humanist's tools of dialogue and rhetoric. In line with the incredulity of postmodern thought towards metanarratives and its correlate that objective truth can never be achieved, "...the principle there is that persuasion makes the community's truth for it . . . . [and] The goal is not indeed achievement of objective truth, but a practical outcome of equity and honor acceptable to the whole community" (O'Donnell 1994).

One way to translate our valued human heritage into a language the modern electronic age can understand and to defend the professional interests of humanists is to rhetorically engage those whose heritage differs. In the process, older conceptions of venerated terms and practices may be radically transformed from our point of view. One key concept in regard to institutionalizing support for electronic text processing concerns what knowledge and skills will be needed to provide that support and how people will obtain them. Many competing interests within and without the academy intersect on this question, but Lanham believes that they may find a common rhetorical ground in Drucker's conception of management as a liberal art and develop a "...new core curriculum in language, the arts, and democratic politics" (Lanham 1993, 114-15).

In *Post-Capitalist Society*, Drucker elaborates in a chapter on "The Educated Person":

> The post-capitalist society—the knowledge society—thus needs exactly the opposite of what Deconstructionists, radical feminists, or anti-Westerns propose. It needs the very thing they totally reject: a universally educated person.
>
> Yet the knowledge society needs a different kind of educated person from the ideal for which the Humanists are fighting. They rightly stress . . . the heritage of mankind. But a bridge to the past is not enough. . . . The educated person needs to be able to bring his or her knowledge to bear on the present, not to mention molding the future. There is no provision for such ability in the proposals of the Humanists . . . without it, the Great Tradition remains dusty antiquarianism. (Drucker 1993, 212)

This conception is not far from what appears to be the new strategic direction of Indiana University's (IU) Office of Information Technologies, whose new Associate Vice President sees a major market to be served by universities such as IU in providing a quality liberal education as well as better training over computer networks to employees of corporations located at distant sites (Caldwell 1994).

Evolutionary Theory and Information Technology

Our literature is permeated with evolutionary terminology, but our arguments continue to be dominated by typological thinking. The basic metaphorical nature of human beings and their language needs to be more widely recognized and accepted. Derrida's deconstructive method can be clarified if we see it as an evolutionary analysis of language. Just as genetically encoded information provides the means for biological reproduction, linguistically encoded information provides the means for cultural reproduction. In both cases, "the possibility of repetition (as the *same,* but repeated and to that extent not *identical*) is definitive" (Bennington 1993, 139). Every biological creature, every literary text, and every scientific theory is both "the same" as other members of its species, genre, or discipline and "different" from them because of its unique inheritance and contextual development. The processes by which these similarities and differences arise is exceedingly complex, but with the assistance of information technology, more adequate theories are being developed (Lenski 1993). The degree to which the evolution of culture and intelligence has been decoupled from our inherited biological being and can be treated as a totally independent system remains controversial (Boyd and Richersen 1985, 1993; Hall 1993; Midgley 1978; Sheehan and Sosna 1991). An evolutionary theory explains the facts of a system

> ...by reference to previous facts as well as to a causal link which . . . may be shown to include (1) a mechanism of preservation and transmission, (2) a mechanism of variety-creation, (3) a mechanism of selection, and which includes or may be enhanced by introducing (4) a mechanism of segregation between different "populations" . . . . The emergence of an evolutionary process presupposes that none of the individual mechanisms becomes too dominant. If preservation dominates, the result is a stasis . . . while a dominance of variety-creation leads to non-deterministic chaos. (Andersen 1994, 14)

Modern history may be defined as a process in which the capacity for variety creation has been expanding exponentially. Technology has greatly extended our cultural ability to invent and transmit tools and behaviors with which we can creatively manipulate our environment. The resulting diversity forms a vast cultural pool of variants that may potentially prove adaptive in the face of unknown future challenges. It also threatens to overwhelm existing social mechanisms that attempt to preserve our inherited wisdom and to select out for breeding the most "fit" new varieties.

Systems have extremely powerful self-regulating properties; we like to think that our society will neither stagnate nor collapse but will be able to adapt itself in an orderly and healthy manner. One important way to do this is to regulate the evolutionary processes within our society by organizing that society according to principles based upon a valid and systematic understanding of society. Either the decisions that we make to allocate our always limited resources will be principled and virtuous or they will be arbitrary and ineffective because they are based upon false knowledge and values. Interestingly enough, the rise of the very electronic technologies whose expansion has created that flood of information threatening to inundate all of us, also

> has exposed the centrality of information processing, communication, and control to all aspects of human society and social behavior. It is to these fundamental informational concepts . . . that we social scientists may hope to reduce our proliferating but still largely unsystematic knowledge of social structure and process. (Beniger 1986, 436)

THE RISE OF A POSTINDUSTRIAL INFORMATION SOCIETY
AND THE ECOLOGY OF ACADEMIC LIBRARIES

Libraries as Social Institutions

Libraries are tertiary, information-processing institutions whose cultural programs serve the needs of the larger social organizations within which they are embedded. The processes and procedures of modern academic libraries, although largely under the control of professional library staffs, have been designed primarily to support their parent institutions' programs of research, teaching, and service. These programs in turn, although largely under the control of various academic faculties, ultimately derive their definition from the demands of the broader community for the "products" of a higher education. Up until recently, the interdependent institutional cultures of humanities faculties, university presses, and library staffs in American academia were relatively autonomous and isolated from the mass culture of the industrialized society surrounding them. Academic culture was, and in part still is, a "book culture" based upon the authority and craftsmanship of individual authors and scholars and justified by classical arguments about the ability of literature and a liberal education to produce virtuous citizens.

Library Economics and Knowledge Work

Retired library administrator Allen Veaner quotes a colleague who expresses the consensus among library directors about the radical effect that the new academic ecology is having on libraries:

> Concisely summarizing how radically librarianship's milieu has changed within a few years, Charles Lowry, director of libraries at the University of Texas, Arlington, urged professionals to recognize that the library has shifted from a labor-intensive craft workshop [with a primarily local clientele] to a capital-intensive, high-technology, light industry [with a national market]. . . . To cope with turbulent change, academic librarianship has to surrender any remaining disconnectedness, laissez-faire autonomy, and dedication to ownership of materials. Higher education now has the opportunity and the tools to transform the library into a people-centered outreach agency with powerful interinstitutional linkages. This transformation is not only proper but essential; if it fails to materialize, the way is open for other agencies to seize the library's domain, as has already occurred in some graduate schools of library and information science. (Veaner 1990, 454)

This situation has arisen because the application of information technology to the production and use of literary texts involves the absorption of academic scholars, publishers, and librarians into the postindustrial information society. That society was not created by literary scholars seeking better ways to interpret literary texts but by industrial capitalists attempting to solve control and regulation problems raised by the speed and complexity of modern mass production, distribution, and consumption. The process basically began when

> commercial capital came to be tied down in the British power-driven industries [so that] profit [began] to depend on the ability not to manage the totality of one's investments but the processing of relatively much smaller investments in raw materials. The faster one moved these investments past one's fixed capital, the greater the returns on one's investment.
> If profit provided the incentive to process matter faster under industrial capitalism, steam power provided the means. As long as the extraction, processing, and movement of matter depended on traditional sources of energy (human, draft animal, wind, and water power) the material economy did not differ markedly in the speed of its throughputs from that of the Middle Ages. (Beniger 1986, 169)

This created a crisis when the artificially increased speed and complexity of production and transportation vastly surpassed the ability of native human intelligence to control them. This control crisis gradually was overcome, first through the invention of bureaucratic organizations and second through the invention of various mechanical information processors and communications devices that eventually led to the creation of the modern computer. Overcoming the crisis of controlling material and energy flows has been achieved at the expense of creating a new crisis as "information processing and flows need themselves to be controlled, so that informational technologies must continue to be applied at higher and higher levels of control" (Beniger 1986, 433-34). Today, under postindustrial capitalism, profit still provides the incentive, but now the need is to process and communicate information even faster, and electronic computer networks provide the means.

Standards and the Growth of a Knowledge Economy

The Internet, as its name implies, interconnects many other networks. Its creation and development was made possible not just by advances in hardware and software but also by the construction of crucial protocols and standards. If the MAchine Readable Cataloging (MARC) standard for the communication of machine-readable bibliographic records has been "the single most important factor in the growth of library automation" (Crawford 1989, 1), then the Transmission Control Protocol/Internet Protocol (TCP/IP) suite of standards for the transmission of information among different computer environments has been the single most important factor in the growth of inter-institutional networking (Gilster 1993, 14). Both developments were made possible by the earlier development of the American Standard Code for Information Interchange, commonly known by its acronym, ASCII (Crawford 1989, 271). Taken together, these and related standards have recently allowed scholars at one institution to easily access both centralized cataloging utilities such as OCLC and RLIN as well as directly access the online public access catalogs of individual libraries throughout the world. In addition, they also have direct access to a variety of scholarly discussion groups and electronic texts. The growth of end-user searching and subsequent democratization of information predicted by advocates of the online database industry previously was thwarted, according to Pfaffenberger (1990, 80), by a technological system whose style captured "the reigning ethos of the world in which it was constructed, namely, reference librarianship and the production of print-based reference media" (Pfaffenberger 1990, 21) and which thereby required the intervention of professional search mediators and which primarily benefited "highly educated. . . [people who] work in fields where there is a perceived advantage to obtaining information in a timely fashion" (Pfaffenberger 1990, 117). It remains a moot question as to whether the Internet will be a more effective means for democratizing information (either inside or outside the academy), or will "by transforming information into a commodity and privatizing information produced by public investments . . . create an information elite" (Pfaffenberger 1990, 172).

As long as the creation, processing, and communication of information depended on traditional sources of control (genetically and culturally inherited human intelligence), our knowledge economy also operated at about the same throughput rate as in the Middle Ages. Until recently, most work with literary texts remained at this speed and scale, constrained by the natural limits of the human brain and supporting social control organizations—such as academic libraries with their craft-based systems of book acquisition, cataloging, and reader services. As we speed up the throughputs of our knowledge economy by the application of electronic technologies, one worries not so much that this process will replace the book as that it will replace human scholars with computer systems just as it has industrial workers. More generally, we may ask: how will electronic technologies change the form and role of human beings in scholarship?

The Microcomputer Revolution and the Growth of Humanities Computing

Commercial software and hardware products developed by the computer industry, and the standards that allow them to be networked, have only recently begun to support humanities computing. Likewise, the skills and knowledge of computing support personnel have focused not on humanistic but on administrative, commercial, and scientific uses. To some extent, these uses do overlap with basic needs of humanistic computing. Thus, standard commercial word-processing and relational database packages can be applied by students and teachers in the humanities to basic writing and data collection tasks. Likewise, the provision of subsidized access to the Internet has allowed individual scholars and organizations to see the potential for expanding scholarly communication by forming electronic seminars such as the HUMANIST (McCarthy 1992). Also, the need to improve the load factor on capital-intensive fiber optic networks exists just as it did during the mainframe time-sharing days, and this is accomplished in many cases by providing campus-wide access to basic scholarly tools such as online library catalogs. These catalogs themselves, of course, have been developed only with the aid of the service utilities and the application of bibliographic control standards.

All this has laid the groundwork for the recent expansion of academic projects in support of humanities computing. In response to the expansion of many new academic organizations devoted to the promotion and support of information technology into the same information territory traditionally inhabited by libraries, a legion of advocates devoted to the organizational survival of libraries has arisen. All of them basically argue that libraries must adapt to this turbulent new environment by imitating the characteristics of those organizational species that appear to have high reproductive potential and by collaborating with a much larger group of organizations in a postmodern environment where space/time has been drastically compressed by the very information technology that forms the reason for our existence (Campbell 1992; Henry and Peters 1993; Lipow 1993; Lucier 1992; McCoy 1993). This pressure to adapt to the future squeezes hardest in the area of library support for the humanities because both libraries and the humanities have heavily institutionalized the value of preserving information from and about the human past as a major source of wisdom about the human condition.

Humanist Scholars and the Virtual Library

Howard Bloch and Carla Hesse, editors for a special issue of *Representations* on "Future Libraries" that grew out of a conference organized by the editors at the University of California at Berkeley on the "Très Grande Bibliothèque and the Future of the Library" (Bloch and Hesse 1993), summarize the intense anxieties, mingled with idealistic hopes, generated by our postmodern condition in relation to libraries and humanistic scholarship:

> Things have been out of control for a long time, only we haven't
> realized it until now; and if the potential loss of the book is linked
> psychologically to the fear of loss of bodily wholeness, self-
> possession, and control, the builders of the future library remind
> us of the ways in which technology also enables control over that
> which we have already lost. . . .
> The electronic library will thus make it possible for readers to
> respond to the dizzying boundlessness of knowledge itself . . . to
> recover the Enlightenment dream of a library that offers not only
> comprehensive or universal access to knowledge but also the power
> to move freely within its perimeters. . . .
> Yet for some, this conception of the library as an ever-expanding
> web of intellectual freeplay is, again, the source of profound anxiety,
> rooted in the fear of losing a cherished liberal conception of cultural
> authority: the self-contained individually authored text, whose
> author can be held accountable to a reading public. The electronic
> library can be viewed analogously in economic terms as signaling
> the displacement of a production-centered culture by a consumer-
> oriented one, with all the cultural conservatism that this might
> imply. (Bloch and Hesse 1993, 5-7)

A great deal of the enhanced knowledge and control that we have
achieved over our natural environment through industrial capitalism
has been achieved not only at the expense of that environment but
also at the expense of dehumanized industrial workers. Both our living
space and our selves have all too often been treated as just another
exploitable, interchangeable "resource"—or at the other end of the
process as a consumption machine. The challenge for companies in
a postindustrial, information age of international competition will be
to treat "people and not machines . . . [as] their most valuable resource . . .
[and to get] humans and technology working together in harmony. . . .
The task therefore is to develop more human-centered systems . . . [that]
retain and enhance human skills, control, and discretion, rather than
taking them away" (Forester 1989, 13) in exchange for money and goods
as orthodox scientific management did under what has been called
"Fordism" (Harvey 1989; Lipietz 1993). The problem with meeting this
challenge in industry comes from the fact that the unpredictable and
unregulated dynamics of international competition may not allow
companies the luxury of "re-skilling" their employees rather than "de-
skilling" or firing them, of offering them self-control and flexibility
in turn for higher productivity, and that the demand for constantly
higher job productivity may itself further diminish the capability of
employees to maintain non-job-related human relationships.

The challenge for scholarly organizations in a postindustrial,
information age of international competition will be to introduce
machines as a valuable resource and to get humans and technology
working together in harmony without destroying the existing human-
centered systems that emphasize human skills, control, and discretion.

DAYS IN THE LIFE OF A KNOWLEDGE WORKER:
THE CASE OF LETRS

Early Developments: 1970-87

During this early period in humanities computing, I came to Indiana University as Associate Government Documents Librarian just as IU librarians were achieving faculty status. I soon decided that my true interests lay not in administration or technical services (little was I to know!) but in subject librarianship. I began refreshing the Arabic I had begun earlier at the University of Chicago, then took two years leave to work as a library consultant and do literary research in Saudi Arabia, after which I pursued a graduate degree in Arabic Language and Literature while working as a reference librarian at IU from 1979 on.

It wasn't until 1986 that I discovered humanities computing, at about the same time our campus computing services did. In that year, I had already chosen a dissertation topic in the Near East Languages and Cultures department—"Arab-English Translation Shifts and the Modern Egyptian Short Story"—that depended heavily on the use of humanities computing methods and concepts. Working with the Multi-Lingual Scholar (MLS) program, I entered texts in the original Arabic that had been translated into English by two or more translators. I then exported these texts from MLS using its character translation capability so that the texts could be imported into Nota Bene in transliterated form where I manipulated them with NB's Text Base program to produce various concordance-style tables, which were then fed into a statistical program. This allowed me to create, for example, comparative histograms of the thematic patterns of the English translations compared to the original Arabic texts. I mention this in part because there was little help available for such work anywhere on campus, and I relied primarily on my membership in the Association for Literary and Linguistics Computing for support. Like others in humanities computing at the time, I was primarily working alone and reinventing the wheel as I went. This experience provided a major motivation for my efforts at institutionalizing support of similar research projects.

The process of industrializing knowledge work also has had a profound effect on the role of library professionals supporting the humanities, and indirectly lead to my current role as Co-Director of LETRS. In the 1950s, the IU Libraries instituted a unique approach to library support for subject specialties. Scholar librarians were hired to be directly responsible for liaison with individual departments and for acquiring materials in their area of specialty. They were independent of any library department, being neither technical service nor public service librarians. The initial concept of the "Subject Specialist" was to hire individuals with subject capabilities and status equal to their faculty clients. Over the years, however, as library expenses, automated technical processing, and access services increased, these subject and area specialists often came to be seen as an expensive luxury and a likely target for organizational downsizing. As individuals attached to no department, they formed an informal group with limited bureaucratic power and diverse professional interests. Thus, when the Near Eastern Languages and Literature Specialist retired in 1987 during a period of unexpectedly intense financial crisis (the incumbent had been half-time Near Eastern Cataloger, an economy previously accomplished after copy cataloging became more prevalent with our participation in OCLC), his position was eliminated instead of being filled. This was the position for which I had been training since 1974.

The elimination of the Near Eastern Subject Specialist position was at that time part of a broader administration plan to restructure the library staff along the lines of what Veaner calls the industrial democracy model, and "to reduce the number of job classifications and permit greater flexibility of assignment" (Veaner 1990, 446). Specifically, an attempt was made to merge the subject and area librarians with the general reference service librarians. As Veaner might have predicted, this attempt to graft an industrial democracy model onto "work in higher education's service sector, where so much of the social structure is based on historical elitism and [where] the output is largely intangible," failed (Veaner 1990, 446). However, for a full year, I was assigned to three jobs: reference and instruction in the Undergraduate Library, general reference in the main Reference Department situated in the Research Collections division, and Near Eastern Languages and Literature Specialist. In the last job, I was supposed to coordinate the work of individuals in other departments assigned part-time to support the collection and processing of Near Eastern materials. With no authority and no resources at my disposal to do this (on top of having conflicting performance goals as a member of two other departments), this was a no-win situation, and I decided to retool. I used my online searching experience gained in the Reference Department and my microcomputer experience gained in my dissertation research to obtain the position of Library Microcomputer Specialist at the Indiana Cooperative Library Services Authority (INCOLSA), the regional agency that represents OCLC in Indiana and took another two years' leave of absence from July 1988 to June 1990. During that period, I developed a training program for bibliographic software, among other duties. In 1990, I returned to IU under a new administration and became involved in providing training in such software, whose capabilities were particularly needed to supplement the lack of any downloading and reformatting capability in the library automation system that had been brought up during my absence.

Since then, under a new administration with a radically different and more open management style, we have in fact accomplished a flattening of our organization, not by replacing it with an industrial democracy model, but by largely eliminating the hierarchically organized middle management layer and extending the concept of librarians as faculty—with all that implies in the way of professional autonomy and collegiality. Major issues remain, but the experiment has created a better internal environment for the collaboration necessary to develop a new service such as LETRS within an external environment of stagnant resources and increased demands.

LETRS is Born: 1991-

By the early 1990s, a variety of corporate actors were helping to promote the conditions that would lead to the creation of Indiana University's Library Electronic Text Resource Service. One major actor was the National Endowment for the Humanities which, with the Mellon Foundation, sponsored the March 1990 Conference on a National Center for Machine-Readable Texts in the Humanities. This conference culminated in the creation of the Center for Electronic Texts in the Humanities (CETH), whose first summer seminar I attended in August 1992, and whose second summer seminar my LETRS Co-Director, Dick Ellis, attended in August 1993. Another very important influence was the Research Libraries Group (RLG), which created a powerful agent for change when it established its Program for Research Information Management (PRIMA) "in 1985 as a response to the changing information environment at research institutions. . . . PRIMA's mission is to explore information resources beyond the traditional purview of libraries and to foster activities that encourage the organization and computerization of new data resources" (Gould 1988, 1). Some of the ways in which RLG specifically encouraged such activities include (1) supporting the work of Marianne Gaunt in creating and maintaining the Rutgers Inventory of Machine-Readable Texts in the Humanities on RLIN; (2) undertaking a survey of *Information Needs in the Humanities: An Assessment,* along with companion surveys of the social sciences and the sciences, as a basis to "determine the relationship between . . . trends [in each discipline] and [its] data requirements . . . [and to] provide a basis for fostering or adopting projects regarded by scholars . . . as valuable" (Gould 1988, 1); (3) undertaking another survey, promoted by "the Research Library Group . . . English and American bibliographers discussion group . . . to determine the way as well as the extent to which text files are supported" (Price-Wilkin 1991b, 11;

Price-Wilkin 1991a, 19-25); (4) sponsoring numerous seminars dealing with the adaptation of research libraries to a changing environment—one in 1985 producing a paper by Timothy Weiskel on "Libraries as Life-Systems: Information, Entropy, and Coevolution on Campus" (Weiskel 1986) that stimulated my developing interest in evolutionary models of social change; and (5) sponsoring workshops specifically devoted to electronic text files in the humanities, especially an ALA pre-conference at Atlanta in 1991. The head of our Reference Department, Ann Bristow, attended this preconference, and brought back information about electronic text initiatives at other universities—including that of Anita Lowry's Electronic Text Service (ETS) at Columbia University. I attended a different preconference, but at some of the main ALA meetings, I heard Richard E. Lucier speak on his concept of "knowledge management" as a way of involving librarians more intimately and effectively in the scholarly communication process. His thoughts on this concept are well summarized in a article appearing in a publication sponsored by another organization dedicated to changing the way we work, EDUCOM (Lucier 1992, 24-31).

For some time, IU's fund managers and subject and area librarians had been trying to figure out how to respond to the few, but significant, requests we were beginning to receive for the purchase of electronic texts—such as the Thesaurus Linguae Graecae (TLG) and the works of Goethe. The time for making a formal proposal seemed to be at hand. We had requests for major purchases of electronic texts, but no way to support the use of such materials; we had before us the model of Columbia's Electronic Text Service and its proof that one could begin with a small investment; and we had a situation in which the Reference Department already was heavily involved in providing support for electronic resources in the humanities with our local area network (LAN) and our connection to online sources such as the American Research on the Treasury of the French Language (ARTFL), the Dartmouth Dante Project, and RLIN. The original name proposed for our service was "Center for Electronic Texts in the Humanities" (CETH), but we discovered just in time that this was to be the new name for the national center for humanities computing at Rutgers and Princeton. Working backwards from acronym to designation, as has become fashionable, we came up with LETRS. Here is the part of our November 7, 1991 initial proposal that lays out our basic assumptions and principles:

> This proposal recommends the establishment of an IU Library Electronic Text Resource Service, to be located in the Research Collections tower of the IUB Library. Such a service would focus the efforts of IU faculty, staff, and students concerned with advancing the use of computing at IU for teaching and research in the Humanities. Within the environment outlined by the Academic

Computing Planning Committee's Computing in the Humanities Subcommittee, the establishment of this service offers a feasible and effective way to begin achieving the many goals and objectives listed by the Subcommittee. The basic approach attempts to maximize the benefits, while minimizing the costs, associated with innovation by building on current structures and established procedures and by working collaboratively to build coalitions among existing organizations, rather than by starting yet another independent project that would compete for limited resources. It is recommended, therefore, that the service be developed in stages, initially located on the main floor of the Research Collections and administered by the Reference Department in cooperation with other library departments and university agencies (Day 1991, 1).

Meanwhile, at Bloomington's Academic Computing Service: 1987-

As at most American universities, IU's computing activities began "...in the support of research in the sciences, but by the end of the 1970s, it was clear that the scope had to expand to include all disciplines and must be better coordinated . . . With the consultation of the Bloomington Campus Computer Use Committee (BCCUC). . . BACS [Bloomington Academic Computing Services] was born" (DeHayes 1987, 1). In 1987, Polley McClure (now at the University of Virginia), was appointed Associate Dean for Academic Computing. One of the first things she did was to review a report of the Academic Computing Planning Committee whose recommendations, if followed would allow IU to "...maintain the gains of the last five years," and become "leaders among liberal arts universities in applying the technology to academic work." These recommendations were to:

>Provide individual workstations for all faculty . . . >Build a high-speed, user-friendly network . . . >Bring the information resources in the University Library onto the network . . . >Integrate computing technology into the instructional program of the University . . . >Establish a Center for Innovative Technology Applications . . . >Strive for excellence in our resources and support for research computing . . . [and] >Strive for national recognition in the application of computing to the humanities. (McClure 1987a, 1-2)

As can be noted from the phrasing of the last objective in particular, the cultural belief of the IU decision-making community was that of belonging to a dominant organizational species. Jacqueline Stewart reports that the participants in project Athena at MIT made a similar assumption, that "we are a world-class institute comprised of world-class people" (Stewart 1989, 290). This manner of stating the goals of humanities computing simultaneously reflects the vague understanding of humanities computing needs that most of these same decision makers had at the time. In the November 1987 issue of BACSpace, McClure wrote as follows:

> Of all our directions, the least clear are those appropriate to take in support of computing in the humanities. Scholarship in the humanities does not lend itself (as do the physical sciences) to the kinds of computing that have historically been the focus of academic computing support. We are making a start in electronic support of the humanities, but we need to know more. In this, scholars in the humanities have a critical role to play: one of helping us define our direction. (McClure 1987b, 1)

Humanities Computing from the Scholar's Point of View

McClure continued her report with a summary of a faculty survey:

> The Academic Computing staff asked Bloomington humanities faculty in a September [1987] survey to define the ideal computing environment. Though many of the 50 respondents expressed frustration at the question, claiming they "didn't know what was out there to help them," the vast majority predicted computing would play an important part in the future of the humanities. The results show the following consensus: >Sixty-eight percent agreed they needed workstations, with word processing capabilities (eighty-six percent), and a printer (twenty-eight percent) in their office. >Fifty-two percent wanted access to electronic libraries; thirty-eight percent wanted workstation tools for managing bibliographies. >Sixteen percent wanted external databases. >Ten percent wanted special character sets. >Eighteen percent said they'd like various teaching aids, including graphics, computer-driven projection systems, and more teaching labs (on the model of the Macintosh lab that is used mainly for teaching English composition). (McClure 1987b, 2-3)

She went on to discuss those humanities computing activities that Susan Hockey outlined in her presentation as defining the field but that the scholars surveyed had not mentioned. McClure listed them as "quantitative text analysis, [converting] material to electronic form [with an] Optical Scanner, . . . style analysis, [and] 'crunching words' in general" (McClure 1987b, 2-3).

In general, it may be said that the problem of providing support to humanists whose work can benefit from the use of computers has been exacerbated by a rapidly changing technology whose potential power cannot easily be harnessed. Scholars and students understandably are reluctant to invest precious money in new equipment and software that immediately becomes outmoded, or to invest precious time and energy into learning how to do something in a new and improved manner that they already can do with assurance in a more traditional way. Likewise, although desktop computing power has been increasing at a phenomenal rate for some time now, along with a similarly spectacular decrease in unit costs, these developments have been driven by the markets for business, personal, and scientific software. Most of the basic hardware, network, and software standards that provide what little stability there is in the computing industry were not designed with humanistic scholarship in mind. Only within the last couple of years, for example, have international standards for the production of electronic texts and for multilingual character encoding finally been promulgated and begun to be incorporated into the type of systems needed for sophisticated scholarship in the humanities.

Nevertheless, early founders of the humanities computing movement recognized the potential power that electronic technologies had for accomplishing many of the traditional but complex information-processing tasks that scholars undertake and for expanding the capacity for scholarly communication. A major figure among these visionaries was Joseph Raben, a 1954 Indiana University Ph.D. in English who subsequently went on to found the journal *Computers and the Humanities* in 1966, later became the first president of the Association for Computers and the Humanities in 1978, and recently founded *Scholar*, an online service for text analysis and natural language applications. He expressed his recognition of the developing interdependency between humanities scholars and a computer-run, postindustrial, information society in an interview for *Contemporary Authors:*

> The motivation to establish a journal to further the interaction of computers and humanities research was a recognition that each field would ultimately appreciate its need for the other. Complex machinery requires imaginative, inquiring minds to exploit its potential; the humanities require all the aid that technology can supply for the routine functions that support high-level activity: indexes, concordances, bibliographies, text collations, photo-composition. In my editorial and authorial activities, I have sought to explain the benefits of this interaction to appropriate audiences around the world. (*Contemporary Authors* 1989, 385)

Computers were invented during World War II by scientists working for the government. Administrative and commercial uses have dominated since that time. However, traditional scholars have been using computers to strengthen their inherited cultural values and activities since the 1950s. It should come as no surprise that the individual who began this process came from an organization famous for its institutionalization of values. As Susan Hockey pointed out, Father Roberto Busa, at the Instituto Filosofico Aloisianum, in Gallarate, Italy, was the first to use a computer to automatically generate a concordance—indexing four of Aquinas's hymns in 1951. We should not forget that many of the other institutions whose well-being we are concerned with serving in the LETRS project—scholarship, universities, faculty—were invented in medieval Europe.

Theodore F. Brunner, who conceived the TLG in 1971 and continues to manage it, points out that its origins go back to 1572, when "a Geneva scholar, editor, and printer named Henri Estienne—Stephanus, as he is more commonly known to classicists—published a Thesaurus Graecae Linguae (TGL), a comprehensive lexicon" (Brunner 1991, 62).

The electronic text centers being established in universities exhibit a great variety, but in general we all are acquiring a remarkably similar set of texts and tools that are focused on what we at LETRS have been describing as "those valued and enduring works that traditionally have provided readers with culturally significant interpretations of the human condition and have formed the core subject of study in the liberal arts" (Day and Ellis 1993, 7). These texts have largely been produced, again as Susan Hockey pointed out, by independent research organizations—usually with a vested interest in and veneration for a particular linguistic or literary tradition. A major impetus for the founding of LETRS was the request for access in the library to electronic versions of classical texts: the TLG, Perseus, and the Packard Humanities Institute discs. Likewise, we have acquired the major Biblical text packages as well as the CETEDOC CD-ROM of Medieval Christian Latin Texts, a CD-ROM of Judaic Classics, and several versions of the Qur'an and the Islamic Hadith. Prior to forming LETRS, the Philosophy Department successfully submitted a grant to the University Computing Services to finance the purchase of a LAN plus most of the philosophical texts offered by the INTELEX company—noted in "Sidebar 3" of Price-Wilkin's article (Price-Wilkin 1991b, 14).

Beginnings of Library/Computing Services Coevolution: 1987-91

The period from 1987 to 1991 at IU was a period necessarily devoted to the creation of a stable, standard, somewhat easier to use information technology infrastructure. The major area where this resulted in perceived and measurable advances for humanities computing support has been in the provision of online, networked resources. All involve support for traditional scholarly activities but relieve some of the time and space constraints associated with these activities. Creating a campus-wide network hooked into the Internet and heavily promoting the subsidized use of electronic mail has created a critical mass of users and contributed to lively scholarly communication both within and across traditional disciplines via the many siblings descended from Willard McCarty's first HUMANIST electronic seminar list (McCarty 1992). Not only has it allowed fulfillment of the goal to "bring the information resources in the University Library onto the network" but also to connect with a variety of non-IU Library based online resources, beginning with catalogs of other universities and with general scholarly bibliographic utilities such as RLIN and CARL and extending to existing full-text humanities resources such as ARTFL and the Dartmouth Dante Project. On the more local level, joint IU Library/University Computing Services projects have led to the creation of several CD-ROM LANs (recently integrated under library control) which include major commercially available scholarly bibliographic sources such as the *MLA Bibliography* and *Philosopher's Index*.

Marriage at a Young Age: LETRS as a Joint IU Libraries and University Computing Services Project, 1992-

We are now well into the second stage of our project. In 1992, the rapid increase in scholarly communication resulting from the exponential growth of the Internet helped to make LETRS well known as a model for others. An interview about our program (entitled "Belles LETRS" by the interviewer) and other electronic text centers in a special issue of *Liberal Education* on "The Future of the Book" came about via such publicity (de Klerk and Deekle 1993, 46-48). Competition among institutions of higher education for resources, prestige, and a reputation for innovation has become intense. It was in such an atmosphere that the administrations of both the IU Libraries (IUL) and University Computing Services (UCS, formed by a merger of BACS and Administrative Computing) had already decided that as other universities began to take the lead in providing support for humanities computing, internal cooperation and coevolution made more sense as a survival strategy than competition. LETRS was already established by the Library but was greatly in need of technical and financial support for hardware and software if any campus-wide initiative was to succeed. UCS had an established network and resources to purchase hardware and software but few resources organized to support the actual content and activities of humanities computing. A jointly sponsored expansion of the LETRS facility in the Library was proposed, and an internal facility funding grant to the Research and University Graduate School was submitted and accepted in September 1993. Room was made for the new facility on the first floor of the research collections and services tower of the main library by moving the subject card catalog into the author/title catalog area. The center was constructed in January 1994 out of modular components with glass-paneled walls facing the public areas. It contains a seminar room and small traditional library, offices for the two co-directors, three research carrels, and a public computing area with room for sixteen workstations. We have been averaging about thirty patrons per week since the facility opened.

LETRS is a true partnership administered by two co-directors, one from each organization. Six graduate students with advanced skills in humanistic subject areas and languages, as well as computer ability, were hired as consultants. Our major difficulty has been in learning how to tap the resources of the full-time staff of each organization. The LETRS co-directors have no hierarchical authority over our co-workers. Only Dick Ellis has officially been appointed by UCS full-time to the LETRS project. I am still a member of the Reference Unit library faculty with additional duties beyond those of LETRS. Thus, we have evolved what can best be described as a matrix organization. It has taken over a year of negotiations and trial groupings to finally arrive at the suggestion of having a joint steering group consisting of the two co-directors and three other individuals from each organization that will meet once every other week to track the status of projects and communicate developments. Members of this steering group all have the authority needed within their own organizations to get things done in most of the areas where LETRS needs assistance. On alternate weeks, the IUL and UCS representatives meet separately to discuss issues from their own organizations' points of view. Selection responsibilities have begun to be integrated into normal library operations as was envisioned in the original 1991 proposal. Perry Willett, Librarian for Comparative Literature, English and Theatre, has been designated collection development coordinator for LETRS. We have yet, however, to develop a true collection policy. Likewise, a faculty advisory committee appointed last September has met only twice and has had some of the same difficulties as did the earlier advisory and survey groups in focusing on exactly what type of support we can and should provide.

Basic hardware support for the LETRS facility was institutionalized early on by integrating it into the system of UCS-supported public computing sites so that when something breaks, routine procedures for repair can be activated. Developing policies and means for the provision of software support has not been so easy. One of the reasons LETRS was created was that humanities tools do not easily fit into the model of industrial productivity that the computer services have inherited. Almost none of it is standard or widely used. In terms of labor costs and service to patrons, we are facing the same type of problems that led industrial capitalism to invent bureaucratic organizations and automated data processing—per unit costs are too high to be justified by performance criteria. Similar economic issues, of course, lie at the root of the development of the Text Encoding Initiative. At the same time, academic libraries in general are being hard pressed to operate more efficiently as a result of increased patron demands, rising materials and labor costs, and heavy infrastructure investments. Visions of virtual libraries spawned by the logarithmic increase in Internet use are pulling libraries in the same direction that our problems are pushing us. The same economic forces that led information utilities such as OCLC and RLIN to take on a central role in bibliographic data processing, now are leading academic libraries to construct cooperative organizations designed to modify their existing systems of cultural preservation and scholarly communication—based upon locally processed and accessible collections of print media—by building new systems based upon globally distributed and accessible collections of electronic media. As a result, LETRS has developed the following official "LETRS Support Policy" that follows basically the same technical model and the same economic reasoning presented by John Price-Wilkin at this conference:

> *Level 1—SGML Scholarly Electronic Texts in the Humanities:* Recognizing that one of the priority goals of the Bloomington Libraries for 1994/95 is to increase access to full-text scholarly information over the campus network in cooperation with University Computing Services, LETRS will provide full support for electronic texts in the humanities that have been acquired by IU Fund Managers and are in Standard Generalized Markup Language (SGML) tagged format—the encoding standard supported by the Association for Computers and the Humanities (ACH), the Association for Literary and Linguistic Computing, and the Association for Computational Linguistics (ACL).
>
> *Level 2—Non-SGML Scholarly Electronic Texts in the Humanities:* Recognizing that not all electronic texts relevant to humanities scholarship are available in SGML format, LETRS will work with IU Library fund managers on a case by case basis to provide whatever support can be arranged. Some of these electronic resources will be supported by the fund managers or LETRS staff and others will simply be made available to the end user.
>
> *Level 3—Humanities Computing Software Tools:* Recognizing that many different types of software may be useful and necessary in order to take full advantage of electronic text resources, LETRS may make available, but can not guarantee support for, some demonstration software tools that may be of special interest to scholars and students in the humanities. Examples of such software include: programs for various levels of text analysis, management, markup, production, and retrieval; computational linguistic and language learning programs; and multi-lingual word processing programs. (Library Electronic Text Resource Service 1994).

CONCLUSION

Industrial society primarily used land, labor, and practical knowledge to add value to its production of material goods and was organized around a rudimentary form of automation called mass production, which concentrated authority in managers and professionals who did the knowledge work and concentrated practical, supervised labor in the workers and staff. Under this system, pure knowledge workers in academic institutions enjoyed a certain isolation from the resultant mass culture—although we tended to copy the internal professional-staff dichotomies. Postindustrial society uses immaterial and theoretical knowledge as the basis for the production of services and is organized around more flexible, democratic work groups among its knowledge workers while perhaps lowering the status in many cases of its second class service workers—and decreasing job stability and security at all levels. Because of the preeminence of privileged information and innovative knowledge as a competitive advantage, institutions of advanced research and higher education such as IU are being drawn much closer into the central economic system and its norms of efficiency and productivity. One aspect of this is our desire, our need, to invest heavily in very expensive technological infrastructures, which require extensive interaction with commercial suppliers and represent not only a high initial capital investment but high continuing upgrade costs as well as human resource support and maintenance costs.

The main significance of LETRS, I believe, is that by coming together and articulating a vision of the future linked to the advancement of values long venerated by the tradition of humanistic scholarship, we have been able to draw on an incredible outpouring of support and enthusiasm. In practice, this has meant that we have been able to mobilize resources from many organizations to create a major facility that we are calling a humanist's laboratory—located in what has long been considered to be the heart of the university, and staffed by people whose primary commitment is to support the humanistic use of new information technology. In addition, we function as a forum, a node, and a service center to connect the needs of scholars with the many resources that already exist for serving those needs but that have remained unfocused in the past because no one viewed them from an integrated perspective. Our capacity to continually adapt to changing conditions will depend upon how well we can facilitate the development of a stable community of interest among the many different groups that have so recently begun working together. Can this collaborative style of knowledge work go beyond the current ad hoc stage and institutionalize its core values in the daily life of the university? Will it help to integrate new, computer-based research and teaching methodologies into the curriculum? Will it assist the process of recruiting new staff members throughout the university who have the skills and attitudes needed to maintain the traditional humanistic disciplines while advancing the practice of those disciplines through the application of relevant new methods? Will it lead to the establishment of procedures for reallocating and attracting resources to more effectively and efficiently put the power of computers and networks in the service of humanistic scholarship and liberal learning? How we answer these questions in practice depends, in large part, upon our relationship with all those other organizations and individuals outside IU who are actively defining the field of humanities computing and who are concerned with the production, dissemination, and interpretation of electronic texts.

REFERENCES

Andersen, Esben Sloth. 1994. *Evolutionary Economics: Post-Schumpeterian Contributions.* London: St. Martin's Press.

Beniger, James R. 1986. *The Control Revolution: Technological and Economic Origins of the Information Society.* Cambridge, Mass.: Harvard University Press.

Bennington, Geoffrey. 1993. Deconstruction. *The Blackwell Dictionary of Twentieth-Century Social Thought,* ed. William Outhwaite and Tom Bottomore. Oxford: Blackwell.

Bloch, R. Howard, and Carla Hesse, eds. 1993. Introduction. Special issue on "Future Libraries" of *Representations,* no. 42: 1-12.

Bolter, Jay David. 1991. *Writing Space: The Computer, Hypertext, and the History of Writing.* Hillsdale, N.J.: Lawrence Erlbaum Associates.

Boyd, Robert, and Peter J. Richerson. 1985. *Culture and the Evolutionary Process.* Chicago: University of Chicago Press.

Boyd, Robert, and Peter J. Richerson. 1993. Culture and Human Evolution. In *The Origin and Evolution of Humans and Humanness,* ed. D. Tab Rasmussen, 119-34. Boston: Jones and Bartlett.

Brunner, Theodore F. 1991. The Thesaurus Linguae Graecae: Classics and the Computer. *Library Hi Tech* 9(1): 61-67.

Caldwell, Lee. 1994. The National Information Infrastructure (NII): National Directions and Local Initiatives. Paper presented at the Sixth Indiana University Libraries/University Computing Services INforum, 20 April, Studio 6, IU Radio/TV Building, Bloomington, Indiana.

Campbell, Jerry D. 1992. Shaking the Conceptual Foundations of Reference: A Perspective. *RSR: Reference Services Review* 20(4): 29-35.

Contemporary Authors, New Revision Series, 12. 1989. s.v. Raben, Joseph.

Crawford, Walt. 1989. *MARC for Library Use: Understanding Integrated USMARC.* 2d ed. Boston: G.K. Hall.

de Klerk, Ann, and Peter V. Deekle, eds. 1993. The Future of the Book in an Electronic Age. Thematic issue of *Liberal Education* 79(2): 1-52.

Day, Mark Tyler. 1991. Proposal for the Establishment of an IU Library Electronic Text Resource Service (LETRS). Reference Department, Indiana University Libraries, Bloomington. Typescript.

Day, Mark Tyler, and Richard Ellis. 1993. The LETRS Center: Building Computing Support for the Humanities. *University Computing Times: Indiana University* (October): 7-10.

de Man, Paul. 1979. The Epistemology of Metaphor. In *On Metaphor,* ed. Sheldon Sacks, 11-28. Chicago: University of Chicago Press.

DeHayes, Daniel W. 1987. The Challenge to Be Met. *BACSpace* (February): 1-4.

Drucker, Peter F. 1993. *Post-Capitalist Society.* New York: HarperCollins.

Forester, Tom, ed. 1989. *Computers in the Human Context: Information Technology, Productivity, and People.* Cambridge, Mass.: MIT Press.

Gallie, W. B. 1955-56. Essentially Contested Concepts. *Proceedings of the Aristotelian Society,* n.s., 56: 167-98.

Gilster, Paul. 1993. *The Internet Navigator.* New York: Wiley.

Gould, Constance C. 1988. *Information Needs in the Humanities: An Assessment.* Stanford, Calif.: Research Libraries Group.

Hall, John A. 1993. Culture. *The Blackwell Dictionary of Twentieth-Century Social Thought,* ed. William Outhwaite and Tom Bottomore. Oxford: Blackwell.

Harvey, David. 1989. *The Condition of Postmodernity: An Enquiry into the Origins of Cultural Change.* Oxford: Blackwell.

Henry, Charles, and Paul Evan Peters. 1993. The Transformation Potential of Networked Information. *College & Research Libraries News 54*(9): 512-13.

Lanham, Richard A. 1993. *The Electronic Word: Democracy, Technology, and the Arts.* Chicago: University of Chicago Press.

Lenski, Gerhard. 1993. Evolution. *The Blackwell Dictionary of Twentieth-Century Social Thought,* ed. William Outhwaite and Tom Bottomore. Oxford: Blackwell.

Library Electronic Text Resource Service. 1994. LETRS Support Statement. Indiana University, Bloomington. Duplicated.

Lipietz, Alain. 1993. Fordism and post-Fordism. *The Blackwell Dictionary of Twentieth-Century Social Thought,* ed. William Outhwaite and Tom Bottomore. Oxford: Blackwell.

Lipow, Anne Grodzins, ed. 1993. *Rethinking Reference in Academic Libraries.* Institute Facilitator Louella Wetherbee. The Proceedings and Process of Library Solutions Institute, no. 2. Berkeley, Calif.: Library Solutions Press.

Lucier, Richard E. 1992. Towards a Knowledge Management Environment: A Strategic Framework. *Educom Review 27*(6): 24-31.

Lyotard, Jean-François. 1984. *The Postmodern Condition: A Report on Knowledge.* Trans. Geoff Bennington and Brian Massumi. Vol. 10. Theory and History of Literature. Minneapolis: University of Minnesota Press.

McCarty, Willard. 1992. HUMANIST: Lessons from a Global Electronic Seminar. *Computers and the Humanities 26*(3): 205-22.

McClure, Polley A. 1987a. The Crossroads for Academic Computing. *BACSpace* (March): 1-3.

McClure, Polley A. 1987b. The Future of Academic Computing: The Humanities. *BACSpace* (November): 1-3.

McCoy, Jacquelyn. 1993. Re-engineering Academic and Research Libraries. *College & Research Libraries News 54*(6): 333-35.

Midgley, Mary. 1978. *Beast and Man: The Roots of Human Nature.* Ithaca, N.Y.: Cornell University Press.

O'Donnell, James J. 1994. Review of *The Electronic Word: Democracy, Technology, and the Arts,* by Richard A. Lanham. *Bryn Mawr Classical Review* [Online]. Available: ftp ftp.lib.Virginia.Edu Directory: /pub/alpha/bmcr/94/94-6-13.

Pfaffenberger, Bryan. 1990. *Democratizing Information: Online Databases and the Rise of End-User Searching.* Boston: G.K. Hall.

Price-Wilkin, John. 1991a. Text Files in RLG Academic Libraries: A Survey of Support and Activities. *Journal of Academic Librarianship 17*(1): 19-25.

Price-Wilkin, John. 1991b. Text Files in Libraries: Present Foundations and Future Directions. *Library Hi Tech 9*(3): 7-44.

SCHOLAR: An Online Service for Text Analysis and Natural Language Applications. Contact: jqrqc@cnyvm.bitnet, Joseph Raben; Subscriptions to: listserv@cunyvm.cuny.edu; FTP archive at: jhuvm.hcf.jhu.edu.

Sheehan, James J., and Morton Sosna, eds. 1991. *The Boundaries of Humanity: Humans, Animals, Machines.* Berkeley: University of California Press.

Stewart, Jacqueline A. 1989. How to Manage Educational Computing Initiatives—Lessons from the First Five Years of Project Athena at MIT. In *The Society of Text: Hypertext, Hypermedia, and the Social Construction of Information,* ed. Edward Barrett, 284-304. Cambridge, Mass.: MIT Press.

Veaner, Allen B. 1990. *Academic Librarianship in a Transformational Age: Program, Politics, and Personnel.* Professional Librarian Series. Boston: G.K. Hall.

Weiskel, Timothy C. 1986. Libraries as Life-Systems: Information, Entropy, and Coevolution on Campus. *College & Research Libraries 47*(6): 545-63.

MARY BRANDT JENSEN

Director of Law Library Operations
Professor of Law
University of South Dakota School of Law
Vermillion, South Dakota

Cohabiting with Copyright on the Nets

ABSTRACT

Although the primary purpose of both copyright and the nets is to expand the publicly available knowledge base, the way each goes about expanding the knowledge base can be quite different. To avoid potential conflicts, net users must understand common misconceptions about what constitutes work in the public domain and what uses are permitted (copyright does not necessarily permit users to do the same things with electronic works as nonelectronic works). Determining if the work is in the public domain, what exactly the copyright holder has given permission to do, and how and from whom to ask permission will reduce copyright conflicts. In addition, understanding that the law is a political compromise between various points of view, that it is complex and often can only be interpreted by experts, and that it is only a starting point for discussion between users and copyright holders will improve both equitable access for users and equitable compensation for copyright holders.

INTRODUCTION

Several months ago, when Brett Sutton first asked me to select a title for my paper, I suggested two titles. I suggested "Cohabiting with Copyright on the Nets" or "Coexisting with Copyright on the Nets." Brett chose *cohabiting*, probably because it sounds sexier and was more likely to attract attention. That may have been the original reason for the choice of title, but as I reflected on what I wanted to say, I came to realize that the term *cohabiting* also expresses what I want to say better than the term *coexisting* does. To coexist with something means to be present in the same place, time, or context. It implies nothing about whether the coexistence is intentional or happens by chance; nothing about whether there is a mutually beneficial relationship (however rocky it may be), an attraction between two entities, or just a coincidence. *Cohabitation* implies a far more complex relationship with attraction, common interests, or some mutually beneficial reason for living in the same place, time, or context. The relationship between copyright and the nets is complex, intentional, and, one hopes, mutually beneficial, although at times it may seem rockier than Charles and Diana's marriage and perhaps as doomed to failure.

The constitutional purpose behind copyright in the United States is to encourage the creation of useful works by giving authors sufficient rewards, incentives, and protection to make it worthwhile for them to continue producing works. Thus, a primary purpose of copyright is to expand the knowledge base available to the public. In many respects, that is also a primary purpose of the nets. However, the way that copyright and the nets go about expanding the knowledge base can be very different. While copyright seeks to expand the knowledge base by encouraging creation through control of distribution to produce rewards, the nets take the approach of increasing knowledge by expanding access and removing barriers to mass distribution. This apparent conflict is made worse by a public whose ideas about copyright often more closely resembles the law of the past than the law of the present. If this rocky relationship is ever to develop into a solid lasting marriage, the people involved are going to have to give up their romantic illusions and settle down to the hard work that is needed to make a marriage survive and work.

ROMANTIC ILLUSIONS

Romantic Illusion #1:
If it is on the nets, it must be in the public domain.

Since I labeled this statement an illusion, it is obvious that I will point out that not everything on the nets is in the public domain. In fact, the opposite is true. Most of the documents, messages, and other works on the net are copyrighted.

Honeymoon Version of Romantic Illusion #1:
If it is posted on an anonymous FTP site, it must be in the public domain.

Even when people realize that just because something is on the net doesn't mean it is in the public domain, most people still tend to think of at least the documents posted on anonymous File Transfer Protocol (FTP) servers as material that is in the public domain. However, users of the nets cannot rely on the fact that a document is posted on an anonymous FTP server as a basis for assuming that there are no copyright restrictions on the use of the document. Anyone can post a document on most anonymous FTP servers. Even if the server is set up so that only selected people can post documents to it, the people who run the servers are often uneducated on the subject of copyright and suffer from some of the same misconceptions as many users of the nets.

Newlywed Version of Romantic Illusion #1:
If it doesn't have a copyright notice on it, it must be in the public domain.

Another common misconception is that if authors want their works to be protected by copyright, authors have to put notices on the works and/or go through other formalities to obtain copyright protection. This used to be the law under the 1909 Act. But under the 1976 Act, copyright attaches as soon as an author's expression is fixed in a tangible medium of expression. All documents that exist on the net are fixed somewhere on someone's storage devices, and so they all meet the fixation requirement. As recently as 1988, an author could lose his copyright if he allowed his work to be widely distributed to the public in the United States without a notice. But even that formality is now gone. When the United States joined the Berne Convention in 1989, the notice requirement was removed from U.S. law. Furthermore, notice requirements never existed in many other countries where a number of the documents on the nets originated or reside.

First Anniversary Version of Romantic Illusion #1:
If it says it is in the public domain, it is in the public domain.

Once people begin to understand that the absence of a copyright notice does not mean that something is in the public domain, they begin to look for notices in files that say that the files are in the public domain or may be copied and freely distributed. This is definitely a step in the right direction, but it is still a naive view. It assumes that the person who put the public domain or permission notice on the document is either the copyright holder or someone with sufficient copyright knowledge to determine when something is in the public domain. Unfortunately, misconceptions about the duration of copyright are as common as misconceptions about obtaining a copyright.

If it appears that the author put the public domain or permission statement on a work, it is usually safe to do those things with the work that the statement specifically authorizes. However, just because the copyright holder gives permission to reproduce or distribute a document under certain circumstances does not mean that the user has the right to reproduce or distribute the document in even slightly different circumstances. For example, if an author gives people the right to distribute copies free of charge, that does not necessarily give a university the right to distribute copies to a class on a cost recovery basis. Such notices rarely place works in the public domain. What they really are is a type of copyright license, and net users must abide by the terms of the license or seek additional permission for whatever they want to do with the document.

One very popular file on the Internet contains a statement similar to the following permission statement:

> Permission is granted to make and distribute verbatim copies of this guide provided the copyright notice and this permission notice are preserved on all copies.
>
> Permission is granted to copy and distribute modified versions of this booklet under the conditions for verbatim copying, provided that the entire resulting derived work is distributed under the terms of a permission notice similar to this one.

This notice does not place this work in the public domain.

If it appears that the public domain statement was placed on a document by someone other than the author, then it is only as reliable as the person or organization responsible for putting the notice on the document. The person or organization may even be immanently reliable in all aspects except their knowledge of the intricacies of U.S. (and in some cases international and foreign) copyright law. This is not a simple area of the law. Because of the amount of time it took Congress to pass the 1976 Act and the way it dealt with the transition provisions, it is easy even for attorneys to make mistakes with certain types of documents unless they are familiar with these provisions.

It is also unsafe to assume that the same rules that are in effect today concerning what is in the public domain will remain unchanged even in the near-term future. Congress recently made changes in the renewal provisions. The European Community is in the process of lengthening the copyright term, and a similar move is under consideration in the United States. The North American Free Trade

Agreement (NAFTA) even restored copyright in certain limited cases to films that had fallen into the public domain.

This is a complex area of the law requiring reasonable caution at all times and expert advice if you want to be absolutely safe.

Romantic Illusion #2:
Copyright permits people to do similar things with works on the nets as it permits with nonelectronic works.

Most people think of copyright primarily as a law governing when you can make a copy of something. But copyright goes far beyond merely regulating reproduction. It also regulates four other types of activities: production of derivative works, public performance of works, public displays of works, and public distribution of works. Because of the way the law defines these activities, it is impossible to use works on the nets without engaging in public displays, public performances, and public distribution. For example, any time a copy of the work is displayed on a cathode ray tube or other viewing device, a display occurs.

Newlywed Version of Romantic Illusion #2:
Even if copyright prohibits some of the things that seem like they ought to be permitted, private uses of works on the nets is okay.

If a work is available for display or performance or distribution in a place open to the public or in a place where a substantial number of people outside the normal circle of a family and its social acquaintances are gathered, the distribution, performance, or display is public. Because the net is accessible from so many places, anything on it, including nearly all performances, displays, or distributions that occur on it, is probably public even if it is password protected. Furthermore, there is no general private use exception in the copyright law.

First Anniversary Version of Romantic Illusion #2:
Exceptions in the law, such as fair use, permit most ordinary uses of works on the nets.

Fair use and the other exceptions in the law apply to works on the nets as they do to more traditional works. But the application does not always produce the results that many people think it should.

First, many people have a very hazy understanding of these exceptions even in the non-network environment. They tend to oversimplify, generalize, and broaden the application of the exceptions. For example, few people realize that the subsection of the law that permits the performance or display of works in classrooms is limited to face-to-face activities. The next subsection that permits transmission outside of a single classroom applies only to nondramatic literary and musical works, and so would not permit the showing of audiovisual material over a closed circuit TV channel much less a wide area network.

Second, people do not take into account the fact that the capabilities of the network naturally encourage people to copy, distribute, display, and perform greater portions of works than the nonelectronic world does. The mere fact that more of the work is involved in an electronic activity makes it less likely that fair use and other exceptions will permit the activity. How many of you have ever FTPed or downloaded only part of a document? You get the whole thing even if you eventually will use only part of it. In fact, it is so easy, you often get all of several files just to make sure you have everything you might need.

Finally, the networked world is a potential source of royalty income for copyright owners. Open access to a work on the networks can substitute to some degree for forms of the work for which the copyright holder is entitled to expect compensation. If network access supplants some of any commercial market for a work, that factor weighs heavily against a finding of fair use.

Thus, even though fair use and the other exceptions are technically no different on the nets than they are in the nonelectronic world, they don't lead to the results that people expect them to lead to on the nets.

BUILDING THE STABLE MARRIAGE

Technique #1:
How to tell if a work is in the public domain.

Figure out when, where, and by whom the work was created or edited. Then apply the following rules of thumb. Do not rely upon statements of others that a particular file is in the public domain unless you know that the person making the statement has done a reliable investigation of the copyright status of the work.

United States
1. Works written by U.S. government officials as part of their official duties are in the public domain. Works written by contractors for the U.S. government are not necessarily in the public domain. Works written by state employees are usually protected by copyright.
2. The actual text of laws, ordinances, regulations, and court opinions are in the public domain. Additional material such as headnotes, references, or annotations which appear in statute compilations and case reporters are usually protected by copyright.
3. Works on which the copyright has expired are in the public domain. But be careful about this rule of thumb. Many people think that

works are in the public domain under this principle when they really are not.

a. Works first published before January 1, 1978, usually enter the public domain seventy-five years from the date copyright was first secured, which is usually seventy-five years from the date of first publication.

b. Works first created on or after January 1, 1978, enter the public domain fifty years after the death of the author. (Nothing will enter the public domain under this rule until at least January 1, 2023.)

c. Works first created on or after January 1, 1978, that are created by a corporate author enter the public domain seventy-five years after publication or one hundred years after creation, whichever occurs first. (Nothing will enter the public domain under this rule until at least January 1, 2053.)

d. Works created before January 1, 1978, but not published before that date are copyrighted under rules b and c above, except that in no case will the copyright on a work not published prior to January 1, 1978, expire before December 31, 2002. (This rule copyrights a lot of manuscripts that we would otherwise think of as public domain because of their age.)

e. If a substantial number of copies were distributed in the United States without a copyright notice prior to March 1, 1989, the work is in the public domain in the United States. (Caveat: Every time a substantially new edition is created, especially if it is a new translation or done by a new editor, a new work is created, so you count from the creation of that edition, not from the creation of the original.)

United Kingdom and a Lot of Other Countries

The general rule is life of the author plus fifty years.

Copyright notice was never required in these countries. So publication without a copyright notice never puts a work in the public domain in these countries.

Whose Law Applies

The law of the country where the potential infringing activity occurs (copying, distribution, public performance, public display, or creation of a derivative work) applies. Thus, if copying is done in the United States, U.S. law applies. If the copies are distributed in the United Kingdom (via a network or otherwise), U.K. law applies to the act of distribution.

Technique #2:
How to tell what the copyright holder has given permission to do.

Permission statements should be read very carefully. Do not read anything into them that is not there. If it doesn't tell you that you can't do something, don't assume that you can do it. Assume that you cannot do anything unless the statement explicitly says you can.

For example, the permission statement quoted under the First Anniversary Version of Romantic Illusion #1 gives permission to copy and to distribute the work, but it does not give permission to copy the work into a larger work that doesn't include a permission statement that is substantially the same as the one quoted. So don't modify this work by stripping off the header that contains the permission statement.

Technique #3:
How and from whom to ask permission to do what you want to do.

You must figure out who the author of the work is. It may be impossible to figure out whether you have requested permission from the right people if you can't figure out who the author is.

You should always ask the author for permission. Copyright nearly always vests originally in the author. It can be assigned to a publisher but only by a signed written agreement that explicitly transfers copyright. Publisher policies that claim to require assignment of all copyrights to the publisher are ineffective unless the author has signed a written agreement transferring copyright. Copyright notices that incorrectly state the name of the copyright holder are fairly common especially in periodicals published by small or specialized presses.

Assignment of specific rights such as the exclusive right to exploit print versions of a work is not the equivalent of an assignment of copyright. For example, if an author sells the print rights to a novel, he has not necessarily sold either the electronic or the movie rights to the novel. So you should always ask the author.

If the author is dead, you need to figure out who his heirs are and ask them.

If the work contains a copyright notice that lists someone other than the author as the copyright holder, you should ask that person as well. In this manner, you will be sure that you have permission from the copyright holder even if you cannot be sure whether a transfer has occurred.

If it isn't obvious who the author is, it will probably be easier to find a different work to use than it will be to get permission to use the work. Sometimes accepting the fact that you cannot safely use a work is necessary to preserve your sanity.

Tell the author or copyright holder exactly what you want to do with a work. If you want to edit a work to make it searchable by Wide

Area Information Servers (WAIS), say so. If you want to create an ASCII version of the work or mark it up with Standard Generalized Markup Language (SGML), tell him that. If you want to post it for anonymous FTP access, tell him that. If you are willing to limit access in some manner, specify the manner in which access will be limited. Don't tell the copyright holder that only a set number of copies will be made unless you have a reliable means to control the number of copies. In short, make sure that any permission you get allows you to do what you intend to do.

Finally, don't assume that a permission given for one use applies to another use. Make sure that the person requesting permission and the person giving permission have the same understanding of what will be done with the work.

Technique #4:
Don't try to make the law what you want it to be.

Far too many people make statements concerning what the law is that are obviously based on what they think a fair, just, or logical result would be. If you are going to cohabit with copyright, you must accept the fact that the law is a political compromise that did not anticipate all the ramifications of electronic networking. You must also accept the fact that what a particular user, copyright holder, or publisher thinks a fair, just, or logical result would be is not necessarily what all users, copyright holders, and publishers think would be a fair, just, or logical result. The law is a compromise between the points of view of the various constituencies who lobbied Congress when it was passed. You can't change it by wishing or complaining. Getting it changed is a long, difficult, and expensive process. The mere fact that you think a change is justified doesn't mean one will or even should occur. Accept the law for what it is and find ways to work within it. If the law says you need permission, get it. If the law says a user doesn't need permission to do something, don't try to prevent the user from doing it through restrictive licensing. If the law is unclear, admit it and work out a reasonable compromise.

Trying to make the law what you want it to be only leads to misunderstandings and bitter emotional battles.

MARRIAGE COUNSELING FOR A STABLE FUTURE

Method A:
For experts only—Try to figure out what the law allows people to do.

It is important for the experts to continue to explore the law and to try to figure out what it does and does not permit people to do on the nets. But this is not an exercise for most laypeople. Copyright law is complex and confusing even when it is applied to technologies that Congress clearly understood when the law was enacted. Applying it to future technologies that Congress only foresaw vaguely and had no way of foreseeing clearly is even more complex and confusing. It is extremely important to start with the actual language of the law itself, particularly the definitions. Words often have different meanings in the law than they do in common usage, and this is particularly true in the realm of copyright law. So a surface reading of the law is not enough. Interpretation of the copyright law often requires careful legal analysis of the text of the law, the legislative history, and case law. Often, there is no clear answer. Sometimes, what the courts decide is wrong and must be corrected by later cases or by Congressional revisions. If you choose to venture into the waters of interpretation of copyright law, go carefully and get expert advice.

Method B:
Intervention and education—Try to persuade all parties that they need to get serious about their copyright education, look carefully at what the experts are saying, question what is being said, and admit their mistakes when they make them.

Because copyright law is so complex and easily misconstrued, it is important that all the parties involved spend some time becoming educated. It is also important that everyone make sure that their information is coming from reliable sources and that they are not misinterpreting what they are being told. And because it is so easy to make mistakes, it is important that everyone be willing to admit mistakes and correct them when they are made. A good relationship must be based on communication, understanding, and agreement. Quick off-the-cuff uninformed judgments have no place in such a relationship.

Method C:
Custody battles are bad for the family—Encourage all parties to quit misusing the law.

Bitter emotional disputes never lead to stronger relationships. In fact, they lead to a total breakdown of the mutually beneficial relationship. The law can't make a family work. It can't make copyright work either, nor can it make the nets work. Only people working together can build a strong mutually beneficial relationship. The law can serve as a basis for that relationship. Copyright law can serve as a starting point for deciding how to balance the rights of users and copyright holders on the nets, but it cannot insure a fair world.

It is possible and at times even easy to misuse the law. I'm sure all of you are aware of situations in which children have been used as weapons in divorce cases. Copyright can also be misused as a weapon in the power games of the net. Users can try to use their view of the law to justify the widest possible uses without compensation. Copyright holders can use it to try to justify licenses that require compensation for nearly every use. But neither approach is good for the net family. Both lead to bitter emotional territorial disputes. If both sides would try to see the other side's point of view and work out reasonable compromises, the family would be a lot better off.

Method D:
Working together—Organize, listen, talk, negotiate, compromise, and settle your differences.

In some ways, Shakespeare was right. Let's kill all the lawyers. At least, let's kill all the litigators. Letting the situation deteriorate to the point where litigation is necessary means that no one will win.

While we are at it, let's kill all the legislators too. If you have to resort to getting Congress to resolve your disputes, you will die of old age or go out of business before you get a resolution.

There is no possible way for either Congress or the courts to move quickly enough to accommodate the speed at which things change on the nets. The only possible way to work out intellectual property matters on the nets is for all interested parties to organize into groups, talk to each other, *listen* to each other, try to see each other's point of view, *compromise,* and settle any differences that arise. None of this comes naturally. It takes work. It is very much like a marriage. If all sides give 100 percent to the relationship working toward the good of all, it works. If everyone only wants to give his share and is most concerned about getting the most for himself, copyright will hinder all of our work.

LORRIE LEJEUNE

Electronic Publishing Specialist
University of Michigan Press
Ann Arbor, Michigan

The Role of the Scholarly Publisher in the Electronic Environment

ABSTRACT

Scholarly publishing has changed as a result of a shrinking market for specialized materials, increased production costs, and advances in computer technology. Publishing on CD-ROM or on the Internet offers reduced production costs, increased storage capability, and enhanced access to information through resources such as World Wide Web and tools such as Gopher, Mosaic, and Storyspace. For publishers to provide high-quality, peer-reviewed, and edited material in an online environment, cost recovery methods must be developed that provide well-designed user interfaces and that ensure network security. The scholarly publisher's imprint will continue to be a sign of quality and credibility, but the online environment also enables scholarly publishers and libraries to redefine their roles in the dissemination of information.

INTRODUCTION

In the not-so-distant past, when a scholar finished a monograph, he or she would pack up the paper manuscript and send it off to a publisher—often a scholarly press—for publication. The press, often but not always affiliated with a university, assessed the project's worthiness by passing it through a rigorous process of peer and university review. If approved, the manuscript was carefully copyedited, typeset, and printed, while a marketing strategy was agreed upon. Nine months to several years after the contract was signed, the finished book

105

would find its way to readers via retailers, libraries, and direct mail (see Figure 1).

The role of the publisher in this process was definitive: the press decided which books were published, how they were produced, and how they would be sold. Printed books and journals from scholarly publishers formed the primary means of scholarly communication until just recently, when the arrival of the Internet changed the rules of this well-defined business.

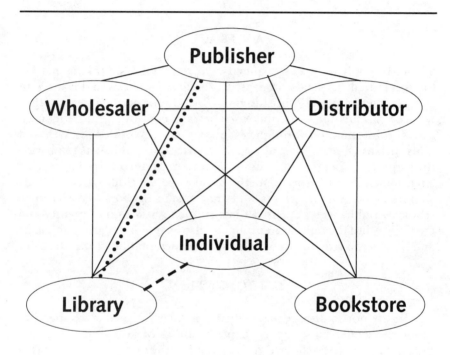

Purchase Transaction
Free Transaction
License or Royalty Transaction

Transactions not included: translations, rights, extracts, permissions, book clubs, etc.

Figure 1. Current sales web[1]

Publishers are standing on the brink of a radical change in how thoughts and ideas—which for lack of a better word I will refer to as "information"—are identified, organized, and disseminated to readers. With the advent of fast microprocessors, inexpensive high-volume storage, and the Internet, with its capacity to transport a digital signal around the world in seconds, information need no longer be linear or packaged in a physical unit—a prospect that both excites and terrifies publishers.

ECONOMIC REALITIES

The dissemination of ideas and research results is the traditional focus of scholarly publishing, with monographs, edited collections, regionalia, and trade titles (for the educated layperson) comprising the bulk of most presses' lists. Over the last ten years, however, scholarly presses have seen their markets for these specialized books shrink as university subsidies, library budgets, and general readership declined. Although scholarly and university press titles comprise 20 percent of all the books published in the United States, those titles earn only 2 percent of the total revenue of books sold.[2] The publisher's expenditures for paper, printing, binding, and warehousing comprise only about 30 percent of the total cost of producing a book, which means that the bulk of the publication costs are incurred by the time the first copy is printed. Combining this factor with the decline in sales, scholarly publishers are feeling a squeeze on two fronts.

What is the outcome of this squeeze? Prices of books have risen. Over the last few years, presses have improved their productivity by making increased use of computer technology, reducing typesetting costs (and time) by taking advantage of authors' word-processing disks, for example, or by substituting desktop publishing methods for conventional typesetting. But the potential savings of time and money are limited, and the option of increasing revenue by raising prices substantially over current levels would only cause a further decrease in sales (which, in this age of shrinking library budgets, would be somewhat self-defeating since libraries are the most frequent buyers of scholarly titles).

THE FUTURE OF SCHOLARLY PUBLISHING

In spite of this apparently gloomy state of affairs, there are a number of bright spots on the publishing horizon, the most compelling of which are CD-ROMs and the Internet.

Publishing on CD-ROM offers a number of advantages over publishing in print and few disadvantages. Like books, CDs can be sold in units, thus the current methods publishers use for marketing, sales, billing, and collection are still applicable. The costs of producing a CD are also relatively low—as little as $1 per unit for 1,000 units or more. The single largest advantage of CDs is the sheer volume of data that can be stored on them; this feature opens up a multitude of publishing possibilities for multimedia and reference works. But needs vary. Libraries and certain scholars benefit most from the storage capabilities of the CD, but publishers of monographs, on the other hand, seek ways to distinguish their projects. The Internet provides the means to do this.

Online publishing via the Internet represents a move away from a unit-based product and presents new challenges. In the spring of 1993, approximately one million people had Internet access; that number has risen to roughly twenty million in the past year.[3] The involvement of telephone and cable companies in computer networking will undoubtedly have an impact on the number of users with access to the Internet in the next few years. Experts are predicting that publishers and libraries alike will see unprecedented demands for online and electronically based information.

How will online publishing fit into the scholarly world? Because the Internet began at universities, its primary user base is still the academic community. As Internet usage expands, these users will continue to be the most experienced, demanding better and more efficient methods for accessing the increasing volume of data over the network. This trend, coupled with the rising costs of books and printed journals, is making publishers, particularly university presses, more willing to put information online.

Providing information online has a number of distinct advantages over offering it in printed form, the most obvious being savings in the costs of paper, printing, binding, and warehousing. Other advantages are less obvious, but potentially more intellectually exciting. The printed book or journal is of necessity a linear entity, in that to put it on paper, it must have a beginning, middle, and end. Using hypertext, for example, an online publication need not be in a linear format. Rather, the user decides the order in which the information is used and how it is used. The notion of hypertext has been with us for years, but only recently, with the advent of the World Wide Web (which is a subset of the Internet or, more specifically, a method of accessing Internet resources using a graphical user interface like Mosaic), Gopher, and hypertext authoring tools, has the hypertext environment offered a realistic and usable alternative to the printed page.

VEHICLES OF ONLINE PUBLISHING

Gopher was the first of the client-server interfaces to allow information to be accessed over the Internet without platform-based conflicts. Information might be stored on a UNIX-based server, but the Gopher client allows a user running Macintosh, DOS/Windows, or even a mainframe to browse through text without needing to know the original platform used to create and store it. Mosaic, the most popular client for the World Wide Web, takes Gopher a step further. Where Gopher is currently limited to an ASCII, text-only environment, Mosaic offers formatted text, high-resolution images, and a simple yet powerful user interface. Links to other documents are clearly indicated in the text (words that indicate links appear in a different color), and moving from one document to another is a seamless process. In fact, users are often unaware that they have accessed servers all over the world as they browse through the menus and move from one linked document to another.

Gopher and Mosaic are examples of interfaces designed for browsing—that is, looking at and obtaining information in a passive manner. In contrast, an excellent example of an interactive tool for creating and manipulating hypertext is Storyspace, which provides the framework or "look" of a document; the initial text and links from idea to idea are placed by the author, and readers are free to explore the linked parts in any order they choose. In many cases, readers are also free (and often encouraged) to add their own text and links to build on what the author has started. This concept of interactive authoring coupled with the immediacy and worldwide scope of the Internet offer nearly limitless possibilities for authors and readers.

At Michigan, we are exploring the notions of hyperfiction, interactive text on the net, and audiovisual and multimedia presentations in drama and the arts, as well as CD-ROM and online versions of one of our major reference works. Our authors are becoming increasingly excited by the possibilities inherent in nonlinear work, and the press is considering publishing simultaneous paper and online versions of at least one new work. We are also pursuing ideas for collaboration with the University of Michigan libraries for online and CD-ROM versions of some of the university's permanent collections. It must be noted that although authors are interested in exploring these new options for presenting their work, the responsibility for creating and marketing these new works still falls, for the most part, on the press.

COST RECOVERY

At the moment, most information accessible via the Internet is free, but that cannot remain the case for long. If publishers are to offer the same kind of high-quality, peer-reviewed, and edited material that is available in print, there must be a cost-recovery mechanism. Unfortunately, the current unit-based model for cost recovery does not translate to the online environment, so a new model must be envisioned. Why hasn't that happened already? The solution to the obvious problem of how to charge and collect for information is contingent on, first, establishing standards and, second, deciding on a technology that will support them. Questions such as "What do consumers want?" and "How much and in what manner will they pay?" must be addressed, as well as those concerning the technical aspects such as "Which user interfaces are most appropriate?" and "How can we ensure network security?"

One potential solution to online cost recovery is a centralized billing server such as NetBill, which is based on an accounting/billing server prototype developed at Carnegie-Mellon. A centralized billing server would provide a basic technological standard with an easy-to-use customer interface and room for a variety of services, product options, and pricing schemes. In addition to providing a seamless environment for accessing information from a wide range of sources (sales of new books, library transactions, periodicals, etc.), the server would also offer a secure online environment for monetary transactions and cyclical accounting and statement services for both customers and information providers.

THE SCHOLARLY PUBLISHER'S CONTRIBUTION
TO THE ONLINE ENVIRONMENT

As electronic and online publishing become more commonplace, the traditional boundaries between authors, publishers, libraries, wholesalers, retail stores, and end-users become blurred (see Figure 2). Authors may wonder why publishers are necessary if they can make their works available over the Internet on their own. Publishers may decide to become online libraries for their own materials if cataloging and storage can be done on a single server. And why shouldn't libraries solicit new works if they can offer widespread dissemination? As Internet usage expands, the potential for overload becomes frighteningly real. There will be far more information available than users can sort through. How will anyone find anything? And most important, how will we determine the accuracy of a given piece of information? We must realize that our current, time-honored methods of information access, verification, and citation will change. The Internet offers the ability to update and change information instantaneously. There is no guarantee that a fact or figure available on John Smith's World Wide Web server today will appear in the same form tomorrow. We take for granted

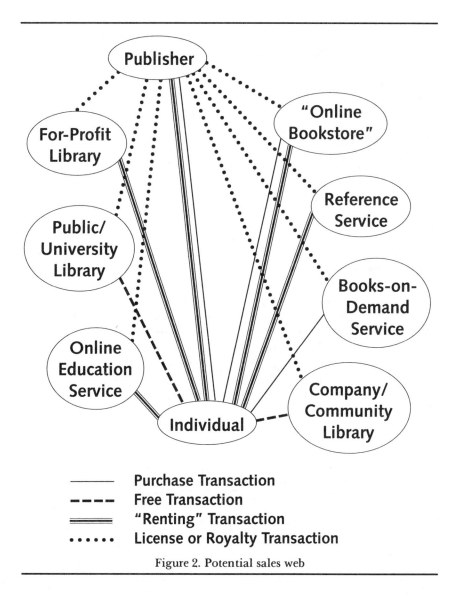

Figure 2. Potential sales web

that the information we confidently cite in our own works is accurate because an unchangeable original is cataloged and stored in a library. This is not true for the Internet. We do not yet have a widely accepted method for archiving, verifying, and referencing works that are published exclusively online.

All this points us to the issue of credibility, which in my mind is the key issue in online publishing. Assuring the reader that the information is what it appears to be and that it can always be found in a given place is the most convincing argument for the continued existence of publishers (and libraries) in the electronic environment. So what is the role of the scholarly publisher in this new environment? It is the same as it has always been: identifying new ideas, information, and works in a given field and then selecting for publication those with the highest potential value to their selected audience. The publisher's imprint is a sign of quality and credibility—a seal of approval indicating that a given work has been chosen from a larger pool of works based on its intellectual merit and value to its audience.

COLLABORATIONS FOR THE FUTURE

The scholarly world is a rapidly changing one, and the effects of these changes will be felt not only by scholarly presses but by individuals and libraries as well. The creation, packaging, and storing of information has long been a compartmentalized process with authors, publishers, libraries, and users each performing their respective functions independently of one another. In the online environment, publishers and libraries must make an effort to collaborate thereby ensuring that information maintains its integrity and continues to flow smoothly in the academic community and to the public. Working together, publishers and libraries will enhance their roles as the disseminators of ideas and ensure their places in the new electronic world.

NOTES

[1.] The figures in this paper are courtesy of Michael Jensen, Electronic Media Manager, University of Nebraska Press, Lincoln, NE.

[2.] Colin Day. 1994. Who will Publish Your Manuscript? or Can University Presses be Taken for Granted? Paper presented March 15, at Michigan State University, East Lansing, MI.

[3.] Larry Jackson. 1994. NCSA Mosaic. Presentation given June 17, at Electronic Publishing Issues II. Annual meeting of the American Association of University Presses, Washington, DC.

JOHN PRICE-WILKIN

Systems Librarian for Information Services
Alderman Library
University of Virginia
Charlottesville, Virginia

The Feasibility of Wide-Area Textual Analysis Systems in Libraries: A Practical Analysis

ABSTRACT

This paper discusses the textual and software resources necessary for
the establishment of a generalized wide-area textual analysis system.
A distinction is made between textual analytical systems and text retrieval
systems. The necessity of using standards and open systems in implementing such systems is emphasized. The paper includes a review of
critical characteristics of generalized analytical software. It is argued
that the resources necessary for the establishment of a service are currently
available. The paper concludes with a discussion of deficiencies in
current resources and standards. The author also includes an appendix
discussing the need to incorporate a recognition of structure in textual
retrieval systems.

INTRODUCTION

I propose to offer an assessment of where we stand in being able
to offer wide-area access to textual analysis resources based primarily
on my experience in providing support for wide-area textual analysis
systems. I will begin by defining what I believe is necessary for the
establishment of a wide-area electronic text service, including what we
mean by a service that supports textual analysis, and will discuss the
relevance of open systems and standards. I will give some attention
to the availability of textual resources—commercially and informally

113

distributed—and will provide a lengthier discussion of the capabilities of textual analysis software needed to take advantage of standardized encoding. And finally, I will briefly discuss the lack of standard mechanisms for access and protocols for search and retrieval.

MODELS AND CONFUSION

Computer-aided analysis of text has a relatively long history, but only in the last few years have we established access mechanisms at the institutional level. There is now a relatively young and promising situation for wide-area support for textual analysis. There are a few widely divergent models for providing resources to communities of scholars, and there is confusion in the marketplace about what resources are appropriate for the analysis of text. Because this discussion is only a consideration of wide-area networking of the resources of textual analysis, I will not consider those cases where the support consists of a text center where the actual work with texts and software is performed. With that consideration in mind, I believe there are three examples. They are ARTFL (American Research on the Treasury of the French Language) at the University of Chicago, the systems developed by Malcolm Brown at Stanford and Dartmouth, and the service offered by the University of Michigan and later expanded at the University of Virginia. Rather than explore each system exhaustively, I will highlight aspects of the three to define the context of this discussion of wide-area textual analysis services. The three models represent different approaches to how materials are accessed, the collections offered, and the encoding of those collections.

ARTFL is probably the first example of a system that offered immediate access to its collection of text processed for access with an analytical system. In 1988, ARTFL moved from offline access to texts and developed their own UNIX search engine and encoding scheme to provide access to their body of some 3,000 titles. While ARTFL's software can also support client/server transactions and is not tied inextricably to the interface with which most of us are familiar, its strategy is to centralize its corpus and provide primary access to the materials through their PhiloLogic interface. Libraries interested in offering access to ARTFL's collections are not burdened with issues such as transforming ARTFL's encoding scheme to meet local needs and deciding on methods of indexing or subsequent encoding. Similarly, they are also not able to define collections in ways that suit local needs by making texts available for use with other software packages or adding markup to facilitate different analytical approaches.

Malcolm Brown led the development of a server protocol and graphical client first at Stanford and then at Dartmouth to gain access to those universities' collections of texts. In both cases, the systems use Open Text's PAT search engine[1] and, for its texts, markup suggestive of Standard Generalized Markup Language (SGML). The client was developed in 1990 at Stanford as Searcher and was elaborated as part of an entire system of information retrieval (Dartmouth College Information System—DCIS) at Dartmouth (Brentrup 1993). The systems at these institutions are oriented toward a protocol that has grown to be an extension of Z39.50. Collections are limited, and development efforts are devoted to effective clients that serve general needs, offer a polished graphical interface, and provide a substantial degree of reliability. Markup is limited to that necessary for the presentation and basic functionality of generalized queries. Specialized access, it could be argued, is not formally supported.

The implementations at Michigan and Virginia differ from the ARTFL and Stanford models in their focus on building SGML-compliant collections and the minimal attention they devote to the development of an interface or client for the resources. They also use PAT. At Michigan, most work was done with command-line access to the PAT software itself, and only later was a vt100 client introduced.[2] Both institutions rely primarily on the Open Text clients but support all clients that can query the PAT search engine, including World Wide Web (WWW) forms-compatible clients such as Mosaic. Collections are actively expanded through traditional collection development activities. At the University of Virginia, the process of applying markup is done collaboratively with Electronic Text Center staff, systems staff, and catalogers, and in almost every effort, the Text Encoding Initiative (TEI) guidelines are used for that process. Work with researchers at both institutions guides the application of markup and indexing for specialized purposes. All of this effort in the construction of texts is reflected in the materials offered through the wide-area services.

A brief digression is useful at this point to consider a resource that contrasts to the initiatives already noted. Chadwyck-Healey markets its texts in two ways: it sells the texts themselves, with SGML, on tape, and it sells the texts on CD-ROM formatted with a modified version of EBT's DynaText software. Both Chadwyck-Healey's textual initiative and EBT's DynaText are laudable—Chadwyck-Healey for undertaking a project with immense potential impact on scholarship in the humanities, and EBT for creating an excellent SGML publishing tool. The combination of these two resources, however, reflects a significant degree of confusion about the needs of textual analysis. EBT's software is designed for publishing electronic texts and does not have significant analytical capabilities. Its sophistication in browsing and formatting information is excellent, and it also provides search capabilities that exploit the SGML tagging. While it is well suited to supporting a document retrieval system, it does not give scholars the ability to easily examine large numbers of occurrences or to search quickly across large collections. The misapplication of DynaText to this project is ironic in that the *English Poetry Database* is perhaps the most substantial resource for literary computing made available to date and needs to be supported by an appropriate analytical engine.

Variation in the implementations of analytical systems is not a bad thing: it means there are choices. The status of software at the heart of the three models discussed a moment ago is perhaps a further indication of the infancy of providing these sorts of services. The software at ARTFL is an in-house effort and is not yet available for implementation outside that institution. The other two models use PAT as their search software: this software is marketed by Open Text as a general-purpose search "engine" and is sold without any apparent awareness of or guidance in how access will be provided to the textual resources. Despite failings in all three of the models, each is an excellent foundation and stands in contrast to the CD-ROM solution provided by Chadwyck-Healey, which simply does not offer tools for analysis. Each is a model of wide-area textual analysis because it provides access to large bodies of texts, facilitates a broad range of analytical functions, and is remotely accessible to all platforms used at those institutions. Two of the three are models that can be easily implemented at other institutions.[3]

Despite this minor chaos, there is an atmosphere of enthusiasm. University libraries around the United States are establishing electronic text centers; Chadwyck-Healey continues to announce the publication of new series in SGML; and rumors of academic text creation projects emerge periodically. The optimistic atmosphere results in part from momentum: the establishment of an increasing number of text centers encourages more people to see this as a viable movement, thus encouraging more university libraries to establish electronic text centers. Other factors are playing an important role: the creation and leadership of the Center for Electronic Texts in the Humanities (CETH) and the development of the TEI guidelines are two profoundly significant factors. Also playing a role is the availability of appropriate software to facilitate services and the growing wealth of textual resources. These are some of the more obvious factors that I see lending weight to a growing mainstream acceptance of computer-aided analysis of text and the development of initiatives for wide-area networking of the resources. Nevertheless, the notion that adequate texts and software are available is not generally accepted. I would like to proceed to examine the nature of these assumptions, beginning by explaining what I see as necessary minimal resources for textual analysis.

TEXTUAL ANALYSIS, NOT ELECTRONIC PUBLISHING

I risk stating the obvious by saying that textual analysis stands in contrast to electronic publishing with tools such as DynaText and full-text electronic document delivery as seen in Project Mercury or TULIP.[4] While electronic publishing projects deliver a fully integrated, ready-to-read *electronic document,* and efforts such as TULIP are designed primarily to expeditiously produce facsimiles of articles or books, textual analysis focuses on computer-aided processes that aid in determining characteristics of text. This is not a case of bad and good approaches: the software used in textual analysis, document retrieval, and electronic publishing will almost necessarily be very different. For example, a textual analysis system must support phrase searching as easily as it does a word search. The notion of stop words is untenable. Absolute precision in retrieval is essential, and probabilistic methods as found in software like Wide Area Information Servers (WAIS), Topic, and Smart are unlikely to be useful. Truncation cannot significantly increase the amount of time needed to retrieve results. And while document retrieval systems return large chunks of text by design and can provide key words in context (KWIC) displays only with difficulty, fine-level results such as the KWIC are a fundamental part of the textual analysis system. These same characteristics may be found in the other systems, but for textual analysis, they are critical.

Consider the following example of textual analysis using the example of the vowel shift in English, e.g., the change from lond to land and lomb to lamb. In all of Old English, there are 262 works that contain the stem "lond" and 1,239 works that contain the stem "land."[5] Only 126 works contain both stems, and in those 126 works, there are 834 occurrences of the stem "lond" (Figure 1a). This is an interesting result for an Anglo-Saxonist. The person who, looking at the complete Old English Corpus, wanted to see all 834 instances of the string "lond" in texts that also have the string "land" almost certainly does not want much broader context than the relevant lines, and definitely does not want all 126 works delivered to his printer so that he can read them later at his convenience. Eight hundred thirty-four is only a moderately overwhelming number of occurrences, but let us expand the problem to include all "on/om" and "an/am" strings. Looking at the more than 300,000 relevant occurrences will be quite a task even in a system that provides KWIC displays or displays of relevant lines, but a system that can further refine the results based on other textual characteristics (e.g., verse works as opposed to glosses) can make this manageable. Figures 1b to 1d represent the results of narrowing the search based on textual characteristics such as genre, language, and period. The raw search results, all taken from the entire Old English Corpus, were retrieved in a total time of less than two seconds. The method and results are not uncommon for a textual analysis system.

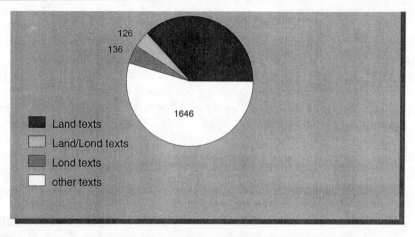

Figure 1a. Distribution of lond and land in Old English Corpus (area of intersection [126 texts] includes 834 occurrences of "lond")

STANDARDS AND OPEN SYSTEMS

Standards and open systems approaches must be a defining part of these efforts to provide the resources of textual analysis to communities of scholars. It is not enough to say that access is improved if a major investment is made in textual resources that will be unusable in two years. The texts must be reusable. It must be possible to use the texts in a variety of types of analysis, with a variety of analytical packages. Additionally, the texts must be accessible to a variety of computing environments. Because of the cost of creating the texts, investing in the texts must be an investment in the future. Selecting texts based on a system's capabilities when that system excludes the possibility of simultaneously using the texts with other tools is to restrict the field of inquiry. To that end, a standards-based encoding scheme and a generally agreed upon tag set must be at the foundation of text creation.

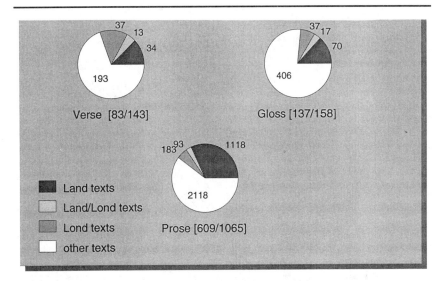

Figure 1b. Distribution of lond and land in Old English Corpus subset (number of "lond/land" occurrences in area of intersection listed in brackets)

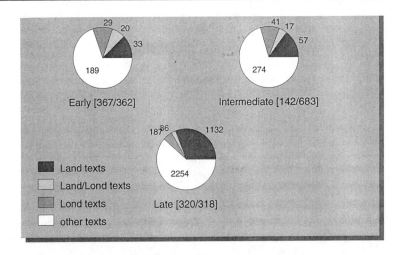

Figure 1c. Distribution of lond and land in Old English Corpus subset (number of "lond/land" occurrences in area of intersection listed in brackets)

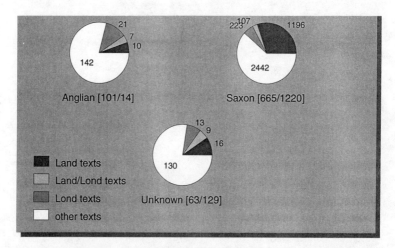

Figure 1d. Distribution of lond and land in Old English Corpus subset (number of "lond/land" occurrence in area of intersection in brackets)

The application of SGML through the Text Encoding Initiative will continue to play a central role in ensuring that resources are produced in a way that makes them flexible and of continuing value. This paper is not the place for an argument of the value of ISO 8879, Standard Generalized Markup Language, especially when the argument has been made so effectively elsewhere (Coombs, Renear, and DeRose 1993). In addition to its value as an internationally approved standard, SGML is ideally suited to supporting textual analysis because it is a descriptive rather than a procedural markup language. That is, it is a language designed to reflect the structure or function of text rather than simply its typography or layout. The difficulty of designing an implementation of SGML to meet a broad range of text-processing needs in the humanities has been met by the Text Encoding Initiative in its *Guidelines for Electronic Text Encoding and Interchange.*[6]

It must also be said that text without markup is irrelevant to this discussion: without markup, questions like the "lond/land" question cannot be effectively asked. For example, without markup, there is no effective, standards-based way of representing the "body" of the text and distinguishing it from descriptive information about the text. There are some alternatives to markup, including, for example, modeling the text's structure through a database or (as HTML and Gopher do) through the use of the filesystem. Reliance on a database (instead of encoding) for representing structure is inadequate because of its proprietary format.

Use of the filesystem—directories and files—to represent structure is quickly overwhelmed by complexity and the amount of information found in thousands of documents.

By using open systems to support access to materials, the textual analysis system can support the widest variety of platforms. An integral part of this is the establishment of access standards for textual analysis. Z39.50 is a capable mechanism for access to bibliographic information, but it will almost certainly fall short when dealing with complex documents and structural relationships (see the Appendix). Short of such a standard, however, an effective strategy is the use of a published or documented protocol. The PAT query language is at the foundation of the Telnet-derived protocol in use at the University of Virginia. Using this strategy, the university has been able to support wide-area access to a commercial X-Windows client (PatMotif), a locally developed vt100 client (URL: file://etext.virginia.edu/pub/clients), a commercial MS-Windows client (PowerSearch), WWW forms-compatible clients such as Mosaic and OmniWeb, a student-developed X-Windows OED client, and the PAT command-line.

WHAT TEXTUAL RESOURCES?

Our needs for textual resources are at least as great as our historical collections, but we have begun to enjoy some benefits from standards efforts and the increasing interest in electronic publishing. The body of material available from the Oxford Text Archive, parsed and in TEI-conformant markup, grows as a result of current efforts in creating new texts and the efforts of Jeffery Triggs,[7] the University of Virginia, and others in the conversion of previously deposited materials. In addition to the Old English Corpus (a complete representation of Old English assembled for the *Dictionary of Old English*), more than 100 works of some quality are available from the Oxford Text Archive, most via anonymous File Transfer Protocol (FTP).[8]

Commercial offerings have begun to have some impact on the collections we build. Chadwyck-Healey's often controversial offerings comprise the largest portion. Their *English Poetry Database* is projected to be completed in late 1994, and already we have more than 1,500 volumes of English verse as a result of it. Forthcoming projects include an English verse drama series, an African-American verse (to 1900) series, and a recently announced *American Poetry Database*. Their *Patrologia Latina Database,* including the 200 volumes of Migne, should also be finished this year. These efforts are notable for the scrupulous (if generic) application of SGML. Also producing SGML texts is Oxford University Press, with a varied and attractive publication list. The University of

Michigan Press will begin publishing works in SGML from the Society for Early English and Norse Electronic Texts (SEENET), late this year. Though not specifically in SGML, high-quality philosophical texts are being published by INTELEX; the University of Virginia is applying SGML to many of these and returning the marked-up versions to the publisher for subsequent resale.

It is remarkable that by the end of the year it will be possible to offer nearly all of England's verse online,[9] to offer all of extant Old English, and to offer significant bodies of Middle English materials. If literary research in the electronic environment has suffered from being limited by the body of material available, this body of "extraordinary language" (as contrasted to the "ordinary language" of everyday speech and writing) should begin to change that. But there are many questions about the quality of the materials.

There are several common criticisms of electronic texts: many electronic texts are based on poor editions, some are poorly transcribed, and (of the ones with SGML) the level of markup will not support the most sophisticated investigations. Many of the criticisms are appropriate, but the problems with many of the currently available electronic texts are opportunities rather than failings.

The choice of editions is frequently made more problematic by issues of copyright, but poor editions have always been part of our collections and have played a role in defining good editions. Scholars working on new editions at the University of Virginia have expressed the hope that electronic texts drawn from poor editions could serve as the foundation for current editorial efforts. Some of the available electronic texts are from editions of the highest quality. Several scholars have contributed the files used in creating scholarly editions (for example, Frances McSparran, who contributed the files for her Early English Text Society *Octovian*). One significant publisher, Library of America, has contributed typesetting tapes of several titles to the Oxford Text Archive. In these instances, we have only the most authoritative sources for exceptional editions.[10]

Limited markup is an opportunity for many interested in more sophisticated forms of analysis: detailed markup is usually a function of a particular type of analysis and so is unlikely to suit all users. One of the advantages of working with standards-based and generally agreed upon markup is that it is possible to build on the work of others. It will be difficult to identify or define a minimum level of markup for electronic texts, but a foundation of structural markup for commonly recognized features (e.g., poems, stanzas, and lines in a volume of verse) will serve most needs.

It is also true that there are poorly transcribed texts that should not be archived. We have received files that the depositor explains are failed experiments with scanning that even the scholar who produced them was not willing to use. Poorly transcribed texts pose an unambiguous threat to scholarship and should be clearly identified and set aside so that they may be used only by those fully aware of the problems inherent in the texts.

A bigger problem than the quality of the electronic texts is the current conditions of use in commercial resources. For example, even with the most liberal license, it is not possible for a scholar to begin work creating a new edition of a work using an electronic edition from a commercial publisher. More typically, it is even difficult to use a given text in two environments (e.g., with a statistical program and a campus-wide textual analysis system) simultaneously. The cost of acquiring these collections along with licensing restrictions is creating a situation where only those affiliated with larger, well-endowed universities have access to these resources. In general, these problems are creating a disjuncture with traditional roles of research libraries, as the libraries are no longer able to serve the role of augmenting the collections of smaller institutions, and the resources acquired cannot be used in the continuum of scholarship where older editions form the basis for newer editions. The economics of publishing are likely to ensure that these situations do not change. We should begin to look at alternative strategies for creating electronic texts for libraries, including creating the texts ourselves.

CONDITIONS NEEDED FOR A WIDE-AREA ANALYTICAL ENVIRONMENT

A system for textual analysis will necessarily be more complicated than a simple document retrieval system because of the operations that are performed. Operations include those mentioned earlier, such as effective phrase searching, easily browsed large result sets, and precision in searching. In addition to those capabilities, a textual analysis system should include other features:

- *Efficient cross-textual analysis:* The system should not constrain the user to searching a single text or a small group of texts with each search. It should be possible to search large bodies of material and quickly get a response (i.e., within seconds).
- *Expeditious results:* Similarly, most searches should yield results in seconds, not minutes. A search of a truncated stem "lond" in the *English Poetry Database* at Virginia takes approximately one second. The same search takes several minutes on the Chadwyck-Healey

CD-ROM, a problem attributable to both the DynaText software and
the organization of data on CD-ROM.

- *Recognition of structure:* Software must be able to examine structural
relationships and, specifically, to locate occurrences of features defined
by their structural placement. (What do we mean by structure? The
organization of a text explicitly and implicitly makes clear elements
of structure such as chapters, paragraphs, poems, stanzas, and verses.
These more obvious elements are often signaled to the reader in
unambiguous ways by headings, but just as frequently, as with stanzas,
they are indicated by conventions generally recognized. Structures may
also be composite or abstract, as in "16c quotations in the OED,"
where the era of the quotation is signaled by a feature of a substructure,
i.e., date.) For example, to examine the vowel shift in the Old English
Corpus accurately, it is necessary to eliminate both the Latin text
within the Corpus and the descriptive information accompanying
the texts. To identify rhyme or other line-end features, it must be
possible to distinguish between text that appears before a carriage
return (e.g., in prose formatted to display on the screen) and a true
end-of-verse.

In addition to these more common forms of analysis, other activities
such as morphological analysis, statistical analysis of occurrence patterns, and general grammatical analysis—i.e., the recognition of
constructions of various types—will need to be supported. We should
expect to see at least as many forms of computer-aided textual analysis
as we would find in print textual analysis.

A single package will not accommodate all sorts of analysis but
can satisfy a majority of the fundamental needs of textual analysis.
Understanding this leads us to other important conclusions. For example, the importance of reusable text, of text whose signals are rendered
in a standards-compliant way, is imperative. Again, it is important that
it be possible to use the same text with a number of different analytical
packages and in a number of different environments. In an environment
where a well-designed general-purpose package serves a core of needs
in a client/server environment, it may be possible that more specialized
activities will move to a post-processing phase supported by specialized
clients speaking to the central server. By using centralized storage and
retrieval from larger bodies of materials, we can make it unnecessary
for scholars to circumscribe their perspectives based on textual resources
that fit on their desktops.

CAPABILITIES OF PAT:
DOES IT MEET THE NEEDS OF TEXTUAL ANALYSIS?

At least one package offers all or most of the capabilities outlined
as critical pieces of a generalized textual analysis engine. PAT offers

extraordinary performance in both word and phrase searching over large bodies of material and can take significant advantage of SGML encoding. (Examples that follow are from the still incomplete *English Poetry Database,* currently a corpus of approximately fifty million words. Most of the searches that follow yield results in approximately one second.)

- *Speed:* As mentioned previously, words and phrases, in a body of more than 1,500 volumes, can be retrieved in a second or seconds. Combinations of words or phrases do not take significantly more time (ex.: "lond" yields 1,559 matches; "lond" "near" "home" yields 8 matches).
- *Phrase searching:* PAT employs an unusual indexing scheme (Pat trees) to orient retrieval primarily to phrases or strings rather than words (Gonnet, Baeza-Yates, and Snider 1991). Called "semi-infinite string indexing," the indexing allows the software to retrieve phrases with essentially the same speed as it does words (ex.: "lond of troy" yields 4 matches).
- *Truncation:* Truncation benefits from the same indexing that aids phrase searching. Stems are easily searched; truncation is eliminated by adding a space to the end of the search (ex.: "lond " and "lond" yield 1,559 and 6,738 matches).
- *Stop words:* Although PAT does support the concept of stop words, minimal index overhead (roughly 75 percent of the total size of the text), low costs for disk space, and high retrieval speeds make it possible to index without stop words (ex.: "to be or not to be" yields 15 matches).
- *Structure recognition:* PAT can generate structures based on tags or tag relationships. For example, the structure "stanza" is created by indexing the space between the <stanza> and </stanza> tags. It can also create structures based on composite or abstract features, such as the structure "rhymed," which consists of all poems including the attribute "rhymed=y," or the structure "C16," which consists of the body of all works published in the sixteenth century or whose authors flourished in the sixteenth century. Examples:

docs poem (i.e., how many poems does the *EPD* include? 64,670)

docs poem not incl "rhymed=y" (i.e., how many unrhymed poems are there in the *EPD*? 2,346)

docs poem incl.20 docs stanza (i.e., how many poems in the *EPD* have more than twenty stanzas? 2,812)

(lond—london) within docs C15 (i.e., excl. London, how many words beginning with "lond" are there in 15c *EPD* poems? 362)

PAT's SGML awareness is flexible. In addition to its ability to index based on tags or tag relationships, PAT is accompanied by a suite of tools extremely valuable in processing texts in SGML. A parsing tool, sgmlregion, can check the SGML validity of a document and can generate rudimentary display specification rules files to view texts in a variety of ways (Figure 3). A structure indexing tool, multiregion, provides a thorough low-level checking of tags and tagging that discovers errors missed by most true SGML parsers.[11]

PAT's support for CONCUR is probably unintentional and centers around its recognition (not enforcement) of SGML. In the following example, pages and page IDs do not always coincide with poems and stanzas. Note that "page 4" ends in the middle of the second poem.

```
<poem>                                                  <page n=4>
<stanza>
<l> From fairest creatures we desire increase,</l>      <l> From fairest creatures we desire increase,</l>
<l> That thereby beauties Rose might neuer die,</l>     <l> That thereby beauties Rose might neuer die,</l>
<l> But as the riper should by time decease,</l>        <l> But as the riper should by time decease,</l>
<l> His tender heire might beare his memory:</l>        <l> His tender heire might beare his memory:</l>
</stanza><stanza>
<l> But thou contracted to thine owne bright eyes,</l>  <l> But thou contracted to thine owne bright eyes,</l>
<l>Feed'st thy lights flame with selfe substantiall fewell,</l>  <l> Feed'st thy lights flame with selfe substantiall fewell,</l>
<l> Making a famine where aboundance lies,</l>          <l> Making a famine where aboundance lies,</l>
<l> Thy selfe thy foe, to thy sweet selfe too cruell:</l>  <l> Thy selfe thy foe, to thy sweet selfe too cruell:</l>
</stanza><stanza>
<l> Thou that art now the worlds fresh ornament,</l>    <l> Thou that art now the worlds fresh ornament,</l>
<l> And only herauld to the gaudy spring,</l>           <l> And only herauld to the gaudy spring,</l>
<l> Within thine owne bud buriest thy content,</l>      <l> Within thine owne bud buriest thy content,</l>
<l> And tender chorle makst wast in niggarding:</l>     <l> And tender chorle makst wast in niggarding:</l>
</stanza><stanza>
<l> Pitty the world, or else this glutton be,</l>       <l> Pitty the world, or else this glutton be,</l>
<l> To eate the worlds due, by the graue and thee.</l>  <l> To eate the worlds due, by the graue and thee.</l>
</stanza></poem>
<poem><stanza>
<l> When fortie Winters shall beseige thy brow,</l>     <l> When fortie Winters shall beseige thy brow,</l>
<l> And digge deep trenches in thy beauties field,</l>  <l> And digge deep trenches in thy beauties field,</l>
<l> Thy youthes proud liuery so gaz'd on now,</l>       <l> Thy youthes proud liuery so gaz'd on now,</l>
<l> Wil be a totter'd weed of smal worth held:</l>      <l> Wil be a totter'd weed of smal worth held:</l>
</stanza><stanza>
<l> Then being askt, where all thy beautie lies,</l>    <l> Then being askt, where all thy beautie lies,</l>
<l> Where all the treasure of thy lusty daies;</l>      <l> Where all the treasure of thy lusty daies;</l>
<l> To say within thine owne deepe sunken eyes,</l>     <l> To say within thine owne deepe sunken eyes,</l>
<l> Were an all-eating shame, and thriftlesse praise.</l>  <l> Were an all-eating shame, and thriftlesse praise.</l>
</stanza><stanza>
<l> How much more praise deseru'd thy beauties vse,</l>  <l> How much more praise deseru'd thy beauties vse,</l>
<l> If thou couldst answere this faire child of mine</l>  <l> If thou couldst answere this faire child of mine</l>
<l> Shall sum my count, and make my old excuse</l>      <l> Shall sum my count, and make my old excuse</l>
<l> Proouing his beautie by succession thine.</l>       <l> Proouing his beautie by succession thine.</l>
</stanza><stanza>                                         </page><page n=5>
<l> This were to be new made when thou art ould,</l>    <l> This were to be new made when thou art ould,</l>
<l> And see thy blood warme when thou feel'st it could.</l>  <l> And see thy blood warme when thou feel'st it could.</l>
</stanza></poem>
<poem><stanza>
<l> Looke in thy glasse and tell the face thou vewest,</l>  <l> Looke in thy glasse and tell the face thou vewest,</l>
<l> Now is the time that face should forme an other,</l>  <l> Now is the time that face should forme an other,</l>
<l> Whose fresh repaire if now thou not renewest,</l>   <l> Whose fresh repaire if now thou not renewest,</l>
```

Figure 2. Flexible views, along with display specification language.

PAT offers a solution to a challenging problem in SGML, a sort of support for CONCUR. Briefly, CONCUR is a feature of SGML designed to support tag relationships that do not nest in a predictable way.[12] For example, pages do not coincide with chapters, always beginning within a chapter, and finishing within a chapter. SGML packages available today rarely support CONCUR. Because PAT and supporting tools can generate structures selectively, rather than necessarily processing all tag pairs in one pass, it is possible to index two conflicting streams of tags in different processes, thereby avoiding the conflict (Figure 3).[13]

PAT's Quiet Mode is a complete language suitable for client-server communication. This
sample of communication with the *Oxford English Dictionary* demonstrates a search of a word
and then a co-occurrence search, followed by a display of ten sampled hits with 250 characters
of context. The dialogue is marked with "Client" communication and "Server" response, and
results are numbered, for readability.

```
Client:   "lond "
Server:   <SSize>13210</SSize>
Client:   "lond " near "home"
Server:   <SSize>38</SSize>
Client:   {Quieton raw}; {Printmode 1}; pr.250 sample.10
Server:   <PSet>
1.    <Start>187380797</Start><Raw><Size>250</Size>
      A> <W>Charit. Lond.</W> 31 <T>The Home for Confirmed
      Invalids. </T></Q><Q><D>1863</D> <A>S. Low</A> <W>Charit.
      Lond.</W> Index 312 <T>Home for Aged Annuitants.
      </T></Q><Q><D>1897</D> <W>Whitaker's Alm.</W> 282 <T>Dr.
      Barnardo's Homes for Orphan Waifs
      </Raw>
2.    <Start>26391928</Start><Raw><Size>250</Size>
      D>1723</D> <W>Lond. Gaz.</W> 6127/3 <T>The Mayor..having
      appointed Carew Davis..Pumper of all the Bath-waters.
      </T></Q><Q><D>1836</D> <W>Scenes Commerce</W> 162 <T>The
      Bath water is hot.</T></Q></PQP><PQP><Q><D>1795</D> <A>W.
      Lewin</A> <W>Insects Gt.
      </Raw>
      [six occurrences deleted]
8.    <Start>309187934</Start><Raw><Size>250</Size>
      D>1867</D> <W>Lond. Rev.</W> 22 June 696/1 <T>To restore our
      rivers to their former prolific condition, it is
      indispensable that salmon-passes should be provided.
      </T></Q><Q><D>1899</D> <W>Daily News</W> 4 May 11/2 <T>In
      1863 a salmon pass or ladder
      </Raw>
9.    <Start>48322082</Start><Raw><Size>250</Size>
      <W>Old Home, Lond. Suburb</W> (1879) 244 <T>A calm variety
      of incident.</T></Q></QP></S6></S4><p><S4><#>2</#>
      <S6><DEF><LB>Comb.</LB>, as
      <IL><LF>calm-minded</LF><SF>calm-minded</SF><MF>calm-minded<
      /MF></IL>, <IL><LF>calm-mindedness</LF><SF>-mindedn
      </Raw>
</PSet>
```

Figure 3. Pseudo-CONCUR

PAT also has failings. For example, it does not yet support regular
expression searching. That is, single character internal truncation,
variable character substitution (e.g., "m[aoe]n" retrieves "man" "mon"
and "men") is not yet possible. By indexing for left-hand truncation,
one introduces annoying problems in other areas and quadruples index
sizes.[14] And the software is supplied without guidance for implementing
a service in a campus-wide environment (i.e., the expectation seems
to be that every potential user will have an account on the host machine).
Still, PAT's design intelligence is one that accommodates many research
needs while accommodating needs of long-lived documents, i.e.,
documents in SGML.

LEVELS OF USE AND WORK PERFORMED:
UNIVERSITY OF VIRGINIA AND
UNIVERSITY OF MICHIGAN

In 1993, the first full calendar year of use at the University of Virginia, nearly 1,700 University-affiliated persons logged 7,533 total sessions. A session may last only a few minutes or several hours, and may involve one or several databases. Overwhelmingly, sessions were logged by students and faculty from the School of Arts and Sciences. This finding is distinct from that at the University of Michigan, where the second largest user group was from the School of Engineering. The difference between the two universities is explained at least in part by the requirement, at the University of Michigan, for every user to acquire an account on the host machine. At Virginia, the mode of access is much more barrier-free and allows for serendipity. Supporting random, unpredicted use is a critical part of support for a textual analysis system.

The types of uses reported here are anecdotal (conveyed to the author in personal e-mail communication) but are meant to represent the complexity of research supported and the limitations of the current system.

Case 1

A University of Michigan scholar interested in Middle English dialect explored characteristics of the texts through PAT's recognition of structure. "One scribe copied [the *Owl and the Nightingale*, Cambridge], but the language shows that two scribes, with different dialects, copied an antecedent version, and that their work can be identified through his handiwork." E. G. Stanley has defined those sections as lines 1-900 and 961-1183 (being the work of one scribe) and 901-60 and 1184-end (as the work of the second scribe). Using the software and its recognition of structure to define those sections, she was able to save the divisions (under the names C1 and C2) and "contrast the two spelling systems."

Case 2

All of Austen's novels and many of her letters are available through the systems at Michigan and Virginia. A philologist at Michigan leads a discussion group that often uses the collection to look at questions of historical language change. One interesting instance is the passive construction with "being" as in "the house was being built." Late in the nineteenth century, this construction began to displace the earlier preferred construction, "the house was building." Austen's *Sanditon* was completed by another writer, and a comparison of the novel with Austen's other writings finds a clear preference for the passive "[was/were/am/is] being" where it is absent in the works authored solely by Austen.

Case 3

A medievalist at the University of Virginia was asked by a student completing a dissertation on *Piers Plowman* "whether the parallel terms/phrases *Do Wel, Do Bet,* and *Do Best* were ever used as infinitives rather than as simple nominals made from the verb form. The verb form has usually been taken essentially to be imperative when it carries a purely verbal sense. . . ." By searching the A, B, and C texts of *Piers Plowman,* he was able to provide the student with "all the instances of each, each in a ten-line context . . . , and the result was [the student] solving one of the important cruxes of the poem."

Case 4

An Anglo-Saxonist at the University of Virginia was completing an edition of a text and decided he should include those words that occurred only in the text he was editing in a glossary. Using the University's online version of the Old English Corpus, he was able to identify each of these. "[T]hough because grammatical inflection often changes the root form of a word (e.g., man, men) and medieval spelling is variable (e.g., hit, hyt), it was often necessary to do more than one search." This quickly led him to the conclusion that support for regular expressions, e.g., "m[aoe]n*" to yield all words beginning with "man," "mon," or "men," is a critical factor currently lacking in the system. However, he reported that he "got more ambitious than that. The Old English Corpus consists of poetry, prose, and glosses to Latin texts, and these three types of texts employ lexicons that are in some ways specialized. That is, there are words that are used only in poetry, and, somewhat surprisingly, words that are used only in glosses. There are prose words that are not used in poetry, though they are used in glosses. My text was, I was already aware, unusual in that it contained a large number of words that were otherwise attested only in glosses, and not just any glosses, but a particular set of them, glossing Latin texts that my author seemed particularly to like. So I was interested in finding those words that were attested, outside of my text, only in glosses." While the Old English Corpus is marked for three types of text (prose, verse, and glosses), it became clear to the scholar that more in the way of classification will be necessary: "Then some folks would like other groupings. Historians might like to be able to rope off the charters in the same way, for example, or the legal texts; some might like to search just the medical texts."

From the perspective of the institution hoping to provide access to the resources of textual analysis, there is much that is promising. Textual collections are available, and the climate for collaborative development of resources is positive. The standards for defining those textual resources are mature and well articulated. Software to accommodate many types of analytical work is available. An open systems orientation is possible with some of the incipient clients and the server code written to take advantage of PAT and ARTFL's PhiloLogic. Still, much is lacking.

WHERE FROM HERE?

PAT can serve as a foundation for current efforts and future developments but lacks some important capabilities. It must begin to support regular expression searching. Open Text should supply server code (rather than relying on login-based transactions and personal accounts on the host machine for all users) that is as carefully tested and reliable as PAT itself. It also needs competition from other packages.

A search and retrieval protocol that is aware of document structure is needed. Such a protocol would resemble Z39.50 in facilitating a wide range of standardized operations for heterogeneous clients but would differ from Z39.50 in its ability to exploit complex documents.

A related need is a standard query language. Such a query language would function like Z39.58 (the Common Command Language) and would probably only be used by developers in creating clients. A standards-based query language would have the benefit of supporting the development of clients that would speak in a predictable way with a textual analysis server, making possible queries such as "limit searches to the body of the text that has a header with faulkner in author" or "locate verse groups that contain more than one line with the phrase 'were driven'."

Of course, my conclusions about the requirements for software and my sense of the types of uses are not drawn from a detailed analysis of research habits but instead from work with faculty at Michigan and Virginia. For the most part, this is a necessary compromise in beginning to establish services such as this. We are frequently several steps ahead of our constituencies in understanding the limitations and the possibilities of the technology. We know, for example, that Z39.50 is critical in moving our bibliographic systems forward, but the standard and its client/server operation will mean virtually nothing to those who will benefit most from it. We need to create an environment so that the questions of needs can be asked not in a vacuum but with an understanding of the potential of the technology. A thorough analysis of faculty research needs is still necessary. The environment created at the University of Michigan and the University of Virginia can serve as a foundation for that sort of needs analysis, but I am convinced that the resources offered through current systems in those institutions can also serve as the foundation for effective research today and tomorrow.

APPENDIX

ACCESS THROUGH STRUCTURE

Document Structure

A persistent and fundamental problem of creating and accessing libraries of material on the Internet is the matter of the structure of documents. Documents, whether wholly textual or compound documents, exhibit aspects that we generally call "structure." A monograph is comprised of parts, chapters, or essays. A journal is comprised of volumes, issues, and eventually articles. Articles, essays, and chapters are comprised of sections. Compound documents exhibit similar, though less predictable, features. Structure is widely recognized and is used to frame the meaning of documents. Despite this, paradigms for the transfer of information in a networked environment have either eschewed the notion of structure entirely or have represented rudimentary structures through the filesystem's directory and file paradigm. That is, large, complex documents are passed in their entirety from server to client, or coarse levels of structure in the document are modeled by fragmenting the document into directories and files. Both models of document transfer are inadequate for a variety of reasons. Current network capacity often fails to provide sufficient bandwidth to support fluid transfer of large documents; current workstation capacity is frequently overwhelmed by documents of even moderate size. And while both network capacity will increase and workstation capabilities will develop, the user of large documents is not able to navigate easily in these large bodies of text and will frequently want small, well-defined portions. The other alternative currently being used by Gopher and HTML/HTTP, fragmentation of documents into directories and files, is equally untenable, as we build large collections of documents and face the need to transfer even more precisely defined subsections of documents (e.g., entries in a large glossary). An effective means of recognizing and transferring structural features of documents is perhaps the most significant impediment to making large bodies of material available in a networked environment.

Most other problems of access to digital libraries depend on the more fundamental problem of developing a model of access to structured information.[15] The resolution of issues such as copyright, accounting, authentication, and data redundancy will continue to leave unresolved this problem of effective access to documents. Several solutions to these other problems have been proposed, tested, and some are in wide use. Billing servers and model copyright and use agreements such as the Coalition for Networked Information (CNI) Project READI have been offered as possible solutions to these problems. Kerberos and the corresponding Distributed Computing Environment (DCE) implementation of this authentication scheme may be a wholly adequate means of assessing the identity and rights of a user querying a large document server. However, without a resolution of issue-structured access, none of these proposed solutions can be widely used or tested.

Related Standards

The NISO standard, Z39.50, promises to revolutionize access to bibliographic databases. Through the standardization of the organization of bibliographic information and the protocols through which client and server communicate, we have begun to see the disappearance of traditional models of host-based access to bibliographic information. Those traditional models made inevitable the loss of the amenities of the local computing environment, amenities such as a sophisticated user interface and reasonably easy capture of information. Systems for retrieval have proliferated, despite the promulgation of a Common Command Language (Z39.58). In a very short time, graphical user interfaces for database navigation, searching, and information retrieval have been developed. Similarly, intercommunication between dissimilar systems has begun to take place, making differences between systems less significant and the choice of a user interface the governing factor.

A relatively simple extension of Z39.50 from a bibliographic environment to document retrieval is unlikely to take place. We will not be able to force all documents into a similarly well-defined structural representation: unlike a document, the bibliographic record is one-dimensional and has a predictable and relatively small set of possible fields. Similarly, the dimensions of the bibliographic record do not pose the challenges that are posed by a document. Nesting of elements (e.g., the third section of the first article within the second issue of the fifth volume) is a defining feature of the document. Because such an extension of Z39.50 to the document is unlikely, a similar protocol designed around the needs of the document is necessary. At the same time, we can see in recent developments around Z39.50 some of the great promise held for the establishment of such a protocol.

A Model of Structured Access

A model of access to and transfer of structured documents must be developed. The model should utilize information about the structure carried explicitly in a statement of the document's grammar. Each document might declare conformance to a specific Document Type Definition (DTD) in the interaction between client and server. The statement of conformance would be passed from client to server upon initial request for a document by the client. DTDs minimally convey information about the constituent parts of a document, and the relationship between those parts within the document. In the first interaction between client and document, the client browser will offer a virtual table of contents based on the highest level(s) of structure reflected in the DTD. A book DTD might offer the choices of parts, chapters, and sections, arrayed hierarchically in the browser. A more generic DTD might express those options as subdivisions of the body of the text where level one divisions (e.g., "div1") would be subdivided by level two divisions (e.g., "div2").

DTDs can be registered with the ISO, expediting this process. Built into the client would be the basic structural components of most widely used DTDs, including those from the American Association of Publishers (AAP), the American Mathematical Society (AMS), and the TEI.[16] In most of these cases, structure names will be resolved in the browser as natural-language names (e.g., "Chapter" rather than "chap"). In other cases, such as the more generic situations that prevail in TEI DTDs, generic structural divisions will be expressed by their tag names with available attribute values and will be arrayed in a similar hierarchical subdivision to facilitate browsing.

User requests would be mediated by the client in order to retrieve the relevant structure's contents. Upon being presented with a structure map or virtual table of contents, two operations would be immediately possible. By selecting one portion of the browser (e.g., a bullet opposite an entry), the server would provide the client with a list of substructures of the selected structure as found in the document. By selecting the name of the structure (e.g., "Chapter 1"), the contents of the structure will be passed to the user's client. Should the individual making the request desire to receive the contents of the entire document, this will also be possible. In this way, efficiencies of network and workstation capacity and reader ability will be maintained.

A Structure-Aware Query Language

Just as Z39.50 benefited from the Common Command Language (Z39.58), the proposed representation of structure can benefit from the articulation of a query language that is structure aware. Such a language must be capable of expressing nested relationships and must be capable of distinguishing between structures and text strings. So, for example, the language must be able to respond both to "give me the bibliography of the third chapter in part two" and "show me articles in the Journal of X where the author uses the phrase 'the indeterminacy of language'." A standards-based query language would make it possible for a developer to create a client that could speak in a predictable way with a textual analysis server, thereby effectively encouraging the development of many different types of clients supporting many different functions. These might range from simple browsers of electronic text to specialized post-processing clients where lemmatization or statistical analysis might take place based on locally defined rules of no consequence to the server or its search engine.

NOTES

1 PAT is available from Open Text Corporation, 180 King Street South, Suite 550, Waterloo, Ontario N2J 1P8, Canada. Tel.: 519-571-7111; Fax: 519-571-9092.

2 It is not my intention to discuss the hardware needed to make such a service available, as the options available have changed so substantially in such a short period of time. The RS/6000 Model 320 Michigan first used to make its service available cost approximately $15,000, while disk drives cost nearly $3,000 per gigabyte. Currently, a similar (and still appropriate) server costs less than half that of the 1989 Model 320, and disk drives cost approximately $750 per gigabyte. RAM continues to be a disproportionately large part of the cost: while 32Mb is satisfactory, in order to support large indexing and many simultaneous users, 64Mb is more appropriate. Any of a number of workstation class UNIX computers is well suited to this task.

3 Project Mercury is described in Mark Kibbey and Nancy H. Evans. 1989. The Network Is the Library. *EDUCOM Review* 24(3): 15-20. The TULIP project has been discussed in Karen Hunter and Jaco Zijlstra. 1994. TULIP the University Licensing Project (for delivery and use of journals). *Journal of Interlibrary Loan, Document Delivery & Information Supply* 4(3-4): 19-22.

4 The vt100 client was developed by Yuzhen Ge and John Price-Wilkin, working from a model of menuing in other Open Text applications and elaborating code written by Paul Pomes at the University of Illinois at Urbana-Champaign. The software is provided freely and without support. For more information about retrieving the software, please see the file "announce," available via anonymous ftp in the "pub" directory at etext.virginia.edu.

5 A careful construction of this search would eliminate false drops. In this example, only *London* is removed from the "lond" set. The searches used are:

docs body incl (lond—london)
docs body incl land
1 ∧ 2
(lond—london) within 3

6 The first preliminary draft of the guidelines was published in 1990. The second draft, known as P2, has been published subsequently in fascicles and is available via anonymous FTP from file://sgmll.ex.ac.uk/tei/p2. A complete, revised edition (P3) was published in 1994 (Association for Computers and the Humanities et al. 1994).

7 Triggs is the Director of the Oxford English Dictionary's North American Reading Program and can be reached at triggs@bellcore.com.

8 While the Old English Corpus is not available via anonymous FTP, most of the Oxford Text Archive's SGML-conformant materials are from black.ox.ac.uk, in the ota directory.

9 Of course, many works of English verse will not be included in the *English Poetry Database*. Chadwyck-Healey's source, the *New Cambridge Bibliography of English Literature* is not exhaustive for the period covered, works published only in periodicals will probably not be included, and works published in the twentieth century are omitted entirely.

10 It is also the case that scholars have found these resources important in their work. I believe it is because there is such intrinsic quality in many of the resources (from both good and bad editions) and because they are educated users of the resources, using caution where caution is appropriate.

11 Multiregion reports occurrences of "mangled tags" such as the double "<<" at the end of the title: "<header><fileDesc><title>The Feasibility of . . . <</title> ." The double "<<" may be valid content, according to the Document Type Definition (DTD), but is clearly a mistake.

12 This is an admittedly superficial description of CONCUR. At one point, Goldfarb (1990, 177) describes CONCUR as a "feature of SGML, which allows instances of multiple document types to exist concurrently in the same document."

13 PAT also provides a sort of SGML in its communication with other programs. PAT communicates (for example, through client/server relationships) using what it calls

"Quiet Mode." PAT's Quiet Mode is a structure-aware command syntax to report all results in paired tag sets, making possible a more reliable communication between interface and index (Figure 3).

14 Indexing for left-hand truncation with PAT is problematic. While with texts indexed for right-hand truncation, the user can "turn off" truncation by including a space, as in "lond " it is not possible to search for " lond " when texts are indexed for left-hand truncation. All initial spaces are removed, so that both " lond" and "lond" yield the same results.

15 The structural representation of documents, both compound and flat, has largely been achieved by recent standards developments (ISO 8859, ISO 10744, and ISO 10646). ISO 8859, or SGML, has remained virtually unchanged since its passage in 1986 and continues to be a valuable resource in this area. In 1992, the ISO passed both HyTime, a standard for time-based compound or multimedia documents, and ISO 10646, or UCS, a 16-bit character encoding scheme for the world's alphabets. Specific implementations of these standards—i.e., DTDs, in most cases—are still needed in some areas, but efforts by associations and publishers have largely solved this problem, leaving only the need to elaborate specialized, project-specific DTDs.

16 The AAP DTDs are widely used in publishing and offer markup guidelines for books, journal articles, tables, and formulas. A variant of the AAP DTDs has recently been approved by the ISO as a more general set of publishing DTDs. The AMS DTDs are probably the most widely used scientific DTDs. The TEI DTDs are being elaborated now but consist of a wide array of tag sets for a variety of applications. They are unquestionably the broadest and most versatile DTDs available for electronic publishing.

REFERENCES

Association for Computers and the Humanities (ACH), Association for Computational Linguistics (ACL), and Association for Literary and Linguistic Computing (ALLC). 1994. *Guidelines for Electronic Text Encoding and Interchange*, TEI P3. Ed. C. M. Sperberg-McQueen and Lou Burnard. Chicago; Oxford: Text Encoding Initiative.

Brentrup, Robert J. 1993. Building a Campus Information Culture. *Cause/Effect* 16(4): 8-14.

Coombs, James H., Allen H. Renear, and Stephen J. DeRose. 1993. Markup Systems and the Future of Scholarly Text Processing. In *The Digital Word: Text-Based Computing in the Humanities*, ed. George P. Landow and Paul Delany, 85-118. Cambridge, Mass.: MIT Press.

Goldfarb, Charles F. 1990. *The SGML Handbook*. Oxford, Eng.: Clarendon Press.

Gonnet, Gaston H., Ricardo A. Baeza-Yates, and Tim Snider. 1991. *Lexicographical Indices for Text: Inverted Files vs. Pat Trees*. Waterloo, Ont.: UW Centre for the New Oxford English Dictionary.

Price-Wilkin, John. 1991. Text Files in Libraries: Present Foundations and Future Directions. *Library Hi Tech* 9(3): 7-44.

Price-Wilkin, John. 1992. A Campus-wide Textual Analysis Server: Projects, Prospects, and Problems. In *Proceedings of the Eighth Annual Conference of the UW Centre for the New OED and Text Research*. Waterloo, Canada: UW Centre for the New OED and Text Research.

JAMES W. MARCHAND

Professor
Department of Germanic Languages and Literature
University of Illinois at Urbana-Champaign

The Scholar and His Library
in the Computer Age

ABSTRACT

The advent of powerful high-speed computers and the development of networked information resources have freed the scholar from the limitations of his private library, but new problems have arisen. Lack of standardization in both hardware and software, reluctance on the part of many scholars to master the new technology and resources, and the overwhelming choices facing the adventurous modern scholar present barriers to optimal information retrieval. The library must help resolve many of these problems and must utilize the new technology to store, catalog, retrieve, and deliver information regardless of its format.

THE PRE-COMPUTER SCHOLAR

I am by trade a medievalist.[1] This means that most of the information I use is in the form of the written word, stored for most of my career in books and codices found in libraries and archives. Thus, I have spent a good deal of my scholarly time and energy in and dealing with libraries. Like all of us, including the librarians among us, I have always found the libraries I worked in, from the smallest to the largest, to be inadequate and have cursed the various number systems used (see Lehnus 1980), the lack of analysis of serials, the inadequacy and inconsistency of subject headings, the physical location of collections, in short, all of those things we all complain about in our libraries. To overcome these inadequacies, I did all the things a scholar did in the pre-computer age. I slowly

137

acquired a large library.[2] I bought a Mudge (1917-36), then a Winchell (1967), then a Sheehy (1976) (not to mention Totok and Weitzel [1984], Malclès [1950-58], Kaufman, et al. [1955]), perused them thoroughly, and filled them with marginal notes full of Library of Congress, Dewey Decimal, and Harris numbers. I assiduously looked through the various catalogs of the Library of Congress, the Bibliothèque Nationale, the British Museum, the New York Public, etc. etc. As time went on and things got better, I could depend on the various bibliographies listed in my trusty Besterman (1965-66). I ordered microfilms for myself and acquired such things as Keil's *Grammatici Latini* on microfilm. When microfiche came along, I was able to get Migne's *Patrologia Latina* on microfiche. Already in the dark ages before photocopying, I was able to photograph, to copy by holograph, and to use one of the various peel-aparts available then. Even before one could buy a personal Apeco or Xerox machine, I could send microfilm to Ann Arbor and obtain strip xeroxes by Copy-Flow process; for example, I have all of the manuscripts of Wolfram's *Parzival* photocopied and bound, so that I can overcome the problem of sequential searching, which makes microfilm so hard to use for manuscript comparison. I even have several volumes of articles and excerpts I typed in by hand. I was always trying to lessen the burden of library work, figuring out how to use edge-punched cards, how to make sure I always had a supply of three-by-five cards and a pen at all times in the library.

Fonts were a particular problem for the scholar before 1980. One had to learn to use a quill or one of the metal nibs available commercially (e.g., Speedball) to imitate the hands of the manuscripts (as I did in Marchand 1969). Technology afforded the possibility of typing scripts with the Vari-Typer and later with the IBM Selectric, both with replaceable elements. One could have one's typewriter modified by having font faces soldered on, and there were even people like William Bennett, who had rubber stamps made, or Norman Willie, who was reported to have had a Gothic typewriter made. One could get kits that enabled one to replace keys (Type-It). With the advent of the mainframe, the chain printer afforded the possibility of making some fonts, thus creating characters such as thorn and edh.[3]

For large bibliographical projects, one could make use of edge-punched cards or even of Hollerith cards sorted by machine (see Reichmann 1961). One could shingle old note cards and photocopy them off, making bibliographies sorted as to author, date, subject.

Enough of this litany on the scholar of yesteryear. I was still bound to a great extent to an individual library, to indexes of books, such as the impossible-to-use-but-indispensable indexes to Migne, to an occasional trip to another library. The advent of the high-speed computer with large storage capacity has changed all that, especially the advent in the 1980s of the desktop (then laptop, notebook, hand-held) with hard disk, floppies, large amounts of RAM, incredible input (scanner, voice input) and output (CGA, then EGA, VGA, SVGA; voice; laser printers; color printers) devices, and storage and retrieval devices such as CD-ROM. The present-day scholar is freed from the tyranny of the mainframe, has available to him at his desk or under his tree riches which no Croesus of yesterday could have afforded; we have paradise enow at our fingertips. What is wrong?

As I talk to colleagues around the world, a sense of frustration seems to be prevalent. We know that there are untold riches and programs that would solve our problem, but we do not know how to find or use them. Without waxing too philosophical, I remember an old paper of Heinz von Foerster's in which he pointed out that the metaphors we use in speaking of computers are often awry (von Foerster 1970). The network is not an information superhighway, it is an ocean of pathless pieces of information, a self-organizing system where no one knows his way, and the scholar is awash in this sea of information. All one needs to do is to look at the messages on any list, to talk to any colleague, to look at any of the FAQs available.[4] We need help, and the rest of this paper concerns some suggestions I have. Help will have to come from one of the players in the game. Let us look at them.

THE COMPUTER INDUSTRY

The computer industry itself, and this includes manufacturers of hardware, software, etc., needs to think about the user. Each and every interface has to be learned, and protocols differ widely. If one just asks, for example, how to escape from a program, one will notice that there is a bewildering number of ways. No one uses <Escape>, <Break>, or <Ctrl-C>, as recommended in the programmers' manuals. We find <F1> (WordPerfect), <x> (List), <Ctrl-Z> (FancyFont), <Q> (nn), <q> (XT-Gold), <bye> (FTP), etc. etc. Dana Noonan has complained a number of times concerning the lack of any break key at all, for example when using File Transfer Protocol (FTP).[5]

The lack of standardization in such a small matter as an escape key is symptomatic for the whole industry. We have several platforms— DOS, OS2, Windows, Macintosh, UNIX—each incompatible with the other. One of the greatest problems in an academic office occurs when one of the parts uses a Mac and the other uses a DOS-based machine, and everyone knows the problem of receiving a PostScript document when he has only an HP printer, not to mention such things as Rich Text Format.[6] The industry needs to standardize, but it also must consider the needs of the users more. Recently, we have seen a proliferation of tsr and high-memory programs, programs that require increasing amounts of RAM and memory handlers, and the industry has been slow to handle the situation, so that one receives daily calls from colleagues who are finding that they cannot install this or that program, e.g., the CETEDOC CD-ROM. Those who feel that they cannot do without graphical user interfaces and use Windows, often find their machines locked up, always for no reason. Of course, we do not want to go back to 640K, a 6.7Mhz CPU, and a 20M hard disk, but we do need some consideration.

THE MODERN SCHOLAR

The poorest player in the game is the scholar himself, and the Lord helps those who help themselves. There are many closet Luddites lurking in our midst, as became painfully clear in a recent *New Yorker* bite (Baker 1994).[7] Many scholars seemingly just do not want to give themselves the time to learn about the computer, and this seems only reasonable, if they would just leave it at that. Everyone, however, is in search of a guru, and woe unto you if you get to be known as one; the guru's life is filled with nocturnal and Sunday afternoon phone calls. His knowledge of the field is at best haphazard, frequently erroneous, and always difficult to convey. The fact that yesterday's tools were plug-and-play, right-out-of-the-box, a-child-could-set-it-up devices has led to misunderstanding and mistrust of the computer, where you need an interface and fine tuning for almost everything. Even if, *horresco referens*, the scholar uses an electric typewriter, one just plugs it in and it runs.

If we return to the picture of the pre-computer scholar drawn in the first part of this paper, we will notice that everything has changed for him. Many of his research tools are now available electronically, some online, some on CD-ROM, and the prices are coming down. A scholar with a large RAM and Windows, for example, can purchase for less that $20.00 a CD-ROM called *Languages of the World* and can have available on a hot-key a dictionary of twelve languages to be used, for example, within his word processor (see Marchand 1994). Large dictionaries, such as the *Random House Unabridged*, not to mention the expensive *Oxford English Dictionary*, are available (our mainframe, as do many, has this one online, with a poor interface, but not to complain). For those who have the money, all the Wilson indexes (e.g., *Art Index, MLA*) are available on CD-ROM, as are the Bowker indexes (e.g., *Ulrich, Books in Print*). You can have the Hebrew, Greek, German (Elberfelder), French, Spanish, and Dutch Bibles for less than $20.00, with a search engine and display on the proper screen in the original scripts (*Straight from Heaven*, n.d.).

The modern scholar no longer needs his trusty three-by-five cards. When he goes to the library, he takes his notebook computer and a battery-driven scanner.[8] The results, though not always perfect, are better than my handwritten three-by-fives. If he has larger texts to copy, he can take them to his office and scan them using an optical character recognition (OCR) program. I scarcely ever use a pen or pencil anymore.

The modern scholar has little need to travel to other collections to see what they have or to pore through catalogs. He can get online and search through multiple online public access catalogs (OPACs) to find what is available. I used to copy off tables of contents, and there used to be journals, for example, *Leuvense Bijdragen* and *Lychnos*, that published tables of contents of journals, for those who worked at less-favored libraries to use. With the new CARL UnCover service, I can have sent to me by electronic mail the tables of contents of whatever journals I customarily use and, as usual, get a fax of one if I need to (for a fee).[9] Even at my own library, I can download lists of books on a particular subject, make myself a shelf list, etc., without leaving my desk.

The modern scholar is at no loss for fonts. Even in the days before vector fonts, I was able to clip fonts from manuscripts, generate printed fonts, and place all kinds of fonts on my screen (for examples, see Marchand 1987). Nowadays, I can create or borrow fonts in TrueType format, have them appear on my screen in any Windows application, and print on my trusty old HP Series II.[10] If I do not have a character, I can modify one, borrow one, or create one.

The index problem has been solved. If I want to find a passage in Shakespeare, for example, I do not go to my Bartlett's *Concordance*, look for the multiple occurrences, then go to my shelf, then copy off the passage. I simply interrogate my CD-ROM, using Findtext, call it up with List, and copy it into my document.[11] If I am ever able to afford the new *Patrologia Latina* on CD-ROM, I hope the search engine is fast enough for me to search it instead of using the indexes I cursed a moment ago.

I spoke of acquiring a large library, especially of reference works. As time goes on, I am able to get rid of many of these, having acquired electronic texts either from the Internet or on CD-ROM. The value of CD-ROMs is that they are (1) small, (2) durable, and (3) easily searched. With the advent of the new SCSI CD-ROM readers, I can now actually go out under a tree and take a library of works with me. My scholarly work is made immensely easier by the computer, and I have not even begun to name the ways. It could be easier still, however, and that is where the last player in the game comes in.

THE LIBRARY

We have been accustomed to looking to the library for help in the storage and retrieval, cataloging, and delivery of information. Using the term library in the widest sense, I think we must do so now. The dysfunction between the library and the scholar is proverbial. One of my favorite stories to illustrate this is ancient, but it was told to me by a librarian, David Kaser: The Harvard University librarian about 1900 encounters a friend on the street. The friend asks: "How are things?" "Fine," says the librarian, "There are only two books out of the library and I am out after one of those right now."[12] The computer age has brought us tools which increase the dysfunction (such as the NOTIS system and the "problem patron") and tools which can aid in overcoming it. In this section, I shall seek to identify trouble spots and to make suggestions as to what can be done about them; however, given space constraints, I can only name some of the most acute.

How shall we store our information? Shall we use plain ASCII text or shall we use one of the markup languages recommended? If markup, which one and how much? Note that this decision will determine to a great extent how we will retrieve our information. Note that any intervention on the part of an editor will inevitably distort the information and create noise in the system, which may be difficult to remove. For many texts, plain ASCII will be the first choice.

As just pointed out, the packaging of information contaminates it; we just need to choose that method which distorts it the least. The indexing of information or the use of subject headings, etc., will also inevitably form a barrier between the user and the information; even concordancing will do this. Perhaps, again, the best solution at first will be raw ASCII for texts, with a look-up engine that will find strings. Where codicology is important, as in the study of medieval texts, we will have to resort to other means.

In the handling of visual information, we are just beginning. Of course, nothing can replace the original, be it runestone or codex, but remarkable advances are being made (see Marchand 1992a, 1992b, 1992c).[13] However images are to be accessed by the patron, the library should store them in as rich a format as possible, say TIFF, though this may require an enormous amount of storage. Libraries and archives ought to consider three-dimensional representation and reconstitution of objects, for example, by sintering laser. All the manuscripts in the world ought to be stored in the best digitized manner possible, so that their information is at least partially registered. If images are to be manipulated in any manner, even algorithmically, a TIFF file of the first "photograph" ought to be kept. I cannot go into methods here, but it seems to me that the digital camera has advanced far enough to permit real-time registration and filtration and thus better pictures than have been made so far. It should be obvious also that what has been said up to now applies to audio as well.

Even the best of libraries is of little use if the patrons cannot retrieve the information stored. One of the greatest problems of retrieving electronic texts is knowledge of their availability and accessibility. There are great treasure troves of electronic texts out there whose existence is known to me, but which I cannot access, for example, the Rutgers collection and the Kiel collection. It is to be hoped that projects such as Project Gutenberg, Lysator, and the Online Book Initiative (OBI) will continue to provide access to important electronic texts. God bless the Oxford Text Archive; would that others would follow its lead.

The cataloging of electronic texts is of great importance, and we ought all to have an input into the methods of doing so. Before we can catalog them, we need to know of their existence. I patrol World Wide Web and Gopher-space continuously on the lookout for such texts; it is both disheartening and elating to run into a repository of texts of whose existence you were not aware.[14] The Georgetown initiative, the Center for Electronic Texts in the Humanities (CETH), and lists such as ANSAX-L and MEDTEXTL are grand resources, but we need a more concerted effort. When I see lists of available electronic texts such as that of Wiretap, I am really disheartened.[15]

As I look through OPACs, even using HYTELNET, I find the fact that there is no uniform interface for OPACs an almost intolerable burden. I use OPACs to discover works, to confirm citations, and to make bibliographies. The Committee on Institutional Cooperation (CIC) is to be praised for its efforts in the direction of a uniform interface for its member institutions, but this is only a drop in the bucket. As for capturing a session, I have found that I have to have recourse to a tsr program even in my own library.

Once we have identified sources for electronic texts, what shall we do with them? There is no need, for example, for each library to mirror Gutenberg, OBI, Lysator, and such, since these are available on the net, but each library *must* inform its patrons of their existence and provide an interface for interrogating and/or downloading them. Here, of course, we must also depend on the scholar to know something about the texts involved, such as the fact that "The Awful German Language," by Mark Twain, is found as an appendix to *A Tramp Abroad,* so that one does not have to search for it, or that Schiller's *An die Freude,* found in many different places on the net, is incomplete, lacks umlauts, and is frequently garbled.

There are several problems involving CD-ROMs (Budd and Williams 1993). The first is their cataloging, and I know of no source that lists all CD-ROMs, much less one that evaluates them properly. In order to find which electronic texts are available on CD-ROM, we need to analyze each one, if we can find out about its existence. For example, it is of some importance to the patron to know that *Desktop Library CDROM*, 1st Edition, August, 1992 (Walnut Creek), *DeskTop Bookshop*, (Unica Ltd.), *Reader's Library* (Micro-Mart Computer), and *Library of the Future Series*, second edition (World Library), contain almost entirely the same texts, but this is mentioned nowhere.

One of the most vexing problems for the user of CD-ROMs is the up-front software. That provided with the *St. Thomas Aquinas CD-ROM*, for example, is not of any great use for my purposes. Some CD-ROMs, for example, CETEDOC, are hard to install, and recently the list MEDIBER witnessed a rather sharp exchange between a user of *Admyte*, who could not get it to work, and one of its authors. Providers of CD-ROMs should adopt either a uniform interface or no interface and should take into consideration such things as conflict in memory space. The Apple/PC conflict frequently extends also to CD-ROMs.

Now I come to what is probably the most important point I wish to make, and this concerns the mounting of CD-ROMs and other databases for remote interrogation. As an individual scholar, I own the *OED2, Thomas Aquinas,* CETEDOC, several Wilsondiscs, many, many electronic texts, *Languages of the World, ICAME, Computer Select,* etc. etc. on CD-ROM, so that I can use them sitting at my desk. Some of these my library doesn't even own. This is not right; it is obvious that one cannot expect each scholar to provide himself with such tools. The library should mount for remote access all of the above and more. We have jukeboxes and towers that will hold as many as 100 CD-ROMs, and many come with the software necessary to network them for remote access (Breeding 1994). You should be able to sit at your desk and access the *MLA Bibliography, Books in Print,* the Verzeichnis Lieferbarer Bucher, FRANCIS, and Livres disponibles, etc. without having to get up. Both CETEDOC and Migne ought to be available in the same manner. I do not know what to do about the Greek texts of the Thesaurus Linguae Graecae (TLG) or the Latin texts of the Packard Humanities Institute (PHI), which must at present be rented, but we have to make a start. Nor do I know how we can persuade those holding private collections to release them.

These are just some of the problems we face. We need to agree upon some sort of uniformity: (1) of platform, (2) of software, (3) of entry (how about MARC?) (see Caplan 1993), (4) of bibliographical entry (there are over 100 formats at present in use, not to mention the idiosyncracies of individual libraries) (see Howell 1983, Stigleman 1991), (5) of basic elements (ASCII, extended ASCII), (6) of fonts.

At present, the individual scholar who wishes to make use of the tremendous possibilities the computer offers him must collect his own base of CD-ROMs, electronic texts, bibliographical software, presentation software and hardware, font software, and OCR software. All of this is managed at present at most universities by a system of unorganized gurus. It ought to be done by the *library*.

Here is the crux of the matter; we cannot expect our overworked librarians to do this alone, and I do not mean this in a patronizing manner (I have two librarians in my close family, so that I am not inclined to denigrate librarians). Every library needs a computer resource person, someone who can peruse Gleason Sackman,[16] Yanoff,[17] Noonan,[18] December,[19] *Current—Cites*,[20] etc. and keep up to date, who can install programs and support them, who can show the occasional faculty member how to use a scanner and OCR, in short, a guru. It will be necessary to train such people, for I do not know of the existence of one at present.[21]

I am painfully aware that I have only scratched the surface; there is much to be done, and it would be well if we got at it. *Se non è ben trovato, è vero.*

NOTES

[1] Much of this talk is personal narrative and concerns the library I use the most, that of the University of Illinois at Urbana-Champaign. I feel that much of what I say is generalizable and applies, *mutatis mutandis*, to all of us. What I have to say is too important to worry about the conventions of polite conversation and eschew the first person.

[2] I cannot resist quoting here a snippet I used to give to my students in "Bibliography and Methods" (Marchand 1955, vii):

> ON OWNING BOOKS. "The old-time scholar accumulated his house full of books on a smaller income than that of today's young man. Books were important to him; they were the fabric of his life; he did without other things; he wore his coat a year longer and carried home 20 new volumes. Today's scholar will never be able to afford books, no matter what his income or his wife's income, until he feels that books are at least as important to him as table cloths, toothbrushes, cat food, rugs, whiskey, hats, newspapers, cameras, and all the odds and ends that now come higher on the list. . . . Let us have no nonsense about the library taking the place of books in the home or about the great number of volumes published every year. . . . There is a deep personal and psychological difference between owning a library and using someone else's. It is a little like the difference between owning and renting a house, between belonging somewhere and merely passing through. It might even be the difference between a scientist and a technician or between a scholar and a scholarly technician. . . . We might remember what George Savile, Marquess of Halifax, wrote in 1690 or thereabouts: 'The struggle for knowledge hath a pleasure in it like that of wrestling with a fine woman.' If the scholar or the reader finds pleasure, and not merely duty, in the struggle with learning, then he will want to live with it in his own house and not merely to sample it in the library." August Frugé said it, in the *Saturday Review* for 16 July 1955.

3 For an example of an early use of the print chain, see the cover of *Literary Data Processing Conference Proceedings*, (Bessinger, Parrish, and Arader 1964) and the explanation on the title page.

4 FAQs, lists of Frequently Asked Questions, are archived by rtfm.mit.edu, in the pub/ usenet/news.answers subdirectory. One of the best ways to find out about a subject is to download and read the FAQ on it.

5 For example: *Network-News*, no. 12 (November, 1993), p. 5: "Wishlist for the user: 1. A break key. How many times have you waited for the system to tell you it couldn't locate anything when you already saw the typo?" Amen.

6 There are, of course, bridge programs. One can use MacinDos to read and write to some Mac disks, and the Macintosh people have tried to make the Mac operate like a PC on occasions. GhostScript is an excellent add-on for reading and printing PostScript files, but these are add-ons, and they just add to the confusion.

7 This note, featuring an attack on electronic cardfiles and a *plaidoyer* for a return to the card catalog, caused a flurry of remarks on HUMANIST and BI-L, the list devoted to bibliographic instruction.

8 With most notebooks and Artec's WalkScan/256S, for example, one can have under six pounds of equipment, and one does not need an extension cord or an outlet.

9 See InterNIC net-happenings, April 6, 1994. Carl UnCover intends to provide the table-of-contents service free.

10 For information on TrueType fonts, specs, etc.: FTP ftp.microsoft.com in the subdirectory /developer/drg.

11 Findtext is a grep-type program created by Jeff Prosise. A copy may be obtained from the disk included with his book, *PC-Magazine DOS 6 Techniques & Utilities* (Prosise 1993), or from *PC-Magazine's* bbs. List is by Vernon Buerg. It can be obtained from most bulletin boards.

12 For a somewhat harsher view of this dysfunction, see Smith 1990, tempered somewhat by the rebuttal of Phyllis Franklin (1993). The preservation of primary materials and the threat to their existence by imaging technology is another story (see Tanselle 1993).

13 Also posted for FTP in the following groups: HUMANIST, IOUDAIOS, and RELIGION.

14 For example, the texts by John of Trevisa deposited at FTP: blackbox.hacc.washington.edu, subdirectory /pub/text/trevisa, including the Gospel of Nicodemus, the Defensio Curatorum, De Regimine Principum, and Polychronicon. Neither I nor any of the 500 members of MEDTEXTL were aware of their existence, and some of us were actively engaged in work on Trevisa. Occasionally, it happens that one finds a trove and forgets the address. There are a number of works in Slavic languages deposited on a server somewhere in California.

15 The *Catalog of Available Online Books* scarcely scratches the surface of what is available, though I suppose we should not complain about such a pioneering effort.

16 Gleason Sackman is the editor of InterNIC net-happenings, an excellent newsletter for keeping up with what is going on on the network, including E-D-U-P-A-G-E, ALAWON, EDUCOM, The Internet Hunt, and many others: net-happenings@is.internic.net; subscribe at listserv@is.internic.net.

17 Scott Yannoff, *Special Internet Connections*. Updated every week or so, this short list (usually five or six pages) provides access information and brief notes on about 100 popular, new, or interesting network resources. To subscribe, contact Scott Yanoff at yanoff@csd4.csd.uwm.edu. You can also retrieve past issues by FTP: csd4.csd.uwm.edu, /pub/inet-services.

18 Dana Noonan's Nnews, available from ftp.nodak.edu, subdirectory /nnews. There are a number of files, with various dates. I would get them all.

19 Another excellent keeping-up source is from John December, known as the December lists: ftp.rpi.edu, /pub/communications/internet-cmc.

20 *Current—Cites*, available from ftp.lib.berkeley.edu, in the subdirectory /pub/ Current.Cites; there are a number of files, well-labeled. This is a very good source, leaning towards library, with summaries of articles from a number of journals. Also available in *InterNIC-Happenings*.

21 On the University of Texas's experiment with an "interactive online librarian," see Billings et al. 1994. See also McLaughlin 1994 (Syracuse) and Gunning, Myers, and Bailey 1993 (Houston).

REFERENCES

Baker, Nicholson. 1994. Discards. The New Yorker, 4 April, 64-70, 72-76, 78-80.

Bessinger, Jess B., Jr., Stephen M. Parrish, and Harry F. Arader, eds. 1964. *Literary Data Processing Conference Proceedings.* Armonk, N.Y.: IBM.

Bestermann, Theodore. 1965-66. *A World Bibliography of Bibliographies.* 5 vols. 4th ed. Lausanne: Societas Bibliographica.

Billings, Harold, T. F. Carver, J. D. Racine, J. Tongates, and S. Ploof. 1994. Remote Reference Assistance for Electronic Information Resources over Networked Workstations. *Library Hi Tech 12*(1): 77-86.

Breeding, Marshall. 1994. Networking Made Easy. *CD-ROM World 9*(1): 70-71.

Budd, John M., and Karen A. Williams. 1993. CD-ROMs in Academic Libraries: A Survey. *College & Research Libraries 54*(6): 529-35.

Caplan, Priscilla. 1993. Cataloging Internet Resources. *PAC Systems Review 4*(2): 61-66. Available e-mail: Listserv@UHUPVM1.BITNET Message: GET CAPLAN PRV4N2

Catalog of Available Online Books [Online]. 1993. Available: gopher@wiretap.spies.com

Franklin, Phyllis. 1993. Scholars, Librarians, and the Future of Primary Records. *College & Research Libraries 54*(5): 397-406.

Gunning, Kathleen, J. E. Myers, and C. W. Bailey, Jr. 1993. Networked Electronic Information Systems at the University of Houston Libraries: The IRIS Project and Beyond. *Library Hi Tech 11*(4): 49-55, 83.

Howell, John Bruce. 1983. *Style Manuals of the English-Speaking World: A Guide.* Phoenix, Ariz.: Oryx Press.

Kaufman, Isaak M. 1955. *Russkie biograficheskie i biobibliograficheskie slovari.* Moscow: Kul'tprosvetizdat.

Lehnus, Donald J. 1980. *Book Numbers: History, Principles, and Application.* Chicago: American Library Association.

Malclès, Louise-Noëlle. 1950-58. *Les sources du travail bibliographique.* 3 vols. in 4. Genève: Droz.

Marchand, James W. 1955. On Owning Books. *PMLA 70*(5): vii.

Marchand, James W. 1969. Gotisch. In *Kleiner GrundrisB der germanischen Philologie bis 1500,* 94-122. Berlin: Walter de Gruyter.

Marchand, James W. 1987. The Use of the Personal Computer in the Humanities. *Ideal* 2: 17-32.

Marchand, James W. 1992a. The Computer as Camera and Darkroom. *Offline, 37(January 30).* Available: gopher.upenn.edu Directory: Center for Computer Analysis of Texts (ccat.sas) File: Electronic Publications and Resources.

Marchand, James W. 1992b. The Computer as Camera and Darkroom. *Religious Studies News 7*(2): 23-24.

Marchand, James W. 1992c. The Computer as Camera and Darkroom. *CSSR Bulletin 21*(2).

Marchand, James W. 1994. Inexpensive CD-ROMs. *Offline, 44.* Available: gopher.upenn.edu Directory: Center for Computer Analysis of Texts (ccat.sas) File: Electronic Publications and Resources.

McLaughlin, Pamela W. 1994. Embracing the Internet: The Changing Role of Library Staff. *Bulletin of the American Society for Information Science 20*(3): 16-17.

Mudge, Isadore Gilbert. 1917-36. *Guide to Reference Books.* 3d through 6th editions. Chicago: American Library Association.

Prosise, Jeff. 1993. *PC Magazine Dos 6 Techniques and Utilities*. Emeryville, Calif.: Ziff-Davis.

Reichmann, Felix. 1961. Notched Cards. In *State of the Library Art*, vol. 4, part 1, ed. Ralph R. Shaw, 9-54. New Brunswick, N.J.: Graduate School of Library Service, Rutgers.

Sheehy, Eugene P. 1976. *Guide to Reference Books*. Chicago: American Library Association.

Smith, Eldred. 1990. *The Librarian, the Scholar, and the Future of the Research Library*. New York: Greenwood Press.

Stigleman, Sue. 1991. *Bibliography Formatting Software*. Chapel Hill, N.C.: Institute for Academic Technology.

Straight from Heaven. no date. [Computer program]. Lakewood, Ohio: Most Significant Bits.

Tanselle, G. T. 1993. The Latest Forms of Book-burning. *Common Knowledge* 2(3): 172-77.

Totok, Wilhelm, and Rolf Weitzel. 1984. *Handbuch der bibliographischen Nachschlagewerke*. 6th ed. Ed. H.-J. and D. Kernchen. Frankfurt: Klostermann.

von Foerster, Heinz. 1970. Thoughts and Notes on Cognition. In *Cognition: A Multiple View*, ed. Paul L. Garvin, 25-48. New York: Spartan Books.

Winchell, Constance M. 1967. *Guide to Reference Books*. 8th edition. Chicago: American Library Association.

REBECCA S. GUENTHER

Senior MARC Standards Specialist
Network Development and MARC Standards Office
Library of Congress
Washington, D.C.

The Challenges of Electronic Texts in the Library: Bibliographic Control and Access

ABSTRACT

This paper considers special problems in providing bibliographic control of and access to electronic texts and how they are being addressed by the *Anglo-American Cataloguing Rules,* 2d ed. 1988 rev., and the MAchine-Readable Cataloging (MARC) standards used for encoding bibliographic data on the computer. It summarizes the concepts and development of the USMARC Format for Bibliographic Data, computer files specifications, and identifies particular issues in providing bibliographic control of electronic texts including identification, description, location, and access. It explores attempts to address these difficult issues surrounding electronic texts, particularly in the MARC formats, as libraries are adapting to the growth of the Internet and the wide availability and proliferation of many types of electronic items. The paper reviews specific projects that attempt to provide better description of and access to electronic texts, including the OCLC Internet Resources Project, attempts of the USMARC Advisory Group of the American Library Association to enhance the MARC formats to provide location and access to online information resources, standards under development for locators and identifiers of Internet resources (Uniform Resource Identifiers), and some projects involving access to electronic texts. In addition, the author reviews the relationship between Standard Generalized Markup Language (SGML) and MARC.

149

INTRODUCTION

As computers have changed the way information is made available by making electronic resources widely accessible, the library and research communities have had to adapt to new ways of describing and locating information. Librarians and other information professionals are working in increasingly networked environments, with electronic resources such as online databases or electronic text centers becoming an integral part of their frame of reference. The "library without walls" is indeed becoming a reality, and it is necessary for cataloging rules and format specifications to change as well.

Libraries have a great deal invested in machine-readable cataloging records. Large bibliographic utilities and local systems provide services to institutions for access to library materials through the online catalog. It is desirable to include records for resources available only electronically in the same database as traditional library materials so that researchers can tap this type of information as additional source material. Researchers should be able to find bibliographic citations to relevant material regardless of format or location of the item. Because these electronic resources cannot be accessed in the same way as other materials (i.e., by a location that indicates the library and call number or shelf number housing the material), new methods need to be developed for access.

It is important that standards are developed and used for these new types of locator devices so that records can be exchanged between institutions. Given the growth of availability of electronic texts, sharing bibliographic records will be a necessity so that institutions do not expend valuable resources on redundant cataloging. The Library of Congress, the Online Computer Library Center (OCLC), and various committees of the American Library Association (ALA) have made progress in developing cataloging and MAchine-Readable Cataloging (MARC) standards for describing and providing location information for electronic resources, particularly those available on the Internet, the global network of networks.

CATALOGING CHALLENGES

The *Anglo-American Cataloguing Rules*, 2d ed. (*AACR2*) has generally been adopted as the standard cataloging code in most English-speaking countries (Joint Steering Committee 1988). The rules are revised according to changing needs of the library community by the Joint Steering Committee for Revision of AACR. The Committee on Cataloging: Description and Access (CC:DA), a committee of the Association for Library Collections and Technical Services of ALA, initiates proposals for revisions to the cataloging code and advises the official ALA representative to the Joint Steering Committee (American Library Association 1992, 32). In some cases, specific guidelines are issued to supplement *AACR2*, such as the *Library of Congress Rule Interpretations* (Hiatt 1990) or various guidelines for cataloging specific types of material (e.g., *Guidelines for Bibliographic Description of Reproductions*).

Electronic texts pose special problems in using the cataloging rules, partly because the rules often assume that the cataloger is physically examining an item "in hand." In addition, electronic texts often contain minimal information from which to create a catalog record. Those available by remote access are even more difficult to catalog because of the absence of a physical item to examine. Chapter 9 of *AACR2* provides the standard for cataloging computer files and is intended for the bibliographic description of "files that are encoded for manipulation by computer," including both computer data and programs, either stored on carriers available for direct access or by remote access (*AACR2*, rule 9.0A1, 221).

Sources of Information

Electronic texts, particularly those available remotely, often do not contain adequate information for the cataloger to be able to completely describe the item bibliographically. Applying the concept of "chief source of information," which is used to determine the title and authorship statement in AACR2, requires flexibility because of the difficulty in determining what is that chief source. The cataloging rules direct the cataloger to the title screen or screens; in the absence of a title screen, information may be taken from "other formally presented internal evidence," such as menus or program statements. Additionally, the cataloger may use the physical carrier or its labels, documentation, or accompanying material, or the container (Olson 1992, 1). If the item cannot be physically examined (i.e., it is accessible remotely, as is the case with electronic texts available in online databases), the rules do not give much guidance.

Another problem arises when the electronic text is in a format that is not eye-readable, so that the cataloger cannot examine the item at all (for instance, in a compressed or PostScript format). In these cases, often the filename and size of file may be the only available information for descriptive cataloging. The rules discourage the use of filename or data set name as the title proper, but in some instances, it is the only possible title (*AACR2*, rule 9.1B3, 224).

Identification

Determining whether an item is a new edition of a previously issued item is difficult at best when considering electronic texts. This decision determines whether a new bibliographic record is created, and *AACR2* supplemented by the *Library of Congress Rule Interpretations (LCRI)* guide the cataloger in making this determination. An edition in terms of computer files is defined in *AACR2* as "all copies embodying essentially the same content and issued by the same entity" (*AACR2*, 617). Does one consider a computer file that has been compressed the same edition as one that is uncompressed? In other words, does one catalog the item as it is intended to be used or as it is encoded? In addition, with electronic texts, it is not often clear how the item was issued because of a lack of sufficient information, so that issuing body cannot determine the item's identification.

The *LCRI* for rule 1.0 provides general guidance on determining whether a new manifestation of an item constitutes a new edition, thus requiring a new bibliographic record. After consulting the definition of edition (as specified above for computer files), the cataloger is instructed to consider the item a new edition if it meets the specified criteria; among these, if there is an explicit indication of changes of content, if certain portions of the bibliographic record are different (e.g., title, edition, physical description), or if there are variations in the publication area, unless they are only minor variations as defined. For electronic texts, this section does not always assist the cataloger because of the scarcity of information about the item, the difficulty in determining what the chief source is, and the focus in the rules on an item that the cataloger physically holds. In addition, the publication area takes on a new meaning for electronic texts, since many of them are not "published" in the traditional sense. Further, using the criterion that the physical description varies to require a separate record is irrelevant for those electronic texts that are available remotely, since the rules specify that a physical description is not given when there is no physical item (*AACR2*, rule 9.5, 231). Even the title cannot be relied upon to determine whether it is a new edition, since in the electronic world it is very easy to change a filename or even data in a file, and the filename could be the only information to construct a title for the item.

Other characteristics of electronic texts compound the difficulty in deciding whether the item is a new edition. Is an ASCII text of a work a different edition than the PostScript version? Or, for that matter, is the scanned version different than the text itself? Will it serve library catalogs to create separate records for each manifestation, or should a hybrid type of record be created containing information on all those available? When stored on a network, the same electronic text may move from one host to another as computers are in and out of service and files are copied to different sites. The content of the electronic text may not change, but its location or its filename may. Being able to determine if two items are actually the same in content becomes problematic in the electronic world.

As catalogers gain more experience in cataloging electronic texts, some of these questions might be answered. Perhaps how catalogers handle editions may depend upon the use of the data or the system constraints. Some of the questions concerning cataloging of electronic texts may be compared to the issues concerning the cataloging of reproductions. The handling of reproductions in online bibliographic systems has been problematic. Some institutions favor the use of holdings records linked to the bibliographic record for the original, while others favor separate bibliographic records with certain fields added for aspects of the reproduction. It may take time and experimentation for institutions to decide which approach works best for electronic texts.

USMARC STANDARDS FOR ELECTRONIC TEXTS

Although many navigational tools exist for accessing electronic texts over the Internet, librarians are interested in describing and providing access to electronic information resources within the USMARC record structure so that records for these resources can reside in the same database as other library materials. In addition to the description (identifying what the information is, whether it might suit the researcher's needs), the user requires location information (where can I obtain a copy of it?) and access information (how do I get a copy?). If records for electronic information resources are accessible in the same format with other library materials, the systems can process them in the same way. In addition, these records can then be shared between systems in the same way that other USMARC records are.

In the USMARC environment, systems exchange records so that duplication of effort is minimized. Because of the difficulty of identifying and describing electronic information resources, it would be of great benefit for institutions to exchange information about this type of material. If perhaps the institution providing the service or data contributed records about that data for exchange between libraries (as now many types of bibliographic records are exchanged), users might more easily be able to locate information they need. For instance, an institution making a library catalog, discussion list, or database accessible could provide the record that describes and gives location and access information for the service. Using the USMARC format would be appropriate for the library community because of the format's familiarity and flexibility, as well as the desirability of incorporating these types of records within the existing frameworks.

USMARC Format Background

The USMARC formats are standards for the representation and communication of bibliographic and related information in machine-readable form. The *USMARC Format for Bibliographic Data* contains format specifications for encoding data elements needed to describe, retrieve, and control various forms of bibliographic material. Most systems use their own internal formats for storing and displaying bibliographic data but use USMARC, a *communications* standard, to exchange data between systems. The USMARC formats are maintained by the Library of Congress's Network Development and MARC Standards Office in consultation with various user communities (Library of Congress 1989, 2). The USMARC Advisory Group and the Machine-Readable Bibliographic Information Committee (MARBI) of ALA consider proposals for additions and changes to the formats and discuss USMARC issues.

USMARC formats other than the bibliographic format were developed to satisfy additional needs of libraries. The USMARC Holdings Format is a carrier for holdings and location information. It includes copy-specific information for an item; information peculiar to the holding organization; information needed for local processing, maintenance, or preservation of items; and information required to locate an item including holdings organization and sublocation. The USMARC Community Information Format, recently approved as a provisional format, is a carrier for descriptions of nonbibliographic resources to which people in a particular community might want access. These include programs, services, organizations, agencies, events, and individuals. The USMARC Classification Format contains authoritative records for library classification schemes, and the USMARC Authority Format is a carrier for authoritative information on standard forms of names and subjects.

USMARC Computer Files Specifications

In the early 1980s, a MARC specification was developed for communicating information about machine-readable data files within the USMARC Bibliographic Format, describing both the data stored in machine-readable form and the programs used to process that data. The data elements were intended to be used to describe both data files and computer software. Data elements needed for the description of these files were integrated into the USMARC Bibliographic Format under the broader term "computer file"; many of the data elements were defined in *AACR2*, Chapter 9. The Computer Files record specifications were developed before the widespread use of the personal computer, particularly for data files such as census tapes and raw data maintained by large computer centers. Later, data elements were added to accommodate software, after microcomputers began to gain attention, and more attention was given to physical form, particularly physical and technical details about the software (Crawford 1989, 124). The specifications are generally adequate for description of machine-readable files and software but, before several changes in 1993, were limited in providing information on access. Since information in electronic form requires special description, location, and retrieval information, the Network Development and MARC Standards Office has been considering how to enhance the USMARC formats to accommodate online information resources. These enhancements should improve the ability to locate and access electronic texts.

ENHANCING DESCRIPTIVE AND ACCESS INFORMATION TO ELECTRONIC TEXTS

The USMARC Advisory Group recognized the need for accommodating electronic information resources by considering two discussion papers about the topic, Discussion Paper No. 49: *Dictionary of Data Elements for Online Information Resources,* discussed in June 1991, and Discussion Paper No. 54: *Providing Access to Online Information Resources,* discussed in January 1992 (Library of Congress, Network Development Office 1991a, 1991b). Participants attending the meetings agreed that USMARC should be expanded to accommodate description and access of machines as resources on the network as well as data files on the machines, and that further work needed to be done. It was agreed that electronic data resources (e.g., electronic texts, software, or databases) might be more amenable than online systems and services (e.g., File Transfer Protocol [FTP] sites, online public acccss catalogs, or bulletin boards) to bibliographic description using current *AACR2* computer files cataloging rules and the USMARC Bibliographic Format with minimal format changes.

As part of its Internet Resources Project, funded by the U.S. Department of Education, Library Programs, OCLC investigated the nature of electronic textual information accessible via the Internet (Dillon et al. 1993, 2). A group of representatives from OCLC, Online Audiovisual catalogers (OLAC), Library of Congress, and MARBI reviewed work on the project, examined sample documents collected, and planned a cataloging experiment of Internet resources. The experiment was intended to test and verify the applicability of the cataloging rules and the USMARC Bibliographic Format, computer files specifications, and provide sufficient data to determine what changes needed to be made to *AACR2* and USMARC to accommodate these materials.

The cataloging experiment was held during May and June 1992 and involved the cataloging of 300 computer files collected from Internet sites, half of which were all types of electronic texts and the other half randomly selected text, software, and data. Each file was cataloged by three different catalogers. After a call for participation was issued and distributed electronically via the Internet, a group of catalogers was selected to participate and given instructions for cataloging.

Results of the experiment indicated that *AACR2* and the USMARC format generally accommodate the description of Internet resources but that clear guidelines needed to be developed to assist catalogers. The following were some of the areas that needed modifications in the format: more choices in identifying the type of file in the USMARC fixed field (coded) area, guidelines for the appropriate and consistent use of note fields, and standards for including location and access information to find and retrieve the item.

Two initiatives resulted from the analysis of the OCLC Internet Resources Cataloging Experiment: the drafting of guidelines for the use of *AACR2* cataloging rules for Internet resources, presented to ALA's CC:DA, and a proposal for changes in the USMARC bibliographic format to address the deficiencies.

Cataloging Guidelines

Draft cataloging guidelines were formulated by the cataloging experiment planning committee and submitted to ALA's CC:DA. The guidelines were intended for OCLC users preparing bibliographic descriptions of items from the Internet but are also applicable to anyone performing cataloging of electronic resources. They review special provisions in *AACR2* for materials available by "remote access" and attempt to give guidance for preparing bibliographic description of difficult parts of the catalog record. The guidelines have been reviewed by a task force of CC:DA, and some changes have been requested (Dillon et al. 1992, B1-B19). The following summarizes some of the more problematic areas of the cataloging rules that the guidelines address:

● *Published vs. Nonpublished.* The guidelines suggest that electronic journals be considered published, since they are distributed electronically by a formal mailing list, even if they do not carry formal publication information. Many other electronic texts are similar to manuscript material and are to be considered unpublished. However, if the item carries a formal statement of publication similar to that on a title page, it may be considered published. In case of doubt, the cataloger is to consider the work unpublished.

- *Chief Source.* For remotely accessible electronic texts, the guidelines suggest that the chief source is the title screen or other information that displays on the terminal or on a printout. This section was later revised to include any first display of information, the Subject line, or the header to a file. In addition, it was changed to address the situation where a file is unreadable without processing (e.g., a compressed file) and suggests taking the information from the file after it has been processed. The title is to be taken from the chief source if possible and must always be present; it is supplied by the cataloger if necessary.

- *File Characteristics.* Although a section in the guidelines addressed the portion of *AACR2* Chapter 9 dealing with file characteristics, the changes suggested to the cataloging rules have been withdrawn. The guidelines suggest that number of records not be used for Internet resources in the file characteristics area of the cataloging record, since the information may vary greatly from the form in which it is received to the form in which it is used and stored. Since number of records is related to the way it is stored at a particular location, the guidelines recommend including this data element in the location and access information area.

- *Notes.* The guidelines instruct the cataloger in the use of notes and give examples of the types of notes that might be included.

- *Location and Access.* The guidelines instruct the cataloger to use the new USMARC field 856 for location and access information for all information necessary for accessing the electronic resource.

Accommodating Online Information Resources in USMARC Formats

As a result of the earlier discussion papers on accommodating online information resources in USMARC and the OCLC Internet Resources Cataloging Experiment, the Network Development and MARC Standards Office submitted a proposal to the ALA USMARC Advisory Group for changes to the bibliographic format, computer files specifications. The paper intended to address those deficiencies found in the cataloging experiment for describing and locating electronic resources. Proposal 93-4 (Changes to the USMARC Bibliographic Format [Computer Files] to Accommodate Online Information Resources) included three recommendations. First, it proposed the addition of new codes in the fixed field area for "Type of computer file" for bibliographic data, font, game, and sounds. In addition, it called for changing a few definitions. Among those proposed was the use of the word "text," which it considered confusing, because many electronic files include text (e.g., instructions for software). The term "document" was suggested to limit the use of this code to textual material that is intended to constitute a document, whether represented as ASCII or image data. The intent of the file (as document, rather than graphic) would then be expressed in the code. The second recommendation was to broaden the descriptors in the File Characteristics area (USMARC field 256) to allow for more specific terms. Finally, the third portion of the proposal was to add a new field to the USMARC bibliographic and holdings formats for electronic location and access, to allow for the encoding within the record of all information needed to locate and make accessible an electronic resource. Proposal 93-4 dealt only with the subset of online information resources called "electronic data resources" (e.g., electronic texts, databases, or software), rather than online systems and services, because only a few modifications would be necessary to current format specifications.

Proposal 93-4 was discussed at the ALA Midwinter meeting in January 1993, and the USMARC Advisory Group made modifications to the fixed field "Type of computer file" changes. The second recommendation concerning broadening the descriptors was deferred pending its consideration by CC:DA, because it affected area 3 of *AACR2* Chapter 9. (After consideration by a CC:DA task force, this portion of the cataloging guidelines was withdrawn, so it will not be reconsidered by the USMARC Advisory Group.) Field 856 (Electronic Location and Access) was approved as a provisional field with several modifications; after institutions use the field in catalog records, its status as provisional will be reconsidered.

Field 856 is intended to give the user the information required to locate and access the electronic item. It has been noted that the MARC record is deficient in providing nonbibliographic information except in 5XX note fields, which may or may not be searchable by systems, and that it is thus unsuitable to aid in the direct retrieval of electronic texts (*CETH Newsletter* 1993, 13). The proposal attempts to allow for the retrieval of the electronic text (as well as any other electronic resource), perhaps directly if systems are programmed to use it for automatic transfer. Of particular interest in the development of the proposal was the electronic journal or newsletter, because of the phenomenal increase in the number being issued and the need for better bibliographic control of them.

During the initial planning of the OCLC cataloging experiment, participants felt that the capability of machine access to the item should be provided for those items that are self-identifying (i.e., do not require interactive searching). All data elements that a user needs to know to make the connection, locate the document, and retrieve it should be included in the catalog record. In the case of library catalogs or other databases, the information needed to connect should be given, although only site-specific information about the server to which one is connecting (information that everyone would need to know) is included. Information that might be needed about the client (i.e., the system *from* which the connection is made) is not given and must be dealt with locally. Data elements are parsed and transportable between systems and formats. Although the content of this field was developed with Internet resources specifically in mind, as an outgrowth of the OCLC Internet Resources Project Cataloging Experiment, it is expected that the field can be extended to non-Internet resources.

An electronic data resource can reside in many directories at any number of hosts in several formats. It might be stored as a compressed file and an uncompressed file with different filenames, yet the end result is the same item. These characteristics were considered in the planning of the new electronic location and access field. Location data in the USMARC format properly belong in a holdings and locations field (85X block), which according to the USMARC standard can be embedded in a bibliographic record. The electronic location and access information could be considered comparable to the library location and holdings field for a book, which gives the institution, shelving information, and specific information about the item at that particular location (e.g., copy number, piece designation, or notes). Thus, information applicable to the particular "copy" of the electronic item would be recorded in the electronic location field rather than at the record level in a bibliographic field. Consequently, a separate bibliographic record need not be created if the only difference between electronic items is, for example, the host name making them accessible, the compression used, or the filenames. This type of information can be considered "copy specific" and recorded in a separate electronic holdings and locations field of the bibliographic record. A separate record is made only if the intellectual content of the item is different.

Field 856 functions as a locator for an item and includes various data elements in separate subfields that are sufficient for the user to locate and access the electronic resource. The indicator after the tag value shows the access method (e.g., Telnet, FTP, electronic mail, or other) for locating the resource and determines how the rest of the field is used. Data elements that are descriptive in nature are included in the other bibliographic fields in the record. The separate subfields allow for parsing of elements so that they can be maintained, accessed, or, if desired, searched separately. They also permit special displays to be generated by the system if it is programmed to do so. The field is repeated for different locations, filenames, or access methods. Figure 1 shows the

---

856 Electronic Location and Access (R)

(Contains the information required to locate an electronic item. The information identifies the electronic location containing the item or from which it is available. Field 856 is repeated when the location data elements vary (subfields ǂa, ǂb, ǂd) and when more than one access method may be used. It is also repeated whenever the electronic filename varies (subfield ǂf), except for the situation when a single intellectual item is divided into different parts for online storage or retrieval.)

Indicators

First Access method
(Contains a value that defines how the rest of the data in the field will be used. If the resource is available by more than one method, the field is repeated with data appropriate to each method. The methods defined are the main TCP/IP protocols. Subfield ǂ2 may be used to specify others not defined in the indicator)

0	Email
1	FTP
2	Remote login (Telnet)
7	Source specified in subfield ǂ2

Second Undefined
ｂ Undefined

Subfield Codes

ǂa	Host name (R)	ǂn	Name of location of host in subfield ǂa (NR)
ǂb	IP address (NR)	ǂo	Operating system (NR)
ǂc	Compression information (R)	ǂp	Port (NR)
ǂd	Path (R)	ǂq	File transfer mode (NR)
ǂf	Electronic name (R)	ǂs	File size (R)
ǂg	Electronic name – End of range (R)	ǂt	Terminal emulation (R)
ǂh	Processor of request (NR)	ǂu	Uniform Resource Locator (R)
ǂi	Instruction (R)	ǂx	Nonpublic note (R)
ǂk	Password (NR)	ǂz	Public note (R)
ǂl	Logon/login (NR)	ǂ2	Source of access (NR)
ǂm	Contact for access assistance (R)	ǂ3	Materials specified (NR)

EXAMPLES OF FIELD 856 (for files that can be transferred using FTP):

856 1ｂ ǂawuarchive.wustl.edu ǂcdecompress with PKUNZIP.exe ǂd/mirrors2/win3/games ǂfatmoids. zip ǂxcannot verify because of transfer difficulty

856 1ｂ ǂaseq1.loc.gov ǂd/pub/soviet.archive ǂfk1famine.bkg ǂnLibrary of Congress, Washington, D.C. ǂoUNIX

856 1ｂ ǂuURL: ftp://path.net/pub/docs/urn2urc.ps

Figure 1. Subfields defined in field 856; (R) means repeatable, (NR) means nonrepeatable

---

subfields defined in field 856; Figure 2 shows how the field might display in an online public access catalog (OPAC).

The Network Development and MARC Standards Office prepared two proposals for adding data elements to field 856 for discussion at the meeting of the USMARC Advisory Group in February 1994. Because of a desire to be able to communicate information that links a

---

TITLE: North American Free Trade Agreement
PUBLISHED: 1992

PRODUCER: United States. Office of the U.S. Trade Representative.

SUBJECTS: Free trade--United States.
Mexico--Commercial treaties.
Free trade--Mexico.
Free trade--Canada.
United States--Commercial treaties.
Canada--Commercial treaties.

ELECTRONIC ACCESS:
Access via GOPHER or telnet. For assistance contact Law Library Reference, 607 255-7236.
DOMAIN NAME: fatty.law.cornell.edu
FILE TRANSFER MODE:
ASCII
FILE SIZE: 2020 bytes

CODED MARC FIELD:

856 12 ‡afatty.law.cornell.edu ‡m Tom Bruce ‡n Cornell University Law School ‡q ASCII
‡s 2020 bytes ‡z Access via GOPHER or telnet. For assistance contact Law Library Reference,
607 255-7236

Figure 2. OPAC brief display

---

bibliographic record with an electronic object, whether an image, text file, or any other type, the American Memory Program at the Library of Congress suggested the addition of two subfields that are currently recorded in a local field (Library of Congress, Network Development Office 1993). Other projects are also considering the use of the electronic location field to link bibliographic records with other electronic resources. VTLS, a library system vendor, has developed a multimedia product called InfoStation, which uses a local field in bibliographic records to link sound and image files and plans to use the standard field 856 to do this in the future. The system uses the information in this field to find the file and display the image associated with the bibliographic record. The Research Libraries Group (RLG) has launched the Digital Image Access Project, a collaborative project to explore the capabilities of digital image technology for managing access to photographic collections. Eight RLG institutions are attempting to improve access to collections for shared access across networks. A project at Cornell University Engineering Library is attempting to build a multimedia network to enhance the undergraduate engineering curriculum. Using Cornell's NOTIS system, a Telnet session is initiated to the Iowa State University catalog through another server. The computer uses a unique number contained in a MARC field, which is matched in the database on the remote server, and FTP enables the transfer of image files needed.

In addition, the second proposal concerning field 856 considered in February suggested the addition of a subfield for recording the Uniform Resource Locator, a standard under development (Library of Congress 1993b). MARBI, a subgroup of the USMARC Advisory Group that votes on proposed changes to the USMARC formats, approved the new subfields.

In the development of field 856, it has been questioned whether it is desirable to store in a USMARC record such information as an electronic location, given the volatility of electronic objects on a network. However, it could be used in a variety of ways. Institutions may wish to store only the unique part of the locator that could identify it and then use a lookup table on a remote server to determine where and in what form the electronic object is located. If a system were programmed as such, the system then could generate the other pieces of the 856 field (e.g., host name or path) for display in an online public access system. In this way, only the unchangeable piece would be stored in the USMARC record, and if other pieces of information change, they can be generated on the fly.

Uniform Resource Identification

The Uniform Resource Locator (URL), newly defined in field 856 of USMARC, is one of a family of standards being developed by the Internet Engineering Task Force (IETF) called Uniform Resource Identification (URI). The following is a list of specific standards under development to identify, describe, locate, and control networked information objects on the Internet:

- *Uniform Resource Locator (URL):* address of an object, containing enough information to identify a protocol to retrieve the object.
- *Uniform Resource Name (URN):* a persistent, location-independent identifier for an object, similar to an International Standard Book Number (ISBN) or International Standard Serial Number (ISSN) in the *library* and publishing worlds, providing a unique element to identify it (Mitra 1994).
- *Uniform Resource Citation (URC):* a set of meta-information about an electronic resource, which may include, for example, owner, encoding, access restrictions, or location. Similar in library terms to a bibliographic record. (The group developing this is currently considering renaming it "uniform resource characteristic.")

The URL is the most fully developed of the standards but is still a draft Internet standard, although it is already in widespread use. It allows systems to "achieve global search and readership of documents across differing computing platforms, and despite a plethora of protocols and data formats" and is "a universal syntax which can be used to refer to objects available using existing protocols, and may be extended with technology" (Berners-Lee 1993). Elements of the draft URL standard are contained in separate subfields of field 856 in USMARC; in the URL, the elements are strung together with separators between them. If an institution wishes to use the URL as it has been established, the new URL subfield could accommodate it. An institution may wish to record only the URL, rather than use the separate subfields, record both parsed elements and the URL, or record only the parsed subfields. Recording the elements in separate subfields may be useful to create a display or to verify the separate data elements even if the URL is also used.

The Uniform Resource Name (URN) will "provide a globally unique, persistent identifier used both for recognition and often for access to characteristics of or access to the resource." It may identify "intellectual content or a particular presentation of intellectual content," depending upon how the assignment agency uses it. A resource identified by a URN may reside at many locations under any number of filenames and may move any number of times during its lifetime. The URL identifies the location for an instance of a resource identified by the URN (Sollins and Masinter 1994). The URN is still under development, and not all issues have been resolved. When it is finalized, it will provide the type of bibliographic control similar to that of the ISBN or ISSN to uniquely identify a resource. It will have an impact on the decision as to when to consider a resource a new edition and thus create a separate record.

The Uniform Resource Citation (URC) is under discussion, and a draft standard has not been fully developed. Participants in the IETF-URI group have begun to develop requirements and functional specifications.

Other USMARC Computer Files Specification Developments

Also approved in February 1994 by the ALA MARBI Committee was a proposal to add a fixed field (i.e., one that has a fixed length and is used for coded data) to record physical characteristics of computer files in coded form. Often, it gives information in coded form that has an equivalent note or other field in the record for the same information in textual form, thus facilitating indexing and retrieval. The field was particularly needed for serials, because of the increased numbers of serials being published in different media, particularly CD-ROM and electronic journals. The ability to retrieve serials on the basis of their physical form has been an important goal. This new fixed field for computer files will include coded data on category of material (i.e., computer file); specific material designation (e.g., tape cartridge, magnetic disk, CD-ROM laser optical disc, or remote file); original versus reproduction aspect (not clear how this will be used, but valid in other physical description fixed fields); color (e.g., monochrome or color); and sound (sound or no sound). Since bibliographic records for electronic texts would be encoded using the specifications for computer files, this new data element could be useful for their identification.

Interactive Multimedia Guidelines

Another development in the use of the USMARC formats is the attempt to provide cataloging and USMARC coding for interactive multimedia. Because of the very specific definition of "interactive multimedia," it may be of limited use in the bibliographic control of electronic texts. Interactive multimedia are defined as follows:

> Media residing in one or more physical carriers (videodiscs, computer disks, computer laser optical discs, compact discs, etc.) or on computer networks. Interactive multimedia must exhibit both of these characteristics: 1) user controlled, non-linear navigation using computer technology; and, 2) the combination of two or more media (audio, text, graphics, images, animation, and video) that the user manipulates to control the order and/or nature of the presentation. (American Library Association 1994, 8)

However, it has been reported that the number of these types of materials is quickly growing. After conducting a cataloging experiment, the Interactive Multimedia Guidelines Review Task Force recommended the use of the USMARC Bibliographic Format, computer files specifications, until format and cataloging rule changes might be made to accommodate this specific type of material. The ability to record coded descriptive elements about more than one aspect of an item (e.g., sound recording and computer file) will be available under format integration, which integrates the tag sets for bibliographic records for materials in different physical formats, and will be implemented in late 1994 and 1995; this development is of benefit to the description of interactive multimedia.

Accommodating Online Systems and Services in USMARC

The Library of Congress's Network Development and MARC Standards Office has also explored accommodating online systems and services in the USMARC format. This effort has included the presentation of several papers to the USMARC Advisory Group; another is expected to be presented in June 1994 proposing to add fields to the bibliographic format for those data elements needed for online systems and services that are not currently included in the bibliographic format. Since these records would be created for nonbibliographic data, some extension of the format is necessary.

With the development of tools such as Gopher, Wide Area Information Servers (WAIS), and Archie on the Internet to locate information resources, one might question the need for describing these resources in USMARC. There are a number of directory services now accessible on the Internet as well. However, available Internet tools are not always efficient for pointing to the resource. Many do not give any indication of which servers they actually searched and which were unavailable for one reason or another, and they do not discriminate between various versions of the data in terms of usefulness or completeness. They are poor at locating known items as opposed to possibly relevant things. In addition, the subject analysis available in USMARC records is lacking in these other tools. Library users are not all familiar with (nor should they be expected to be familiar with) tools like Gopher. Such tools could complement rather than replace USMARC records as a source for locating electronic texts and other online resources.

Creating records within USMARC for online services would provide not only access but also organization. Librarians' knowledge of online resources can be used to provide, within library catalogs, pointers to Internet services and resources. In addition, librarians can select the online services that are important to include in catalogs, just as they select books. Discriminating between online resources that might be useful to the library user rather than forcing the user to select from the overwhelming number of sources available on the Internet is a service that libraries should provide.

Making this type of directory information for online systems and services accessible in the USMARC environment would allow for such information to be available and integrated within the same systems as other records. Bibliographic citations to electronic texts could point to the USMARC record for the online service, and only that record would need to be kept current in terms of its electronic location. A subject search could give the user not only records for printed items but also records for electronic items and the systems that provide them.

OTHER PROJECTS INVOLVING
ACCESS TO ELECTRONIC TEXTS

American Memory Program

The American Memory Program is "the Library of Congress's pioneering effort to share some of its unique collections with the nation via new electronic multimedia technology" (Library of Congress 1993a). American Memory makes archival collections available in electronic form. The program offers original printed texts in machine-readable form, which allows for detailed searching of the contents of a collection as well as the bibliographic records describing these items. For manuscript materials, images of the original may be displayed so that researchers can examine the original item's appearance. For photographs and films, analog videodiscs have been used, although the Library expects to convert these materials to digital form. A hierarchical combination of collection, item, and finding aid level records describe each collection. The bibliographic record is stored in an internal MARC format, with links to other related records if appropriate, and a link to the reproduction of the item described. Thus, the user can call up the bibliographic record, which describes the item, and can view either the ASCII text (which has been converted from the original) or the image of the printed original if desired.

The American Memory Program uses an "electronic call number" as its link to the converted text and image. In the past, a local MARC field 938 was used. Since the project wanted to use a standard MARC field, especially to communicate the data on electronic location, it will convert all local 938 fields to 856 fields, particularly after the approval of two new subfields in field 856 to accommodate other data elements needed for the program. Access to the electronic text is possible because of a unique number that resides in the electronic location field. That unique number is also the filename, which is derived from an acronym for the collection and an item number. The additional information, such as the computer where the file resides, directory on the computer, and compression information (data elements that all have defined subfields in field 856), are not stored in the record. Instead, the unique element, in this case the filename, is stored in that field, and a look-up table tells the system the other information. Consequently, if the host name or directory changed, the unique number will provide the link to find the necessary information to locate the item.

The American Memory Program has converted text, which is minimally encoded with SGML to retain any information that might be lost in conversion and to facilitate searching. SGML is also used to link page images to text images. The filename of each page image is in coded form at the head of each page of the electronic text, allowing for a linkage; the filename for the image file is an extension of the filename of the converted electronic text.

The American Memory Program has great potential for enhancing access to archival collections and bringing historical collections to anyone with a computer. However, because it has lost congressional funding, program planners are soliciting private donations to continue the program.

Electronic Cataloging-in-Publication Project

The Cataloging in Publication (CIP) Division of the Library of Congress embarked on a project in February 1993 to explore the viability and practicality of an online link between the Library of Congress and publishers participating in the CIP program. The CIP program is a cooperative effort between publishers and the Library of Congress to provide cataloging in advance of publication for most mainstream titles published in the United States. The advantages of acquiring CIP data electronically include greater efficiency, time savings in the transmission of CIP applications, greater accuracy in the CIP record, and the establishment of the foundation for an electronic library of electronic books (Celli 1994).

The Electronic CIP Project enables publishers to provide the full text of galleys for forthcoming titles and thus provide catalogers with ample text to perform accurate subject analysis. In addition, portions of the electronic galleys supplied under the program could be used in the bibliographic record; for example, a relatively simple block and copy command can move the contents data into the note portion of the catalog record. A few publishers have participated in the project, and Library of Congress staff expects more to do so. The project is still experimental, and future efforts will involve the use of SGML.

The Electronic CIP Project has the potential to provide the foundation for an electronic library of texts primarily because of the twenty-three-year relationship that has been established between the Library of Congress's Cataloging-in-Publication Program and publishers. Over 3,500 publishers participate in the CIP program, which provides cataloging for over 48,000 titles a year. Consequently, as a result of its CIP program, the Library of Congress is ideally positioned to develop a system for acquiring archival masters of electronic manuscripts representing much of the U.S. publishing industry. Much needs to be accomplished for this to happen, but as more and more traditional print publishers develop electronic versions of their titles, it would be relatively easy to develop a significant collection of electronic texts at the Library of Congress. However, many questions will need to be answered, including copyright and royalty issues, and questions about distribution and access. In addition, the concepts of publishing and what constitutes a published work need to change in an electronic world, which may affect the future of the project.

Government Information Locator Service (GILS) to MARC Mapping

The Government Information Locator Service (GILS) has been established to help the public locate and access information throughout the U.S. government. Although this is a locator system to identify databases and services that provide information, rather than a locator system to electronic texts themselves, it is of importance in terms of its use of extending the MARC format to provide for access to electronic information resources. Federal agencies are organizing GILS as a component of the National Information Infrastructure (NII) (*Government Information* 1994). It is intended to make government information available electronically by identifying, describing, and providing access information to locations where information resides. Federal agencies will be responsible for participation in GILS by providing locator records for Federal agencies.

GILS will use the information search and retrieval standard known in the United States as ANSI/NISO Z39.50 (known internationally as ISO 10162/10163). Locator records are to be available in three specified formats, one of which is USMARC. Consequently, an effort has been underway to map GILS data elements to the USMARC Format for Bibliographic Data. Data elements have been defined, and appropriate fields have been indicated. In most cases, no new fields are needed to accommodate the data, but some USMARC definitions have been expanded.

Because of the work that has been done on accommodating online information resources in USMARC, the GILS project to expand USMARC to nonbibliographic data has not required substantial rethinking or newly defining fields in the format. The mapping has made extensive use of the new field 856 for electronic location and access.

RELATIONSHIP BETWEEN SGML AND USMARC

There is a common misconception that SGML could replace the MARC formats in which libraries have invested considerable time and money. This misconception is based on the observation that most SGML documents contain information that is bibliographic in nature. The SGML tags used in the header and front matter of a full-text document often have a one-to-one relationship with the MARC tags defined for the same information in bibliographic records. Although there are similarities between SGML and MARC, those who jump to the conclusion that MARC can be abandoned in favor of SGML are overlooking important differences in the design and intended use of each standard.

SGML and MARC are alike in that they provide a standard structure for machine-readable information. They are both system independent in that they may have different implementations, and the data are in a format that can be exchanged between systems. Each standard is nonproprietary, which means that they can be implemented without having to pay a royalty to the original developers. The structures for MARC (ISO 2709; also, ANSI/NISO Z39.2) and SGML (ISO 8879), as international standards, provide the basic framework for bibliographic and full-text systems that have gained worldwide acceptance and use. Conformance to standards increases the marketability of products and facilitates the exchange of information between a variety of sources.

SGML and MARC are different in the functionality they were designed to support. The structure and syntax associated with SGML-encoded documents were designed to make the processing of full-text data system independent. SGML uses a Document Type Definition (DTD) to define the tags and the syntax associated with them. Depending on the level of markup, the SGML encoding can support a wide variety of print and/or display features. SGML markup will also support context-sensitive retrieval, based on indexing of data encoded with specific SGML tags.

SGML is intended to facilitate the processing of large amounts of data, while the MARC record structure was developed for bibliographic data. MARC data are typically concise and dense, packing a great deal of intelligence into a small number of characters. The average MARC record is only 1,500 characters, whereas even the shortest full-text document involves many times that number of characters. The MARC formats, which are implementations of the standard MARC structure (ISO 2709), define data elements designed to make optimum use of small amounts of data in a machine environment. These data elements easily support the print and display needs of bibliographic data and the complex indexing and sophisticated retrieval needed for bibliographic data.

MARC is highly standardized and accepted worldwide. The precision and consistency needed for cataloging data have promoted the development of standardized cataloging rules for both description and choice of access points and the implementation of the MARC record structure which reflects these rules. In the United States, only one "DTD" for MARC is used, that is one tag set and syntax (USMARC). This high level of acceptance of one tag set and syntax is one of the reasons MARC is so successful and has the support of so many national libraries and computer system vendors. In comparison, there are some sixty DTDs for SGML. Anyone with a MARC system can usually read in and process USMARC data. Export of bibliographic data in either the USMARC or UNIMARC format is also an almost universal capability of bibliographic systems. Full-text systems do not enjoy this level of standardization and will not, even with the advent of SGML, until a small number of implementations of SGML have become well established.

Library catalogs have no need to change the way bibliographic data are encoded or processed. The capability of MARC records to provide links to full-text SGML documents (or other nonbibliographic entities, like image or audio data) has prevented libraries from seriously considering any other encoding for bibliographic data other than MARC.

MARC and SGML have shown themselves to be compatible, and each has its own use in the computer age. It is important that experts in each structural standard and system implementors be aware of the needs and uses of the other so that library materials in machine-readable format and bibliographic information about them can be easily integrated. Rather than embed text in MARC records, the bibliographic records can be linked to SGML-encoded text. For instance, the American Memory Program, as described above, uses links between the MARC bibliographic record and other electronic resources to access full text that contains SGML coding or images in non-ASCII format.

The Text Encoding Initiative (TEI) guidelines, a specific application of SGML that defines an encoding and interchange format for electronic texts, can assist in their cataloging and identification (Gaunt 1994, 8). As described above, electronic texts often lack a usable chief source of information on which to base the description, and the TEI header can provide needed information for the text not found elsewhere.

CONCLUSION

With the tremendous growth of the Internet and the wide availability of electronic information resources, libraries must adapt to a changed world and reevaluate what bibliographic control and access really means. Electronic information resources have become critical to scholarship and research, and librarians need to use their many years of experience organizing and providing access to information to adapt traditional library tools to this new electronic world. "The library community needs to extend traditional descriptive catalog practices to networked resources—in essence, to permit bibliographic description and control of such resources in order to incorporate them integrally into library collections . . . and to improve access to them" (Lynch 1993).

The nation's existing infrastructure of libraries and library systems can continue to provide service in the quest for information in the future. Librarians provide value-added service by selecting the materials to be described and providing access to them; this is particularly important in the electronic world, where anyone can "publish" a text if he/she has access to a network. Not all of the items available electronically deserve to be cataloged, and librarians can provide this service as they have for years with printed and other items (Dillon et al. 1993, 35).

The *AACR2* cataloging rules and USMARC format have served us well in our quest to identify, describe, and locate library material of all sorts, and it can do the same for electronic texts. An enormous amount of time, money, and intellectual effort has been expended on the library infrastructure that serves our nation's scholars, students, and the general public. New tools, such as Gopher, Mosaic, and World Wide Web, have been developed to facilitate access to networked information resources, but they do not provide the same function as the service provided by libraries in cataloging these materials. Not only do librarians select materials deemed worthy to be controlled bibliographically, but also they provide detailed subject analysis, generally through controlled subject thesauri, that is not available through those Internet tools. As anyone knows who has used the tools to locate items by subject, the keyword access that is available is not an efficient method, given the vast quantities of data. As efforts are being made to create directory services, it will be of great benefit to provide description and access to this material within the familiar USMARC environment using the National Information Standards Organization's Z39.50 standard for information retrieval.

The library community has made great strides in adapting existing cataloging rules and format standards to accommodate electronic information resources. This work will continue and will attempt to remain consistent with other efforts to standardize electronic locators and identification. Only by experimenting with new approaches now being developed will librarians be able to make informed decisions about the difficult problems encountered in the bibliographic control of and access to electronic texts. Already, many library catalogs are available by remote access, and thus bibliographic records for electronic resources will be widely available. As information technology changes rapidly, libraries need to continue to provide improved description and access to electronic information using existing, although modified, formats and cataloging rules.

REFERENCES

American Library Association. 1992. *ALA Handbook of Organization and Membership Directory 1992/1993*. Chicago: American Library Association.
American Library Association. Committee on Cataloging: Description and Access. Interactive Multimedia Guidelines Review Task Force. 1994. *Guidelines for Bibliographic Description of Interactive Multimedia*. Chicago: CC:DA, ALA.
Berners-Lee, Tim. October 1993. *Uniform Resource Locators (URL): A Unifying Syntax for the Expression of Names and addresses of Objects on the Network* [Online]. This is an earlier draft that is no longer available. Current draft is Berners-Lee, Tim; L. Masinter; & M. McCahill, eds. 1994. *Uniform Resource Locators (URL)*.

Available by Anonymous FTP to: ds.internic.net. Directory: internet-drafts. File: draft-ietf-uri-url-07.txt.

Celli, John. 1994. The Electronic CIP Project. *Collections Services News* 2(6): 1-2.

CETH Newsletter. 1993. *1*(Fall): 13.

"Conference Reports: ACH-ALLC93, Georgetown University, Washington, D.C., June 15-19, 1993: Documentary Electronic Texts (Panel)." 1993. *Ceth Newsletter 1*(2): 13.

Crawford, Walt. 1989. *MARC for Library Use: Understanding Integrated USMARC.* 2d ed. Boston: G.K. Hall.

Dillon, Martin, Erik Jul, Mark Burge, and Carol Hickey. 1992, November. Guidelines for Bibliographic Description of Internet Resources: Draft. In *Assessing Information on the Internet.* Dublin, Ohio: OCLC Online Computer Library Center.

Dillon, Martin, Erik Jul, Mark Burge, and Carol Hickey. 1993. *Assessing Information on the Internet: Toward Providing Library Services for Computer-Mediated Communication.* Dublin, Ohio: OCLC Online Computer Library Center.

Gaunt, Marianne I. 1994. Center for Electronic Texts in the Humanities. *Information Technology and Libraries 13*(1): 7-13.

Government Information Locator Service (GILS): Draft: Report to the Information Infrastructure Task Force. January 22, 1994. Available by Anonymous FTP to: 130.11.48.107 of ridgisd.er.usgs.gov. Directory: pub. File: gils.doc.

Hiatt, Robert M., ed. 1990. *Library of Congress Rule Interpretations.* Washington, D.C.: Cataloging Distribution Service, Library of Congress.

Joint Steering Committee for Revision of AACR. 1988. *Anglo-American Cataloguing Rules.* 2d ed. rev. ed., Michael Gorman and Paul W. Winkler. Chicago: American Library Association.

Library of Congress. 1989. *The USMARC Formats: Background and Principles.* Washington, D.C.: Library of Congress.

Library of Congress. Network Development and MARC Standards Office. 1993a. *American Memory: Multimedia Historical Collections from the Library of Congress.* Washington, D.C.: Library of Congress.

Library of Congress. Network Development and MARC Standards Office. 1993b. *Proposal 94-3: Addition of Subfield $u (Uniform Resource Locator) to Field 856 in the USMARC Bibliographic/Holdings Formats.* Washington, D.C.: Library of Congress, Network Development and MARC Standards Office.

Library of Congress. Network Development and MARC Standards Office. 1991a. *Discussion Paper No. 49. Dictionary of Data Elements for Online Information Resources.* Washington, D.C.: Library of Congress, Network Development and MARC Standards Office.

Library of Congress. Network Development and MARC Standards Office. 1991b. *Discussion Paper No. 54. Providing Access to Online Information Resources.* Washington, D.C.: Library of Congress, Network Development and MARC Standards Office.

Library of Congress. Network Development and MARC Standards Office. 1993. *Proposal 94-2: Addition of Subfields $g and $3 to Field 856 (Electronic Location and Access) in the USMARC Holdings/Bibliographic Formats.* Washington, D.C.: Library of Congress, Network Development and MARC Standards Office.

Lynch, Clifford A. 1993, March 24. *A Framework for Identifying, Locating, and Describing Networked Information Resources: Draft for Discussion at March-April 1993 IETF Meeting* [Online]. Available at: http://www.acl.lanl.gov/URI/archive/uri-93ql.messages/15.html.

Mitra. February 21, 1994. URN to URC resolution scenario. Version 0.3 [Online]. Available at: http://www.acl.lanl.gov/URI/archive/uri-94ql.messages/86.html.

Olson, Nancy B. 1992. *Cataloging Computer Files.* Lake Crystal, Minn.: Soldier Creek Press.

Sollins, K., and L. Masinter. March 18, 1994. *Specification of Uniform Resource Names.* This is an earlier draft that is no longer available. Current draft is Sollins, K., & L. Masinter. September 1994 (expires March 10, 1995). *Requirements for Uniform Resource Names.* Available by Anonymous FTP to: ds.internic.net. Directory: internet-drafts. File: draft-ietf-uri-urn-req-00.txt.

ROBERT ALUN JONES

Professor of Sociology, History, and Religious Studies
University of Illinois at Urbana-Champaign

Durkheim's Imperative:
The Role of Humanities Faculty in the
Information Technologies Revolution

ABSTRACT

The arrival of powerful information technologies in the traditional humanistic disciplines has done far more than simply add to the tools available for research and instruction. Those who have embraced these technologies have also experienced a significant disruption of their traditional roles within the academy, producing confusion and disorientation as well as excitement and innovation. Some of the reasons for this confusion are discussed, and one example of two "restabilized" roles for humanities faculty—the work of the Advanced Information Technologies Group at the University of Illinois—is described. The conclusion explores some of the advantages of this new kind of division of intellectual labor.

INTRODUCTION

Almost ten years ago, approaching a full year's sabbatical and fashionably open-minded to the promise of new information technologies, I bought my first computer. I thought that it would help me to finish the book that I was writing and possibly impose some order on my life as well. The book is still unfinished, and my life has been chaos ever since.

But this is not another of those tiresome assessments of whether or not these technologies really do increase human efficiency—inquiries

173

that almost always seem to me to be posed in a manner that guarantees one extreme conclusion or the other. Rather, I'll here be concerned with the effects of advanced information technologies on the traditional role of scholars and teachers in the humanities and also with the way these technologies have altered the conception of that role held by the scholars and teachers themselves. These are questions I've thought about frequently in the last decade, as I retired my beloved Montblanc fountain pen, learned to word-process, discovered hypertext, built a hypermedia lab, traveled with and for Apple to endless trade shows and conferences, signed nondisclosures, wrote internal and external proposals, obtained grants, went broke, was orphaned by vendors, built another lab, evangelized faculty, antagonized administrators, logged-in, e-mailed, searched, retrieved, linked, Gophered, WAISed, PHed, FTPed—and generally had the time of my life.

Not surprisingly, I've tried to think of these questions within the context of my own role as a scholar and a teacher—specifically, as an historian of social theory. Occasionally, for example, I've thought of Plato's famous definition of justice, in the *Republic,* as "the performance of one's proper function" or "minding one's own business," wondering simultaneously if the scripting of HyperCard stacks is, in fact, the proper function of an historian of social theory. In more practical and materialist moods, I've thought that Adam Smith's observation, in *The Wealth of Nations*—i.e., that "the greatest improvements in the productive powers of labour, and the greatest part of the skill, dexterity, and judgement with which it is anywhere directed, or applied, seem to have been the effects of the division of labour"—might easily be construed as a utilitarian injunction to leave this nonsense to the Office of Computing Services or Instructional Resources (whatever the obvious and alarming consequences of such resignation might be). This economic argument, of course, is extended by post-Darwinian arguments into a law of nature—e.g., the apparent correlation between the functional specialization of the parts of an organism and the extent of that organism's evolutionary development would make specialists—and Stoics—of us all.

But I'm primarily a Durkheim scholar, and whether or not the division of labor is equivalent to justice, contributes to economic utility, or reflects a law of nature, the really important question for him was post-Kantian and ethical: Should we yield to it or resist it? Is it our duty to become thorough, complete, self-sufficient human beings? Or are we to be but parts of a whole, organs of an organism? Those familiar with Durkheim will recall that this way of posing the question was both rhetorical and disingenuous: For his 1893 dissertation on the Division of Labor in Society was dedicated to the proposition that, at least in academic life, the "thorough, complete, self-sufficient human being" was more often a "morally worthless dilettante." The categorical imperative of the modern conscience was *"Make yourself usefully fulfill a determinate function"* (Durkheim 1933, 43). And Durkheim's brilliant contributions to the history and philosophy of education were all, at least indirectly, attempts to reform French secondary education precisely to produce fewer "Renaissance men" and more specialized "organs of an organism" (Durkheim 1961, 1977).

The rhetoric about interdisciplinary research and instruction notwithstanding, I think we can all agree that Durkheim's vision of a highly specialized division of intellectual labor has largely been realized in American higher education. And while such specialization is frequently justified on utilitarian grounds—e.g., to contribute anything new to any discipline, one must master enormous bodies of information, do so in relatively short periods of time, etc.—I think we can agree with Durkheim that there is an ethical dimension as well. The scholar who has not found her niche or domain within the larger discipline is not just an unlikely candidate for promotion and tenure. She is apt to be looked upon as a moral failure as well, a shallow "dilettante" who has not measured up to the standard of Durkheim's imperative.

However subconscious, I believe that it is this moral dimension of the division of intellectual labor that leads many of us to feel discomfort as we survey the detritus of our traditional roles, the havoc provoked by our attraction to and embracement of these powerful technologies. Our complaints, of course, are always couched in the more mundane language of economic utility—e.g., the time wrested from our research, articles and books still unfinished, promotion and tenure delayed or denied, etc. But there is also an inarticulate sense, surely in other minds but also in our own, that we have betrayed our academic calling, digressed, wandered from the straight and sure path to scholarly achievement and distinction. In fact, I remember quite clearly the point at which I first became acutely conscious of this kind of role confusion. My wife—who has an undergraduate degree in English literature and graduate degrees in art history and library science—was driving me to the airport on the way to my first EDUCOM meeting where, supported by Apple Computer, I was to demonstrate some hypertext materials for teaching the history of social theory. "My husband," she smiled wickedly as she dropped me off, "the computer salesman."

But such confusion is hardly limited to those occasions on which the commercial world intrudes on the academic. It is at least equally prevalent within the university itself, which suddenly appears as a traditional, conservative institution resistant to new technologies and the organizational changes they require. Important segments of the university community find themselves technologically obsolescent, as they simultaneously and determinedly seek out those activities at which they are least competent. The pain of watching a Nietzsche scholar installing VRAM or upgrading an operating system is surpassed only by that of attending courses on HyperCard taught by hackers and computer-jockeys at our computing services office. A respected member of our own English faculty recently invited ridicule by pointing a mouse at the screen of a Quadra 840av, clicking at it, and wondering aloud why nothing was happening. Nearby, a seventeen-year-old undergraduate shook his head and smiled knowingly: "There is so much," he sighed, not without a certain condescending sympathy, "that they don't understand." Indeed, our condition is not unlike that of Freud's prosthetic god, capable of great things, but not entirely comfortable with the tools that make this possible.

For the faculty member in the humanities, therefore, the embracement of advanced information technologies has sometimes seemed equivalent to a fall from grace. The purpose of this paper, however, is to suggest that there may be some form of redemption, and that it lies in doing those things that we have traditionally done quite well—albeit in a slightly different manner. Like Durkheim's categorical imperative, it encourages a sharp division of intellectual labor, in which the faculty remain the teachers and scholars and nonacademics the service and resource providers. But if we thus look slightly less silly to our colleagues, it offers no escape from our responsibility to confront the implications of advanced information technologies for these more traditional activities. Finally, I think this kind of redemption is available in some form on virtually every major campus in the country, although here it has understandably taken advantage of some of the special resources that exist at the University of Illinois.

THE ADVANCED INFORMATION TECHNOLOGIES GROUP

These resources include the superb University Library, the Graduate School of Library and Information Science, the National Center for Supercomputing Applications (NCSA), one of the most thoroughly networked campuses in the country, and a number of faculty in the humanities and social sciences looking for ways to use advanced information technologies to advance their research and their teaching. With the encouragement of Larry Smarr, director of the NCSA, these faculty members eventually produced a proposal titled "Collaboratorium," based on the notion of collaboration between three different groups of people. The first group comprises the Software Development Group at the NCSA—i.e., the scientists and engineers responsible for the development of tools like NCSA Telnet, Collage, and, most recently, Mosaic. The second group comprises faculty in the humanities and social sciences with what we (for lack of a better term) called "Technologically Enabled Projects" (TEPs)—i.e., research projects that depend upon high-performance computing to seek better answers to questions that scholars in the humanities and social sciences have frequently asked in the past. For example: What can historical census data tell us about the pre-Civil War southern household? Has the American electorate become better informed and more independent since the Jacksonian era? What was the nature and extent of the influence of German social science on the French philosopher and sociologist Emile Durkheim? How do we explain the crowd behavior that periodically results in mass suffocation and death at rock concerts and football games? And the third—more "technologically focused"—group comprises faculty, again in the social sciences and humanities, whose research is focused on the way the tools built by the first group are used by faculty like those in the second group. For example: What kinds of norms about communication, cooperation, and competition among scholars and scientists result from the increased use of collaborative information technologies in the intellectual community? How does the discussion of information and the decision-making process in "work teams" change with the introduction of electronic group support systems into the workplace? Is education really enhanced by using advanced computer technologies like hypertext, hypermedia, and interactive multimedia? If so, how and why? And if not, why not?

It hardly takes a rocket scientist to realize that each of these groups stands to benefit enormously from the presence of, and ongoing collaboration with, each of the other two. It was this assumption, in any case, which led the University's Advanced Information Technologies (AIT) Group, its small but interesting laboratory, and a series of research projects in the humanities and social sciences to allow us to embrace these powerful new tools without violating Durkheim's imperative (Figure 1). But the best way to indicate this is simply to describe three of the more interesting and exciting projects that the AIT Group has supported.

INTERMEDIA, HYPERTEXT, AND COGNITIVE FLEXIBILITY THEORY

The first concerns what is surely the most "hyped" (and perhaps least empirically studied) information technology in higher education

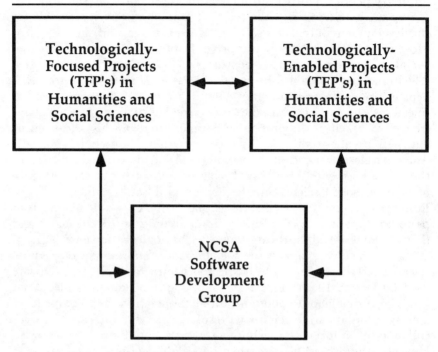

Figure 1. The AIT Lab's research and development groups

today—i.e., hypertext or hypermedia. I confess to some enthusiasm for this technology myself, so much so that, in the late 1980s, I built a hypermedia laboratory to support this kind of instruction—thus imposing on my colleagues the pain of watching a Durkheim scholar installing VRAM and upgrading operating systems (Jones 1988).

My interest in hypertext derived initially from the frustrations encountered teaching the history of social theory to large numbers of first- and second-year undergraduates. These students are, with relatively few exceptions, what I call "interpretive essentialists"—i.e., they are convinced that there is something that every classic text in social theory is Really About, and that this essential meaning can be discovered if they can only break its "hidden code." They are equally convinced that we, as faculty members, possess or at least have access to these codes— a dangerously flattering notion that indulges our self-image as academic "priests" whose prestige derives from the power to dispense the intellectual sacraments. And finally, they think that education is largely a matter of passively receiving these sacraments in the traditional, ritual environment of the lecture hall.

My goal as a teacher, in sharp contrast, is to persuade them that meaning depends upon context, and that there are thus as many possible meanings of the text as there are contexts within which it might be placed. Machiavelli's discussion of the role of fortune in human affairs, for example, might be placed within the larger context of the Renaissance treatment of the classical Greco-Roman conception of the goddess Fortuna, thus illustrating the way that Machiavelli plays on conventional themes while advancing rather unconventional arguments. But it might equally be related to the political conflicts of early sixteenth-century Florence, the Renaissance genre of advice-books for princes, the theme of "moral adaptability" so pervasive in late twentieth-century politics, and so on. We can thus imagine Machiavelli as engaged in a variety of conversations, with both his contemporaries and our own, each of them yielding a different perspective in the history of social and political thought. Hypertext, it seems to me, is a technology for generating precisely these kinds of "imaginary conversations," and thus for undermining our students' tendencies toward interpretive essentialism (Rorty 1984, Jones 1990).

Using hypertext in this way, of course, is to engage in what I've called a "technologically enabling" project, and any views I might have about its success or failure are largely speculative. Fortunately, however, I have a "technologically focused" colleague—Rand Spiro of the Department of Educational Psychology—who is focused on precisely this technology. In his study of advanced knowledge acquisition, Spiro makes a sharp distinction between what he calls "well-structured" knowledge domains and their "ill-structured" counterparts. In the former, the goal of education is typically just to expose the student and establish a general orientation to the field; and here it is appropriate to compartmentalize knowledge, to present clear examples while avoiding pertinent but confusing exceptions, and to employ reproductive memory criteria in assessment. But in ill-structured domains—and surely few domains are more ill-structured than intellectual history—the goal of learning is "cognitive flexibility"—i.e., the capacity to apply multiple, interrelated concepts that involve context-dependent variations to new, diverse, and largely unexpected circumstances; and here, Spiro insists, we must avoid deliberate oversimplification, making a special effort to demonstrate complexity, irony, exception, and contradiction (Jones and Spiro 1992).

Spiro's empirical research suggests that hypertext may be an excellent tool for encouraging the development of cognitive flexibility in ill-structured—but not well-structured—knowledge domains; and it also has some obvious implications for the way programmers like those in the Software Development Group at the NCSA should design tools like Mosaic. Hypertext systems, for example, should encourage the

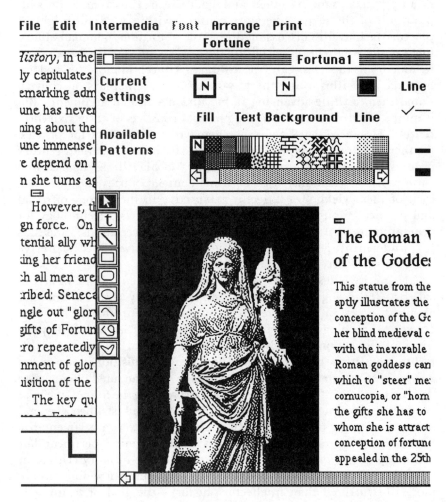

Figure 2. Intermedia, hypertext, and cognitive flexibility theory

learner to see the same text in as many useful contexts as possible. They should also invert the hierarchical authority of the text, allowing the learner to focus on previously peripheral elements, making them central. Systems should include options that permit a re-editing of the text base to successively present to the learner a range of concept applications, as well as information about the nature of the different tailorings of that concept to its contexts, and so on (Figure 2).

IMAGING TECHNOLOGIES AND UGARITIC TEXTS

A second example of this kind of triangular division of intellectual labor comes from Biblical archaeology. In 1928, a Syrian farmer accidentally uncovered some ancient tombs on the Mediterranean coast opposite the northeastern tip of Cyprus. This led to the excavation of the main city at nearby Ras Shamra, which yielded one of the most sensational archaeological finds of the twentieth century—the political and religious texts of the archives of the ancient kingdom of Ugarit. The French excavators uncovered numerous cuneiform tablets, which were written thirteen to fifteen centuries before Christ, in a hitherto unknown alphabetic script. Once that alphabet was deciphered, it was clear that the language of Ugarit belonged, with Hebrew and Aramaic, to the family of Northwest Semitic languages, and also that these tablets constitute the single most important archaeological contribution—far more important than the Dead Sea Scrolls—to our understanding of ancient Canaanite and Israelite religion, society, and culture (Seow 1993, 785-86).

But the obstacles to the accurate interpretation of these texts parallel those facing interpretation of the scrolls. They are in Paris and Syria, they are deteriorating (albeit not quite so rapidly as the scrolls), and like all cuneiform tablets, they are occasionally extremely difficult to read. Transcriptions of the texts combined with facsimile drawings appeared in 1963 and 1976, but neither included photographs of sufficient quality to allow scholars to independently corroborate one reading of the tablets by contrast with another. Scholars have typically chosen one edition of the texts or the other, or moved back and forth between the two editions, depending on which transcriptions and photographs have best supported their own interpretations. The result has been an extraordinary degree of speculative license in Ugaritic studies, flooding the literature with useless reconstructions, restorations, interpretations, and reinterpretations (Pitard 1987, 1992a, 1992b).

But again, the example of the Dead Sea Scrolls affords some grounds for optimism. As director of the West Semitic Research Project at the University of Southern California, Bruce Zuckerman has recently achieved international recognition for his work with multispectral photographs of the scrolls, extremely high-resolution digital scanning of the photographs, and the analysis of the digital images in applications like Adobe Photoshop and Painter X2. Working with Zuckerman, my colleague Wayne Pitard is presently following his example, photographing the Ugaritic tablets in the Louvre this May, scanning the photographs at extremely high resolution, and analyzing the results on a Mac PowerPC 8100 by altering the conditions under which the digital image is viewed. As the project continues, Pitard intends to "publish" the texts electronically, with accompanying explanatory material, quite literally teaching the rest of us how to reinterpret the Old Testament in the light of these Ugaritic materials. Finally, both

Figure 3. Imaging technologies and the Ugaritic texts

Zuckerman and Pitard have already provided anecdotal evidence suggesting ways in which the availability of this kind of evidence, in this kind of environment, might alter the forms of communication and the status hierarchy of an otherwise extremely conservative community of scholars; and this is precisely the kind of thing that sociologists and ethnographers—like my colleague Leigh Star—have recently made the subject of their own, social scientific investigations.

PHILIP KOLB'S PROUST RESEARCH

My third example concerns the greatest figure in twentieth-century French literature—Marcel Proust (1871-1922). We are all aware, of course, that Proust was the author of a single great work—*A la recherche du temps perdu* (7 vols., 1913-27), translated into English as *The Remembrance of Things Past* (1982)—that he was asthmatic, neurotic, and reclusive, spent most of his time in bed, had the walls of his room lined with cork to shut out light and sound, and there took notes and wrote the series of volumes that by 1920 had brought him the Prix Goncourt and international fame. But he was also a brilliant correspondent, and especially during his later years—exploiting his servant and a French postal system that delivered several times each day—wrote as many as twenty letters in a single sitting, to all kinds of people (not just the aristocracy); and he wrote seven days each week. The resulting correspondence provides access, not simply to the greatest literary mind of his generation, but to the more general literary culture of early twentieth-century France.

In 1935, Philip Kolb, a Harvard graduate student looking for a subject for his thesis, received a grant to study at the Sorbonne and work in the Bibliothèque nationale. Kolb decided to write his thesis on Proust, and after he received his Ph.D. in 1938, he returned to Paris almost every year to speak with those who had known Proust, to find and copy pieces of correspondence, to collect information about those mentioned either in *A la recherche du temps perdu* or in the letters themselves, and so on. By the time Kolb died—as professor emeritus of French and a fellow of the Center for Advanced Study at the University of Illinois—he had edited twenty-one volumes of Proust's correspondence (the last completed in the last year of his life) and become, in the phrase of François Crouzet, *l'archéologue de Proust* (Proust 1983, 1989, 1992).

The materials gathered by Kolb during almost sixty years of careful, detailed, inexhaustible scholarship, reside in his unpretentious office in the University Library. Several months ago, with Doug Kibbee and Emile Talbot of the French Department and Joe Hardin from NCSA's

Software Development Group, I received my first guided tour of the Kolb archive from Virginie Green, a graduate student who was Kolb's research assistant. It's difficult to describe the overwhelming impression made by materials of such enormous depth and complexity—especially for a Durkheim scholar, for whom parallel materials are surely beyond our reach. For Kolb had a problem—i.e., almost none of Proust's letters were dated. The solution to this problem was to date the letters through corroborative, external evidence, including every scrap of information about Proust that Kolb could find, but extending to additional information about Proust's correspondents and those mentioned in both the novels and the correspondence. As a consequence, Kolb ultimately forged an enormously subtle web of interrelations among the pieces, creating a huge network representing Proust's social and intellectual milieu.

As each new name appeared in *A la recherche* or the correspondence, for example, Kolb opened a new file—which he then constantly updated—containing information about this individual or family, leaving a single slip of paper briefly identifying the person(s), noting the place(s) where the name appeared, and providing "arrows" to the files containing additional, more detailed information. Similar slips of paper record the specific year, day, and even the time of particular events—including the sending or receiving of letters—providing a more linear, chronological path through the archive; and these, too, "point" to the lengthier documents to which they refer. The Kolb materials, in short, are a giant hypertext, screaming to be digitized. In fact, Kolb himself had begun to use a microcomputer before his death, and both his wife and his daughter assure me that this is a project of which he would have approved. So the AIT Lab has begun committing the Proust materials to machine-readable form, and, as with the Ugaritic texts, we hope to learn much more, not just about Proust, but also about the way in which networked information systems and digital libraries alter the nature of scholarly research, communication, and collaboration.

CONCLUSION

In conclusion, I would like to repeat my conviction that this is the kind of thing that we, as humanities faculty, should be doing. This— not installing VRAM or upgrading operating systems—is Plato's "minding your own business," or Durkheim's "determinate function." We should keep our concentration firmly on the content of our research and our teaching. As we attempt to answer the questions these raise, we will inevitably be led to the adoption of new tools and techniques, and we will need to understand them. But any really deep understanding of these tools and techniques has already become another area of specialized scholarship. What we need, in short, is a reasonable and integrated division of intellectual labor between tool developers, their users in the humanities, and social scientists and humanists studying the use of these tools, in which each group communicates effectively with the other two. Unfortunately, this will require a kind of interdisciplinary collaboration for which the traditional university is ill-prepared, but it will be worth the work necessary to establish it.

REFERENCES

Durkheim, Emile. 1933. *The Division of Labor in Society*. Trans. George Simpson. New York: Macmillan.

Durkheim, Emile. 1961. *Moral Education: A Study in the Theory and Application of the Sociology of Education*. New York: Free Press of Glencoe.

Durkheim, Emile. 1977. *The Evolution of Educational Thought: Lectures on the Formation and Development of Secondary Education in France*. London and Boston: Routledge & Kegan Paul.

Jones, Robert Alun. 1988. Building a Hypermedia Laboratory. *Academic Computing* 3(4): 24.

Jones, Robert Alun. 1990. To "Criss-Cross in Every Direction"; or, Why Hypermedia Works. *Academic Computing* 4(4): 20-21, 30.

Jones, Robert Alun, and Rand Spiro. 1992. Imagined Conversations: The Relevance of Hypertext, Pragmatism, and Cognitive Flexibility Theory to the Interpretation of "Classic Texts" in Intellectual History. In *Proceedings of the ACM Conference on Hypertext*, ed. D. Lucarella, J. Nanard, M. Nanard, and P. Paolini, 141-48. New York: Association for Computing Machinery.

Pitard, Wayne T. 1987. RS 34.126: Notes on the Text. *Maarav* 4(1): 75-86, 111-55.

Pitard, Wayne T. 1992a. A New Edition of the "Rapiuma" Texts: KTU 1.20-22. *Bulletin of the American Schools of Oriental Research 285*: 33-77.

Pitard, Wayne T. 1992b. The Shape of the 'Ayin in the Ugaritic Script. *Journal of Near Eastern Studies 51*(4): 261-79.

Proust, Marcel. 1983. *Selected Letters, 1880-1903*. Ed. Philip Kolb. Trans. Ralph Manheim. London: Collins.

Proust, Marcel. 1989. *Selected Letters, 1904-1909*. Ed. Philip Kolb. Trans. Terence Kilmartin. London: Collins.

Proust, Marcel. 1992. *Selected Letters, 1910-1917*. Ed. Philip Kolb. Trans. Terence Kilmartin. London: HarperCollins.

Rorty, Richard. 1984. The Historiography of Philosophy: Four Genres. In *Philosophy in History: Essays on the Historiography of Philosophy*, ed. R. Rorty, J. B. Schneewind, and Q. Skinner, 49-75. Cambridge: Cambridge University Press.

Seow, C.L. 1993. Ugarit. In *The Oxford Companion to the Bible*, ed. Bruce M. Metzger and Michael D. Coogan, 785-86. New York: Oxford University Press.

TERRY BELANGER

University Professor
University of Virginia
Charlottesville, Virginia

The Materiality of the Book: Another Turn of the Screw

CONFERENCE SUMMARY

This conference has had a wider focus than its title, "Literary Texts in an Electronic Age," suggests: it is difficult to think of the *Oxford English Dictionary* or Michigan's *Middle English Dictionary* primarily as **literary** texts. We were concerned at this conference not merely with literary texts, but with texts of **all** sorts: the prosaic in addition to the poetical, the technical as well as the belles-lettristic, the non-authored book next to the monograph. Our investigations of texts in an electronic age are as relevant to the study of history as to the study of literature: indeed, relevant across a very broad range not only of the humanities but of all prose-based endeavors.

These are the principal themes of this conference, as I understand them:

First, and on a global level, there is consensus among the speakers that we are on the verge of momentous changes in the way we view and use texts both individually and institutionally, and that the scale of these changes is so great as to be cataclysmic, even apocalyptical. The speakers are aware that the history of humankind is the history of change, but I sense widespread agreement among them that the changes in store for us as regards texts in an electronic age are especially cataclysmic, and particularly apocalyptical.

Second, and on a more particular level, we have been concerned here with standards—not so much with standards of excellence as with

187

standards of uniformity, which is not to say that we are not mightily interested in standards of excellence, as well. We are concerned with the need to develop rational and cost-effective standards for the encoding of texts. We are concerned with the need to develop standards for the storage, presentation, and adaptation over time of these texts. And we are concerned with the need to have adequate bibliographic control over these texts.

Third, and also on a more particular level, we are concerned about the roles that the various players in this game will—or might possibly—have: Who will provide the hyper/texts? What kind of instruction will what sort of teachers be able to offer to which students having access to what sort of physical facilities? How will the present professorate learn the skills they are increasingly going to need in order to survive in the classroom? What will publishers publish, and who will pay them to publish it? Where do libraries fit in, if anywhere? Where do campus computer centers fit in? Where do authors fit in, if there still are any? (You will remember the Duke of Plaza Toro's observation that when everybody is somebody then nobody is anybody.)

Fourth, our greatest immediate *collective* concern about the future of texts in an electronic age is access: how will users gain access? How will for-profit and not-for-profit institutions work together—or separately—to provide that access? Who will pay, and how much, and for what, and to whom?

Fifth and finally, our greatest *ultimate* concern is with the effect that the forthcoming, ever-more encompassing electronic environment will have on the way we think and on the way we behave. To what extent will humanistic values end up as sanitary landfill right along with all that used print on paper?

These, then, are the principal themes that I identify in this conference:

- momentous changes just around the corner;
- the need for standards;
- our changing jobs and professions;
- the possibilities and limits of access; and
- the future of humanism in the electronic age.

Let me return to these themes, one by one. First, the fact that momentous changes are in store for us.

It is the invariable prerogative of each generation to convince itself that the changes it must face are greater than all the changes that previous generations have had to face: more change, faster change, harder change, dirtier change. And I think that those of us whose professional concerns are centered in written communication are particularly susceptible to the belief that the current and impending changes in their bailiwicks are uniquely catastrophic. In this respect, Gutenberg has a lot to answer for: we have had more than five centuries of an essentially unchanging technology, but one, so we are assured on all sides, that is done.

By way of putting our communications situation into perspective, consider the transportation industry for a moment, and over just the past two centuries. In the late 18th century, canals were all the cry; and throughout the settled parts of the United States, the race was on to provide cheap and efficient water transportation between the Atlantic seaboard and the Mississippi valley and the Great Lakes. The capital costs of building a canal were staggering—still, they got built.

How long did they last? By the middle of the 19th century, the railroads had become a major threat to canal shipping; and by the end of the Civil War, the canals were done. Think of the thousands of miles of railroad track laid in this country between the 1830s and the end of the 19th century—and of the capital costs incurred in laying that track. Nevertheless, by the middle of the 20th century, the superhighways had become a major threat to rail transportation; and a few decades later, the railroad (at least as a long-distance people-mover) was done.

Enter the airplane. My grandmother, who was born in 1885, died in the early 1970s; she was then in her mid-eighties. She was 17 years old when she heard the news of the Wright brothers' first airplane flight at Kitty Hawk; she lived long enough to see the entry into routine commercial airline service of the Boeing 747, an airplane which is both longer in length and taller in height than the distance and altitude of the Wright brothers' first flight, two or three generations earlier.

There is nothing reassuring in this argument: in the second half of the 19th century, life got tough for the individuals and institutions that depended on the canals for a living; or, later, on the railroads. In contemplating the changes in store for us as regards texts in an electronic age, I think we would do well to remember the story of the two tourists on their first visit to the state of Maine. They wandered into a lobster pound, and there was the owner, busily throwing live lobsters into boiling water. The tourists were horrified, and they complained to the owner that this was cruelty beyond bearing. The owner thought about this for a bit; but then she said, "Oh, they're used to it."

It may be good self-discipline for us all, as we go about the business of constructing our own versions of electronic Doomsday, occasionally to recite a little poem by James Thomson (Mary Brandt Jensen will please correct me if I am wrong, but I believe **this** poem is in the public domain!):

Once in a saintly passion
I cried with desperate grief,
O Lord, my heart is black with guile,
Of sinners I am chief.

Then stooped my guardian angel
And whispered from behind,
'Vanity, my little man,
You're nothing of the kind.'

We will all deal with the changes that come, because we must. Like the lobsters, we'll hate it; but like the lobsters, we'll get used to it.

The second prominent conference theme concerns standards. This is a familiar subject to librarians like Rebecca Guenther, who are trained to consider the implications of the organization of very large files; but as Susan Hockey, C. M. Sperberg-McQueen, and John Price-Wilkin all emphasized in their presentations, the importance of standards to the effective encoding of text is central. Without navigational aids, as Professor Marchand pointed out in his presentation, the Internet is not so much an information superhighway as an ocean of incoherent data. Help will have to come from at least one of the players in the game.

We need to document our work: our encoded texts must tell us where they came from, and provide standardized information about the circumstances of their creation in their headers or elsewhere. In this area, we are making progress. The revised TEI guidelines and the CETH cataloging guidelines are in the press. The Library of Congress is being helpful.

Maurice J. Friedman, the director of the Westchester Public Library and a former colleague of mine at Columbia, likes to say that librarianship isn't **all** glamour; as Mr. Sperberg-McQueen pointed out, text encoding isn't all altruism. Some persons don't want to share their texts, or have used encoding protocols that severely limit or prevent the use of their texts by other researchers investigating other questions.

Whose standards will prevail? I sense a cautious optimism on the part of both Ms. Hockey and Mr. Sperberg-McQueen that the Text Encoding Initiative's advocacy of SGML is likely to succeed, and that we are making real progress in the development of national and international protocols that will discourage redundancy and encourage efficiency in text encoding.

The jury still seems to be out as regards our arrangement for digital imaging, but as Ms. Hockey points out, clearly the future will be with text and image together, even though we have just made a start in this direction, and most of us do not (at least yet) have the kind of hardware we are clearly going to need to handle the large files typical in graphic representation.

Meanwhile, at the lower end of the vineyard, there is Project Gutenberg, growing like a house afire, and no more concerned with

SGML than a skateboarder is concerned with walk/don't walk traffic signals.

The third conference theme on my list concerns the nature and future of our jobs and professions. As a whole, the speakers seem to share a genuine affection for librarians: a number (though by no means the majority) **are**, in fact, themselves librarians (or used to be). None of the speakers directly addressed the likely futures of libraries and librarians at any great length, though Ms. Hockey emphasized the role librarians have to play in documenting text encoding initiatives.

Anita Lowry, Mark Tyler Day, and John Price-Wilkin presented case studies of some of the imaginative ways in which libraries and their staffs are presently coping with the changes being visited on us by the electronic age. Admittedly, at Iowa, at Indiana University, and at the University of Virginia (UVa) alike, their operations are tiny, relative to the size of their institutions and the number of students they serve; and they serve—and can serve—only a small fraction of their potential users. But they will grow, and the wide-area textual analysis systems being developed by Mr. Price-Wilkin and others at UVa are already having an effect that spreads far beyond the walls of the Alderman Library's Electronic Text Center and its next-door neighbor down the hall, the Institute for Advanced Technology in the Humanities. His statement that the e-text initiatives at UVa have been done from internal resources and without external funding, should give hope—and an idea— to many persons in this audience.

Less immediately optimistic was Professor Marchand's estimate of the teachability of one academic department at the University of Illinois in particular and, by implication, a great many other departments in general: his advice to librarians is that they need to jawbone faculty members into an interest in the electronic environment. Robert Alun Jones suggests a middle way for academics: they should continue to concentrate on their own areas of research and teaching, without attempting to establish too deep an understanding of new tools and techniques that have become another area of specialized scholarship. Subject specialists in the humanities and social sciences will need to set up interdisciplinary collaborations, taking advantage of advanced information technologies while still remembering who they are.

The fourth conference theme on my list concerns one aspect or another of access. Speaker after speaker touched on the problems and opportunities necessarily associated with access to electronic resources. Ms. Jensen applies the brakes, giving us a sobering view of the realities of copyright law. Halfway through her presentation I was convinced that we would all end up in jail, as soon as copyright holders found out what we do at home, in ignorance or otherwise, as we busily play a game called "What I Want Copyright Law To Be." But she suggests a sensible solution as an alternative to a replaying by publishers and librarians of the story of the gingham dog and the calico cat (which I will not quote because I cannot remember when Eugene Field died, but I believe it to have been less than 75 years ago). Users of electronic resources can co-exist with the owners and providers of those resources, if they are willing to give up their illusions about copyright and settle down to do the hard work necessary in building this (or any other) stable relationship.

Lorrie LeJeune gives us a level-headed assessment of the view from the scholarly publisher's office. The monograph printed on paper— that mainstay of scholarly publishing—is in its twilight years; scholarly publishers frequently cannot afford to publish monographs, and if they do publish them, scholarly libraries frequently cannot afford to buy them. Like the scholarly library, scholarly publishers are viewing their probably non-subsidized futures (or possible lack of) with interest; and (like scholarly libraries) scholarly publishers have been working hard to ensure a place for themselves in the electronic sun, partly because of their conviction that they add value to the work they publish. It may be true, Ms. LeJeune says, that electronic publishing is the comet and that publishers are the dinosaur; but scholarly publishers have the potential to become electronic safe havens, lending credibility to the works on their lists: and she predicts that credibility is going to become a major issue on the Internet.

The fifth and final conference theme on my list concerns the future of humanism in an electronic age. This theme was particularly well-served at the conference, and for a simple reason. Several of the speakers who discussed humanistic issues took the trouble to draft fully-realized completely-written out presentations (I think in particular of the papers by Professor Robert Alun Jones and of our keynote speaker, Jay David Bolter).

Unlike the other sessions of this conference, Mr. Bolter's speech was a public lecture, attended by a considerable number of persons who were neither registered for this conference nor planning to attend it. Some of them clearly viewed their electronic futures with alarm. Mr. Bolter began by suggesting that he was preaching to the converted: his audience already shared his belief (he suggested) that electronic arrangements were relevant to the study of texts. By the end of the evening, one was not so sure about this assessment: during the question-and-answer period after his formal remarks, a surprising number of questions seemed to be underpinned by the belief that a hypertext future was not likely to be a good thing after all.

At the center of Mr. Bolter's speech is his belief in the importance, in the future as much as in the past, of the use of text for the symbolic representation of ideas. The computer is part of that history of texts.

He reminds us that the history of written communication stretches a long way before the coming of the printing press, and he draws parallels between the pre- and post-Gutenbergian worlds: copyists and annotators of texts during the manuscript period tended to view their base texts with considerably greater flexibility than has been the case since the printing press exerted its fixing influence. Hypertext users have a similar, less formal relationship with their texts. Where we tended to have fixity, in hypertext we have fluidity; where we tended to have strong authorial control (or author/editor/publisher control), in hypertext we have dispersed control. Once we recognize that hypertext is the natural way to write, copyright is going to come under great pressure, as the present frenzy of attempted copyright regulation suggests. Copyright is, indeed, incompatible with hypertext. Society may have to evolve other means of rewarding authorship besides payments made on a basis of copyright possession—means which have existed in the past, for instance during the period of the manuscript book, long before copyright emerged as an important part of text distribution.

Mr. Bolter closed his lecture with what he called a digression on the differences between the technology of writing and the technology of allusion. The original use to which computers were put was numerical, but soon enough this use expanded to include text. Now we must add graphic representation to this list. In dealing with computer graphics we are not dealing with symbolic structures but with perceptual matters. Computer graphics can offer a version of reality itself, and it can do it in three dimensions, as well. This new virtual reality allows the user to occupy changing points of view, and there is the real possibility that the user will confuse virtual reality with actual experience.

Virtual reality can put users into an environment in which they are told that they are seeing the world from the point of view of a dinosaur, or from the point of view of a molecule—but wait, Mr. Bolter said: there is danger here. Knowing what a molecule is likely to do is dependent on a knowledge of mathematics and physics; it is utterly incoherent to ask what it is like to **be** a molecule. Graphic representation finally cannot substitute for symbolic representation, any more than a prose passage can be adequately described by a picture. This is not to say that one cannot comment or enlarge informatively upon the other; but one cannot **replace** the other. We must stay in touch with symbolic representation if we are to stay in touch with 5000 years of human communication.

Mr. Bolter's speech, as it seemed to me, was nicely-constructed and well-delivered. But he shouldn't have mentioned the dinosaur, and he shouldn't have mentioned the molecule. We have all seen what happened to Mr. Bolter on Sunday night happen in a class. The instructor mentions something in passing—just in passing—that for some reason (who knows why?) engages the fascinated attention of the class. A fugue of unstoppable questions and comments erupts, questions and comments which are neither germane to the matter at hand nor relevant to much of anything else. One silly question (or silly comment disguised as a silly question) prompts another and even sillier one. Other persons (including some who would normally know better) join the dance. The result is...well, more amusing for the speaker afterwards than at the time it happens.

During the question-and-answer period after Mr. Bolter's speech on Sunday, there was brisk discussion of the molecule in theory and practice. Can one truly see the world from the molecule's point of view? Does the molecule have a point of view? Regardless of whether or not the molecule has a point of view, should we limit the human imagination by refusing to try to imagine the molecule's point of view? There were a number of ariettas regarding the extent to which a fixed (i.e., printed) text is really fixed that suggested that some members of the audience, *pace* Mr. Bolter, had indeed learned how to see things from the dinosaur's point of view. As a whole, this was a discussion that would have made no mother proud, and I came away from Mr. Bolter's keynote address thinking: speaker 1, audience 0.

The challenge in setting up a conference like this one is not only in getting the right speakers but also in getting the right audience; the importance of the second part of the equation—getting the right audience—is not always recognized. It is by far the harder half of the equation to get to balance.

Certain aspects of the pedagogy of this conference perplex me. Surely the most efficient method for imparting factual information remains the written, not the spoken, word? I take the chief purpose of conferences like this one is to convey ideas too hot, for one reason or another, for the printed word to handle. We should concern ourselves on these occasions with an exchange of values, not the conveying of facts. Thus I relished Michael Hart's presentation; he had values to convey, and he conveyed them. And I very much enjoyed listening to Professor Marchand, who is not afraid to call a spade a spade. But I did feel rather abused when I had to listen to certain speakers filigree their way down a row of bullet points on their overhead projector transparencies. If the ideas with which a conference is concerned are too complicated for the children to understand without the use of such lists, then the conference should be limited to adults. The reverse is also true: if the conference is to proceed at a basic level, then the grownups should be encouraged to go elsewhere.

How well have we done here, as an audience, over the past few days? Well, despite Sunday, pretty well, I think. I wish we had been better, but we did our best, and I hope the speakers do not think that they entirely wasted their time.

As a coda, I would like to return to the title of this talk: "The Materiality of the Book: Another Turn of the Screw." At the University of Virginia this semester, I am teaching a course in the graduate English department called, "The Materiality of the Book." The course concerns itself with some of the ways that the physical presentation of a text can affect its contents and the reader's reactions to those contents. One of our conclusions is that the physical manifestations of those texts can survive an astonishing amount of abuse by their copy editors, printers, publishers, licensers, censors, reviewers, reprinters, emendators, abridgers, adapters, and readers—the physical embodiments of these texts can even successfully withstand later onslaughts by their own authors: it is very hard to destroy every copy of a printed book.

Aristotle would have been perplexed if someone had shown him a manuscript codex copy of his own works, since the codex is a mode of presentation developed only several centuries after his death. He would have been even more perplexed by a pile of printed copies of his works, and no doubt struck almost speechless by Perseus. But those of Aristotle's texts that survived into the 10th century AD or so survive still, and are likely to continue to do so: no hypertext is going to destroy the originals, no matter how many overlays we or succeeding generations plaster over them. As commentators, hypertext creators are in any event still amateurs by comparison to some of Aristotle's medieval and Renaissance commentators. His text survived them, and it will survive us.

Of course we can assume joint authorship status with Aristotle in hypertext. And we can do better than that. We can warn Romeo in time that Juliet isn't really dead. Little Nell no longer needs to die. We can give Genesis itself a happy hypertext ending: everybody can come down from the Tower of Babel speaking flawless SGML. But I once had a sign in my office, put there for the benefit of my very able but very headstrong assistant. The sign read: Of course I can do it. The question is, do I want to.

I am not so sure about the status of the author in the future, but I have considerable confidence in the durability of the authors of the past, and thus of the survival of the values they represent. *Littera scripta manet;* and if Horace didn't say that, then he should have; and in my hypertext, maybe he will.

CONTRIBUTORS

TERRY BELANGER was educated at Haverford College and at Columbia University, where he received his Ph.D. in eighteenth-century English literature in 1970. His doctoral work was on the eighteenth-century London book trade, and he has published extensively on this subject. In 1971, he became associated with the Columbia University School of Library Service, where he established the Book Arts Press as a bibliographical laboratory supporting an extensive program for the training of rare book and special collections librarians and antiquarian booksellers. In 1983, he instituted an annual summer Rare Book School, a collection of courses of interest to students of the history of the book and related subjects. In 1992, he moved the Book Arts Press and Rare Book School to the University of Virginia, where he accepted an appointment as University Professor and Honorary Curator of Special Collections in the College of Arts and Sciences. Belanger is the co-general-editor of Cambridge Studies in Publishing and Printing History. He was Rosenbach Lecturer at the University of Pennsylvania (1986); and he has given the Graham Pollard Lecture of the Bibliographical Society (London, 1988), Malkin Lecture at Columbia (1991), and nearly a hundred other presentations on bibliographical and bibliophilic subjects over the past two decades.

JAY DAVID BOLTER is Professor in the School of Literature, Communications, and Culture of the Georgia Institute of Technology. He is jointly appointed in the College of Computing. His work with computers led to the publication in 1984 of *Turing's Man: Western Culture in the Computer Age,* a book that was widely reviewed and translated into several foreign languages (including German, Italian, Spanish, Dutch, and Japanese). Bolter has lectured at dozens of universities and colleges on the social and cultural impact of the computer. His second book, *Writing Space: The Computer, Hypertext, and the History of Writing,* published in 1991, examines the computer as a new medium for symbolic communication. He is now extending

197

his analysis to include electronic networks (such as the Internet) as well as computer graphics and virtual environments. Bolter is also the developer (with Michael Joyce) of the hypertext system Storyspace. He is now working with colleagues at the Georgia Institute of Technology on multimedia systems for collaborative writing and on the spatialization of text in three-dimensional computer graphics environments.

MARK TYLER DAY is an Associate Librarian, Reference, at Indiana University and Co-Director of its Library Electronic Text Resource Service (LETRS). He holds a B.A. in Political Science, an M.A.T. in Social Studies, an M.A. in Library Science from the University of Chicago, as well as an M.A. in Arabic from Indiana University. Prior to coming to Indiana University in 1972, he held positions at the University of New Brunswick and Princeton University. Since coming to Indiana University, he has worked in the Government Publications Department, Reference Department, and Undergraduate Library, and he served as Near Eastern Subject Specialist. He has also pursued several long-term research and consulting projects, including projects at the University of Riyadh in Saudi Arabia, the American University in Cairo, and the University of Warsaw. He also served as the Library Micro-computer Expert for INCOLSA (Indiana Cooperative Library Services Authority). He is a founding member of ALA's Association for College and Research Libraries Electronic Texts discussion group and is an active member of the Association for Literary and Linguistic Computing and the Association for Computers and the Humanities.

REBECCA GUENTHER is Senior MARC Standards Specialist in the Network Development and MARC Standards Office of the Library of Congress. She received a B.A. in History from Beloit College, Beloit, Wisconsin, and an M.S. in Library Science from Simmons College, Boston, Massachusetts. Former positions include Section Head of the National Union Catalog Control Section, Catalog Management and Publication Division, and Senior Cataloger, German Language Section, Shared Cataloging Division (both at the Library of Congress), and Cataloger, National Library of Medicine. Her current responsibilities include work on national and international library automation standards, including USMARC bibliographic, authority, classification, holdings, and community information formats, and USMARC code lists for languages, countries, and geographic areas. In addition, she has been involved in accommodating online information resources into USMARC formats. She has published several articles on the USMARC classification format and on providing access to online information resources in USMARC.

SUSAN HOCKEY is Director of the Center for Electronic Texts in the Humanities which is sponsored by Rutgers and Princeton Universities and funded by the National Endowment for the Humanities and the Andrew W. Mellon Foundation to act as a national focus for all who are involved with the creation, dissemination and use of electronic texts in the humanities. Before moving to the United States in 1991, she spent sixteen years at Oxford University where her most recent position was Director of the Computers in Teaching Initiative for Textual Studies. She has been active in humanities computing since 1969 and is the author of several books and numerous articles and has lectured widely on various aspects of humanities computing. She is Chair of the Association for Literary and Linguistic Computing and is a member (past Chair) of the Steering Committee of the Text Encoding Initiative.

MARY BRANDT JENSEN is Director of the Law Library and Professor of Law at the University of South Dakota School of Law. She is Moderator of the CNI-COPYRIGHT forum, and from 1989-90 served as Chair of the American Association of Law Libraries Copyright Committee and as Association Liaison to the Copyright Office. She is the author of several articles on copyright in the electronic environment including "Is the Library without Walls on a Collision Course with the 1976 Copyright Act?" (*Law Journal* 85 [Summer 1993]).

ROBERT ALUN JONES is Professor of Sociology, History, and Religious Studies at the University of Illinois in Urbana-Champaign, where he has taught since 1972. His research has been concentrated in three different areas: the writings of the French philosopher and sociologist Emile Durkheim (1858-1917), his contemporaries, and their social and intellectual context; the methodology of the history of ideas, and particularly problems of linguistic context; and the use of advanced information technologies in the humanities, and particularly problems related to the development and analysis of electronic texts. He is also Director of the Advanced Information Technologies Laboratory, a joint project of the National Center for Supercomputing Applications, the Program for the Study of Cultural Values and Ethics, and the College of Liberal Arts and Sciences.

LORRIE LEJEUNE has been actively involved in designing and implementing electronic publishing programs at the university press level for the past seven years. At the MIT Press, she helped establish an in-house system for producing camera-ready copy from a variety of electronic media. As Electronic Publishing Specialist at the University of Michigan Press, she serves as an information resource in electronic publishing, consulting with authors, coordinating production of electronic projects, and investigating and adapting new ways for the Press to take advantage of the latest developments in electronic information technology. She is active in the university press community, teaching workshops on electronic publishing and serving on a number of committees related to issues in electronic and online dissemination.

ANITA K. LOWRY is Head of the Information Arcade at the University of Iowa Libraries. She holds a B.A. in Comparative Literature from Indiana University, an M.S. in Library Service from Columbia University, and an M.A. in Cinema Studies from New York University. Prior to her appointment at Iowa, she was Deputy Head of the Butler Reference Department in the Columbia University Libraries and co-founder and Director of the Electronic Text Service, which was the first facility in an American academic library to be devoted to providing access to electronic texts in the humanities. A long-time member of the Association for Computers and the Humanities and a member of its Executive Council, she is an active proponent, in print and on the podium, of the integration of electronic texts and hypermedia databases into library resources and services.

JAMES V. MARCHAND is Center for Advanced Study Professor of German, Linguistics, and Comparative Literature at the University of Illinois at Urbana-Champaign. He holds a B.A. in Education from George Peabody College for Teachers, an M.A. in German from Vanderbilt University, and a Ph.D. in Germanic Philology from the University of Michigan. He has published in Linguistics, Literary Theory, Medieval Studies, and Computer Studies, including machine translation, image processing, and the use of the computer in the humanities.

JOHN PRICE-WILKIN holds graduate degrees in English and Library Science and has worked for several years in both collection development and automated systems. As part of his responsibilities as Data Services Librarian at the University of Michigan, Price-Wilkin established a wide-area textual analysis system in 1989. He has delivered talks on aspects of textual analysis systems at the annual meeting of the New Oxford English Dictionary, Computers and Libraries, the annual meetings of the Association for Computers and the Humanities, and the American Library Association. Price-Wilkin teaches a course in aspects of the Application of Standard Generalized Markup Language (SGML) and the management of textual resources at the Rare Book

School. Price-Wilkin is currently Systems Librarian for Information Services at the University of Virginia, responsible for systems support for the library's electronic centers.

C. M. SPERBERG-MCQUEEN is the Editor in Chief of the Text Encoding Initiative (TEI), a cooperative international project to formulate and disseminate guidelines for the encoding and interchange of electronic texts intended for literary, linguistic, historical, or other textual research. The TEI is sponsored by the Association for Computers and the Humanities, the Association for Computational Linguistics, and the Association for Literary and Linguistic Computing, and involves the direct participation of about seventy researchers on the working committees and work groups. Since 1987, Sperberg-McQueen has been a research programmer at the Academic Computer Center of the University of Illinois at Chicago, where he has at various times supervised word-processing consulting, maintained CICS for the university's library automation system, developed database systems for university departments, and headed the database and campus-wide information systems group. He is now involved with preparations for the university's Information Arcade.

BRETT SUTTON is a faculty member at the Graduate School of Library and Information Science at the University of Illinois, Urbana-Champaign. He has graduate degrees in Anthropology and Library and Information Science, both from the University of North Carolina at Chapel Hill. His principal areas of interest include the sociology of knowledge, libraries and society, and information technology. Recent publications include "The Rationale for Qualitative Research: A Review of Principles and Theoretical Foundations" in *Library Quarterly,* "The Modeling Function of Long Range Planning in Public Libraries" in *Library Administration and Management,* and "Literacy and Library Development" in *The Encyclopedia of Library History.*

INDEX